Gail Russell

SERIES ON NURSING ADMINISTRATION

EDITORIAL BOARD

SERIES ON NURSING ADMINISTRATION

Volume 6   **March 1994**

Health Care Rationing
DILEMMA AND PARADOX

Editor

Kathleen Kelly, RN, PhD
Assistant Professor
College of Nursing
The University of Iowa
Iowa City, Iowa

Chair of the Board

Meridean Maas, RN, PhD, FAAN
Associate Professor
College of Nursing
The University of Iowa
Iowa City, Iowa

 Mosby

St. Louis Baltimore Boston Chicago London Madrid Philadelphia Sydney Toronto

Dedicated to Publishing Excellence

Senior Vice President and Publisher: Alison Miller
Executive Editor: N. Darlene Como
Assistant Editor: Barbara M. Carroll
Project Manager: Patricia Tannian
Senior Production Editor: Betty Hazelwood
Senior Designer: Gail Morey Hudson
Manufacturing Supervisor: Karen Lewis
Electronic Production Coordinator: Joan Herron

Printed in the United States of America
Composition by Mosby Electronic Production, St. Louis
Printing/binding by Maple-Vail Book Mfg. Group

Mosby-Year Book, Inc.
11830 Westline Industrial Drive, St. Louis, MO 63146

Library of Congress Cataloging in Publication Data

Health care rationing : dilemma and paradox / editor, Kathleen Kelly;
chair of the board, Meridean Maas.
p.   cm. — (Series on nursing administration; v. 6,
March 1994)
Includes bibliographical references and index.
ISBN 0-8016-7521-9
1. Health care rationing—United States.   2. Nursing services—
United States—Administration.   I. Kelly, Kathleen.   II. Maas,
Meridean. III. Series.
[DNLM: 1. Health Care Rationing—organization & administration—
nurses' instruction. 2. Costs and Cost Analysis—nurses'
instruction. W1 SE72Q v. 6 1994 / WY 105 H4334 1994]
RA410.53.H43   1994
362. 1'0973—dc20
DNLM/DLC   93-39824
for Library of Congress   CIP

94 95 96 97 98 / 9 8 7 6 5 4 3 2 1

Contents

Contributors

Bobbie Berkowitz, RN, PhD, CNAA
Chief of Nursing Services
Seattle-King County Department of
  Public Health
Seattle, Washington

Kathleen A. Bower, RN, DNSc
Principal
The Center for Case Management, Inc.
South Natick, Massachusetts

Cecelia Capuzzi, RN, PhD
Associate Professor
School of Nursing
Community Health Care Systems
  Department
Oregon Health Sciences University
Portland, Oregon

John D. Crossley, RN, PhD, MBA
Senior Vice President for Nursing
University Hospitals of Clevelend
Cleveland, Ohio

Carol D. Falk, RN, MS
President
Carondelet St. Mary's Nursing Enterprise
Tucson, Arizona

John Feather, PhD
Director, Western New York Geriatric
  Education Center
Co-Director, Primary Care Resource
  Center
State University of New York
Buffalo, New York

Amy Marie Haddad, RN, C, PhD
Associate Professor and Chair
Department of Administrative and Social
  Sciences
Creighton University
Omaha, Nebraska

Marion Johnson, RN, PhD
Assistant Professor
College of Nursing
The University of Iowa
Iowa City, Iowa

Katherine R. Jones, RN, PhD
Associate Professor
School of Nursing
The University of Michigan
Ann Arbor, Michigan

Meridean Maas, RN, PhD, FAAN
Associate Professor
College of Nursing
The University of Iowa
Iowa City, Iowa

Daniel C. Maguire, STD
Professor of Ethics
Marquette University
Milwaukee, Wisconsin

Edith A. McFadden, MA, MD
Assistant Professor of Otolaryngology
Medical College of Wisconsin
Milwaukee, Wisconsin

Darlene A. McKenzie, RN, PhD
School of Nursing
Community Health Care Systems
  Department
Oregon Health Sciences University
Portland, Oregon

Elizabeth I. Merwin, RN, PhD, CNAA
Assistant Professor of Nursing
University of Virginia
Fellow, Thomas Jefferson Health Policy
  Institute
Charlottesville, Virginia

Barbara Nichols, RN, MS, FAAN
Executive Director
California Nurses Association
San Francisco, California

Leslie N. Ray, RN, PhD
School of Nursing
Community Health Care Systems
  Department
Oregon Health Sciences University
Portland, Oregon

Nancy J. Sharp, RN, MSN
President, Sharp Legislative Resources
Bethesda, Maryland

Susan J. Simmons, RN, PhD
Policy Coordinator
Office on Women's Health
Office of the Assistant Secretary for
  Health
Department of Health and Human
  Services
Washington, DC

Volume 7
Planned Contents

Theme: Health Care Work Redesign

Series Preface

Today's nurse executive needs to stay current in many rapidly changing areas of health care. To meet this demand, the *Series on Nursing Administration* is designed to give nursing administrators new information on current and emerging issues. Developed and managed at the University of Iowa College of Nursing and published by Mosby, it is a quality resource for nurse executives, faculty who teach nursing administration, and students in nursing administration programs. Each year a new volume addresses the most recent issues in this discipline. Thus a subscription to the series will keep readers on the forefront of knowledge and practice.

Every nurse executive interacts with corporate management; with colleagues in other settings, professional groups, the community, and clients; and with nurse colleagues, members of other disciplines, and ancillary personnel. To stay current with developments in each of these areas, the nurse executive reads journals and newsletters, attends continuing education programs, and participates in short-term executive management courses. The most effective method, however, is the sharing of concerns, experiences, and insights with peers. The Mosby *Series on Nursing Administration* formalizes the process of sharing among experts with similar concerns. In every chapter of each volume of the series, expert authors share their experiences and ideas on particular emerging issues. Busy nurse executives can conveniently and cost-effectively keep their knowledge current on a variety of topics by reading this series.

Nursing administration faculty can use the series to keep their teaching and practice alive, current, and timely. Most nursing administration programs have one or more courses that address issues in nursing management. Because these issues undergo rapid change, faculty need a flexible approach to teaching this content. This series offers the instructor maximum flexibility in selecting issues for discussion to fit the needs of a particular class. An instructor teaching a nursing management issues course can use the series as a course text. Students introduced to this series will find it a resource with ongoing value. Faculty teaching undergraduate level administration courses also may use the series to supplement an introductory text on management and leadership.

This series is unique in that it is the first annual series devoted to issues in nursing administration. To ensure that it covers current issues and provides up-to-date information, the series employs a unique publication process involving four groups: a series editor, an editorial board, the authors, and the publisher.

The editor of Volumes 1 through 4 of the series is Marion Johnson, RN, PhD, an assistant professor at the University of Iowa. She has a rich practice base in nursing administration and currently teaches nursing administration at the master's level. Her background, interests, and writing skills make her eminently qualified for the job of series editor.

Kathleen Kelly, RN, PhD, is editor for Volumes 5 through 8 of the series. Kathleen has years of experience as a community health nursing administrator and teaches nursing administration at the master's level. She also administers the Continuing Education Program at the College of Nursing. Her background and current work provide a broad perspective on issues that are of critical importance to nurse executives and managers.

The editorial board consists of faculty teaching in the nursing administration program at the University of Iowa and selected nurse administrators associated with the program. The board meets three or four times a year with the series editor, helps identify the emerging issues and prospective authors, and assists the editor with manuscript review. The University of Iowa's growing program in nursing administration, including study at the doctorate level, makes this an ideal setting to support this publication.

The authors are distinguished nurse administrators and educators chosen for their expertise in particular areas. Although authors have the freedom to pursue an issue as they choose, each is encouraged to address the state of knowledge, future directions, and controversial questions surrounding the issue and to propose one or more options for resolution.

The publisher of the series, beginning with Volume 3, is Mosby. Volumes 1 and 2 were published by Addison-Wesley. Darlene Como, Executive Editor, Mosby, has provided encouragement and assistance with continued development of the series. An annual series is unique in the literature of nursing administration, and we are fortunate that Mosby is committed to its success.

All of us involved in this series believe that it will benefit not only those who teach and practice nursing administration, but the entire nursing profession and, most important, the patients we serve. We welcome your comments and suggestions.

Joanne Comi McCloskey, RN, PhD, FAAN
Chairperson, Editorial Board, Volumes 1-4

Meridean Maas, RN, PhD, FAAN
Chairperson, Editorial Board, Volumes 5-8

Introduction

Driving much of the restructuring and redesign effort in health care delivery today is the concept of reallocating available resources in an effort to maximize quality and access to care while controlling costs. This occurs at a time when resources are constrained by payors and promises of health care reform present an array of unknowns for health care providers. In addition, demographic changes make unprecedented demands for care of the frail elderly and persons with special needs, chronic diseases, and chronically acute conditions.

The effort to allocate resources in a manner that will control cost while serving the greatest needs most commonly is referred to as *rationing*. Whatever the label given this phenomenon, it presents ethical, economic, legal, political, and professional dilemmas for health care providers. Nurse administrators are often on the front lines of the battles that surround these dilemmas.

This volume of *SONA* reviews the development of this concept within the U.S. health care system, explores the dilemmas that are being faced by the health care consumer, provider, and payor, describes the effects of existing and proposed efforts to ration health care, and suggests proactive strategies for nurse administrators and other health care providers faced with the realities of health care rationing. As the volume title implies, the editors and authors address the dilemmas that are integral to any change that involves material resource allocation and calls forth the values, ethics, and politics that surround those decisions. It also recognizes existing and potential paradoxical effects of the very act of rationing, or reallocating, the resources designated for health care.

Volume 6 has been organized to reflect these themes. Section One defines terms surrounding the concept of rationing and the history that has led to the need for rationing and to the controversy surrounding the concept of rationing. It analyzes the key dilemmas that must be confronted if health care rationing is to achieve a degree of acceptance in the U.S. health care culture. Many of these issues are ethical and political in nature, but also included are those issues as elemental as defining quality of care. The horns of the dilemma named rationing are presented as a foundation for the volume.

Section Two provides an in-depth perspective on current efforts to ration health care in a manner that serves the greatest number of needs with the greatest likelihood of effectiveness. State initiatives are described. The perennial issue of paying for prevention care is raised—this time from the perspective of cost and access as desired outcomes. Finally, this section highlights the paradox of episodic health care as it currently is delivered and describes the opportunity health care reform offers for change to a health care continuum. This section recognizes that in the process of solving the current health care crisis through rationing, old problems may remain unsolved and new ones can be anticipated—the truly paradoxical effects of macro-decision making.

The final section offers examples of proactive responses to the health care rationing initiative, as well as recommendations for dealing with barriers to achieving a reallocation of resources that is equitable and tolerated by consumers, providers, and payors. As in each of the *SONA* volumes, nursing implications of the health care development under scrutiny are the focal point. This volume, perhaps more than those preceding it, demonstrates that nurse managers cannot operate in isolation—that their role is practiced in continuous interaction with the macroenvironment and microenvironment. Above all, this volume addresses not *if* but *how* rationing of health care can be ethically, safely, and economically accomplished. It accomplishes this by identifying the questions that must be answered and the balance that must be sought among the dilemmas and paradoxes raised by the realities of rationing of health care.

The editorial board and contributing authors offer this volume as a tool for nurse administrators who assume leadership in the struggle to achieve health care reform that is efficacious and available to all and that retains the best qualities of our current system while responding to the mandate for change.

Kathleen Kelly
Editor

Dilemma and Paradox

A clear understanding of the current state of health care delivery and how it has led to the current focus on rationing of available resources requires analyzing events, defining rationing, and exploring issues that such an approach to health care reform raises for consumer, providers, and payors. The five chapters that make up this section provide such a framework, using a wide variety of literature addressing rationing and related concepts. The intent is to present an in-depth view of the horns of the dilemma of rationing, often called *reallocation of resources* in an attempt to be less offensive.

In Chapter 1 Nichols and her co-authors describe the state of health care costs, access, and outcomes in 1993, define the types of rationing identified in the literature, and review the issues associated with the threat and realities of rationing. Nursing management concerns and implications are highlighted.

Haddad presents ethical implications of health care rationing in Chapter 2. This is presented within the framework of traditional health care. After exploring the ethical arguments for and against rationing, the author provides a valuable tool for nurse managers in her overview of "micro" and "macro" decision making. This is specifically applied to the nurse administrator role.

Chapter 3 explores the dilemma that is uppermost in most discussions of health care rationing—cost versus quality. Berkowitz bases her discussion on the assumptions of universal access and cost control and highlights the elements that define quality. She challenges nurse administrators to develop their potential for contributing to the achievement of quality at a reasonable cost.

In Chapter 4 Sharp offers a stimulating overview of the dynamics of politics, power, and vested interests that affect policy and ultimate assignment of resources. She stresses the vital need for nurses in every role to understand the interplay of these phenomena and the proactive strategies nursing must pursue to influence the policies that will result from the interplay. It is a clear message that nursing must become a major player in the dynamics of politics and power that produce policy.

In the final chapter of this section, Merwin confronts one of the most difficult issues associated with the reality of rationing health care—accountability for allocating resources. This is presented in the framework of events leading us toward rationing, raising the issues of how criteria for accountability will develop, and defining conflicts that will obstruct true accountability for rationing decisions. She assists the reader in considering the question, "Will the fox be guarding the henhouse?"

CHAPTER 1

Rationing Health Care:
What Are the Implications?

Barbara Nichols
Marion Johnson
Meridean Maas

The history of U.S. health care provides a clear roadmap to the current state of affairs in which the question is *how*, not *if* health care rationing will be provided. Definitions of rationing are offered, and issues surrounding rationing of health care are identified. Specific issues for nurses in management roles are highlighted.

Americans pay the most per capita for health care of any industrial nation but have varied access to the most expensive health care system in the world. Despite the expenditure of $650 billion per year, 37 million Americans are not covered by any health insurance plan and Americans are not healthier than people from nations with similar wealth (Lee & Estes, 1990; Sharlett & Reinhardt, 1992; Swartz, 1989; Kitzhaber, 1989). It is a fact that 22 other nations have lower infant mortality rates and 26 have lower rates of death from cardiovascular disease (Wright, 1989; Hoffman, 1989). The United States, on the other hand, has the world's high-

BN: Executive Director, California Nurses Association, San Francisco, CA 94103
MJ: Associate Professor, The University of Iowa College of Nursing, Iowa City, IA 52242
MM: Associate Professor, The University of Iowa College of Nursing, Iowa City, IA 52242

Series on Nursing Administration—Volume 6, 1994

est cesarean section incidence (one in four deliveries) and the highest rates of cardiovascular surgery (Wright, 1989, Hoffman, 1990).

What the $650 billion per year provides is rigorous education for health professionals and advances in science, medical technologies, and pharmacologic therapies, as well as complex organization, delivery, and financing of health care services. The United States has an oversupply of physicians, an underutilization of other health professionals, a glut of hospital beds, limited access to services for large segments of the population, the persistence of soaring health care costs, and rationing of health care services.

As the United States faces a $3.7 trillion national debt, unprecedented economic change, and international challenges, the issue key to the nation's health is how to finance and provide adequate health care services to all citizens equitably. The country's inability to develop a comprehensive health plan to control costs and ensure access to services has culminated in discrepancies in the distribution of health care. Sophisticated treatments and technologies coexist with high infant mortality rates, which are related to lack of access to prenatal and maternity care. The need to make changes in the financing and organization of health care for the most cost-effective delivery is critical. The issue of allocating or rationing scarce or expensive health care services is gaining currency as a practical advantage for delivering health care and services.

HEALTH CARE RATIONING: WHAT IS IT?

Literature on rationing contains varied definitions and perspectives helpful for understanding health care rationing. One distinction is made between price rationing, often referred to as *market rationing*, and non-price rationing. Price rationing denies goods to those who cannot pay the price (Reagan, 1988; Aaron & Schwartz, 1990). It is the basis of our free market system and exists in the U.S. health care system, affecting about 15% of the population (Aaron & Schwartz, 1990). Those affected include the poor, the uninsured, and the insured without coverage for catastrophic expenses. The claim that the United States currently rations care often refers to this type of rationing. One author suggests that price rationing be referred to as "discrimination in access to health care services on the basis of income" (Reagan, 1988), a phrase that captures the essence of this type of rationing.

Non-price rationing refers to the denial of goods or services to those who have the money to pay for them (Aaron & Schwartz, 1990). The decision to deny is based on a judgment rather than on price, and the judgment in turn is based on some criterion. For example, the criteria can be equity and fairness, in which case a society uses equity and fairness standards to distribute health care. The standards to be used can be agreed on by a society (referred to as *collective standards*), by a government, or by an individual—for example, the health care professional. Standards are determined in all of these ways in the current U.S. health care system. Oregon is attempting to define collective standards as a basis for distributing the limited resources available to the state to provide health care services for the poor. The federal and state governments determine standards for Medicare and Medicaid eligibility and coverage. Decisions about the use of organs for transplant often are made by health care professionals, at the individual patient level, or in the development of national standards.

Another method that can be used to make decisions is cost-benefit analysis; that is, are the benefits greater than the costs? The difficulty in applying this method to health care is the need to quantify health care benefits in monetary terms (Hicks, 1985; Pruitt & Jacox, 1991). Although cost-effectiveness analysis can be substituted for cost-benefit analysis, problems remain with identifying quantifiable values for health care outcomes. The federal government is attempting to deal with this problem by funding research that looks at both cost and outcomes to determine the care that is both appropriate and cost-effective.

A second distinction sometimes is made between the allocation of resources and the rationing of resources. In this sense, allocation refers to decisions made at the aggregate level, or macrolevel, and rationing refers to decisions made at the individual level, or microlevel (Evans, 1983). Rationing then takes place within the context of prior allocation decisions (Hicks & Boles, 1984: Specht, 1992) and can be considered an outcome of these allocation decisions. The Clinton proposal for a national health board to establish annual budget targets and core benefits available for all U.S. citizens (Clinton, 1992) is an allocation decision specifying how much money and what services will be provided. Individual rationing decisions are made (1) by state governments when they determine individual eligibility for Medicaid, (2) by health care providers when they determine who receives specific treatments, and (3) by hospitals when they determine who will be admitted.

A third distinction is made between explicit and implicit rationing. Explicit rationing is similar to allocation (the limitation of resources by an external source—in our system the third-party payor) (Mechanic, 1979; Fry, 1983; Specht, 1992). This type of rationing currently exists when health care coverage is limited to certain populations, does not pay for certain treatments, or requires specific criteria be met for the coverage to be effective (Mechanic, 1979). Implicit rationing is similar to microlevel rationing just described—decisions are made at the individual level, usually by clinicians, about which patients get the limited resources. These decisions are necessary because external limitations (explicit rationing) have been imposed or because the resource is scarce (e.g., organs for transplantation, coverage for preventive health care).

WHY RATIONING?

According to economic theory, resources used to produce goods and services are scarce in relation to the aggregate demand for goods and services (Feldstein, 1993). Consequently, some form of rationing takes place in all economic systems; in a free market system such as in the United States, price rationing is used. In other systems, the government may decide how goods and services are distributed. The U.S. health care system was able to ignore this basic economic principle for many years by increasing the price of health care services to allow for the purchase of additional scarce resources and to expand services. Health care for the poor was provided for by shifting the costs of this care to other payors (Ginsberg, 1986).

Rising health care costs, which exceeded general inflation, consumed greater portions of the gross national product (GNP), and were borne increasingly by federal and state governments, fractured the illusion that health care was immune to the economic principles governing other markets. Initial attempts to control costs were aimed at increasing production efficiency and controlling prices, neither of which has proven effective. The strategy that offers the greatest potential for reducing and controlling costs is reducing the amount of care provided, but little is known about how to reduce care without adversely affecting patients (Aiken, 1988). The cost-benefit to cost-effectiveness ratio of various health care interventions is not known; therefore the information needed to eliminate costly interventions whose benefit is no greater than less costly interventions is not available. Because knowledge about intervention effectiveness is not available, rationing has been proposed to reduce health care consumption, control health care costs, and distribute health care services. Movement toward a non–price rationing system assumes that individuals or groups can appropriate scarce resources more efficiently or equitably than a price system (Hicks & Boles, 1984).

RATIONING ISSUES

The current debate about rationing really is not a debate about whether to ration, but a debate about what form rationing should take. Americans have been unable to reach consensus on values that determine resource allocation and distribution of health care services. This has precipitated debate about the use of rationing to decrease health care expenditures and increase access.

In general, arguments for rationing are based on the rationale that unlimited consumption of health care resources is no longer possible. Oregon's proposal represents an explicit form of rationing. Arguments for making rationing explicit are based on the belief that it is more fair to ration on a set of agreed on standards than to ration implicitly through a pricing system or some other mechanism. Implicit rationing occurs, for instance, when individuals without health insurance coverage cannot get services provided for insured individuals (Eubanks, 1989; Capron, 1992). Opponents of the kind of plan proposed by Oregon agree that what really is being recommended is selective explicit rationing—that is, rationing for the poor.

In an attempt to put the best face on "rationing" health care services, it is described by some as setting priorities on how to share fixed services. Others believe that instead of attempting to allocate fixed resources among competing demands, the appropriate response to the current health care dilemma is to provide more health care by investing in the delivery system to make it larger (Rook, 1990).

Clearly, the current approach to rationing reflects the United States' national ambivalence as to whether health care is a right (and thus is a social good) and should be collectively financed or whether it is a privilege, viewed as a consumptive good that should be financed by individual recipients. Answers should be openly debated to design a health care system that is worthy of the nation. Nursing has a stake in this redesign and must address a number of issues if the profession is to be a full participant in that redesign.

ISSUES FOR NURSING AND NURSE MANAGERS

There are a number of implications for nursing and nurses if resources for health care are reallocated to assure equitable distribution of services and there is a shift from cure of illness to the prevention of illness and promotion of health. Clinical practice, nursing education, and the development and application of nursing knowledge will be affected.

Some believe that the opportunities for nurses as primary care providers will increase. This is likely if nursing can demonstrate quality care at costs that are less than for comparable care provided by physicians. Data have been available for some time showing that nurse practitioners can be more cost-effective than physicians in the delivery of certain services (Jacox, 1987). Nursing has been slow to position itself for the recognition of nurses as primary care providers, but the creation of nursing centers and increase in the number of nurse practitioners are two occurrences that have enhanced nursing's potential to provide primary care.

Some of the emphasis in health care delivery is expected to shift from cure of illness to promotion of health. Prevention of illness and promotion of health have been fundamental values in nursing since Florence Nightingale (1858). If more resources are invested in health promotion, nurses in some settings will be in an advantaged position. However, in hospitals there also will be the need to redefine the clinical roles of nurses, to provide education and support for nurses in these new roles, and to reallocate resources to include a new practice emphasis. There will be increased focus on shortened stays and continuity of care. Nurse administrators and managers will need to lead the development of programing for health promotion and continuity of care across organizational and geographic boundaries. This emphasis will create new and expanded roles in managing care. It also has implications for the education and development of staff nurses regarding their scope of responsibility in assessing and planning care, not to mention their awareness of health care delivery options and associated funding.

Use of some resources that have heretofore been available to nurses may be constrained as resources are reallocated for greater emphasis on health promotion and illness prevention. The ability to provide some services, as well as the development and use of some biotechnologies, may be curtailed. The development of knowledge also may feel the pinch if resources for research are less available.

Nurse administrators will be challenged to discover how nurses can be used in all settings to increase the services provided at lower cost. The shift from managing nurses to facilitating the management of care by nurses will continue. Leadership will be needed to design and implement models of practice that enable professional nurses to have greater control over their practice, as individuals and collectively. Ethical issues, discussed in Chapter 2 in this volume, will challenge nurse administrators, clinicians, and educators. The role of nurses as advocates for patients will present difficult dilemmas, focusing on support for individual rights and needs versus the rights and needs of patient groups.

Nursing education will be pressured to increase the number of nurse primary care providers and to put more curricular emphasis on health promotion and prevention of illness. Undergraduate and graduate curricula necessarily will include the knowledge and skills required for nursing case management and managed care. Greater focus will be needed on clinical decision making and skills of negotiation and consensus decision making so that nurses are better prepared for governance of their practice and case management roles. Because resources also likely will be further constrained for higher education, nursing education will be faced with challenges similar to those of nurse administrators and clinicians. How to do more with less and what should be included in curricula that excludes other important content will present difficult decisions for nurse educators.

The question seems to be *how* to ration health care, not *if* it will be rationed. The problem is to ration so that more problems are solved than are created. Central to the concept of rationing is choice by public policy makers. Nursing can have a major influence on that choice if the profession assumes leadership in understanding the concept and articulating the implications of rationing. As a profession, nursing needs to recognize and support a restructuring of health care that enhances access and quality as it controls cost, while it demonstrates the role nurses can play in achieving this goal. The following are some of the questions that must be addressed by policy makers, funding sources, health care providers, and consumers of health care to make rationing decisions. These and other questions are discussed in subsequent chapters in this volume.

• Is health care to be viewed as a right or a privilege?

- If access to basic health care is declared a right, should it be financed federally or locally?
- Will a variety of health care services and providers be paid for their services?
- How will the health care needs of special populations be met?
- What are the ethical and legal issues that need to be addressed to provide accessible, appropriate, affordable care?

REFERENCES

Aaron, H., & Schwartz, W.B. (1990). Rationing health care: The choice before us. *Science, 247*, 418-422.

Aiken, L. (1988). Assuring the delivery of quality patient care. In *Nursing resources and the delivery of quality patient care*. (NIH Publication No. 89-3008, pp. 3-10.) Washington, DC: U.S. Government Printing Office.

Capron, A.M. (1992). Prolongation of life: The issues and questions. In *Improving health policy and management: Nine critical research issues for the 1990s*. Ann Arbor, MI: Health Administration Press.

Clinton, B. (1992). The Clinton health care plan. *New England Journal of Medicine, 327*, 804-806.

Eubanks, P. (1989). Early turmoil for MA universal health-care law. *Hospitals, 63*, 54.

Evans, R.W. (1983). Health care technology and the inevitability of resource allocation. *Journal of the American Medical Association, 249*, 2208-2219.

Feldstein, P.J. (1993). *Health care economics* (4th ed.). Albany, NY: Delmar.

Fry, S.T. (1983). Rationing health care: The ethics of cost containment. *Nursing Economic$, 1*(6), 165-169.

Ginsberg, E. (1986). The destabilization of health care. *New England Journal of Medicine, 315*, 757-761.

Hicks, L.L. (1985). Using benefit-cost and cost-effectiveness analyses in health-care resource allocation. *Nursing Economic$, 3*(2), 78-84.

Hicks, L.L., & Boles, K.E. (1984). Why health economics? *Nursing Economic$, 2*(3), 175-180.

Hoffman, M.S. (Ed.). (1989). *The world almanac and book of facts 1990*. New York: Pharos Books.

Jacox, A. (1987). The OTA report: A policy analysis. *Nursing Outlook, 35*(6), 262-267.

Kitzhaber, J. (1989). *The Oregon Basic Health Services Act*. Salem, OR: Legislative Assembly.

Lee, P.R., & Estes, C.L. (1990). *The Nation's health* (3rd ed.). Boston, MA: Jones & Bartlett.

Mechanic, D. (1979). *Future issues in health care: Social policy and the rationing of medical services*. New York: Free Press.

Nightingale, F. (1858). *Notes on matters affecting the health, efficiency, and hospital administration of the British Army*. London: Harrison & Sons.

Pruit, R.H., & Jacox, A.K. (1991). Looking above the bottom line: Decisions in economic evaluation. *Nursing Economic$, 9*(2), 87-91.

Reagan, M.D. (1988). Health care rationing: What does it mean? *New England Journal of Medicine, 319*, 1149-1151.

Rook, J.P. (1990). Lets admit we ration health care: Then set priorities. *American Journal of Nursing, 90*(6), 39-43.

Sharlett, S.M., & Reinhardt, U.E. (Eds.). (1992). *Improving health policy and management: Nine critical research issues for the 1990s*. Ann Arbor, MI: Health Administration Press.

Specht, J.K. (1992). Implications of the ethics and economics of health care rationing for nursing administration and practice. In M. Johnson (Ed.), *Series on nursing administration, Vol.4: Economic myths and realities*. St. Louis: Mosby.

Swartz, K. (1989). *The medically uninsured: Special focus on workers*. Washington, DC: The Urban Institute.

Wright, J.W. (Ed.). (1989). *The universal almanac 1990*. Kansas City, MO: Andrews & McMeel.

CHAPTER 2

Ethical Issues in Health Care Rationing

Amy Marie Haddad

Rationing, by its very nature, is an ethical issue. This chapter explores the ethical implications of rationing for nursing using traditional, principle-based ethics. Utilitarian and deontological ethical theories are applied to specific dilemmas unique to nursing practice. The differences between rationing decisions in medicine and in nursing are examined. The chapter closes with an examination of the types of allocation decisions commonly encountered by nurse administrators.

The literature in health policy, economics, and ethics is replete with discussion and debate about what is essentially the two-fold problem in health care—increased cost and increased number of uninsured individuals (Wiener, 1992). Although there is some disagreement about what percentage of the gross national product should be spent on health care in comparison with other social goods, most agree that there is a limit to what can be spent on health care. Given this, health policy discussion today almost always moves to an exploration of the "R" word: *rationing*, an expression that was studiously avoided in the past (Kapp, 1989).

Associate Professor and Chair, Department of Administrative and Social Sciences, Creighton University, Omaha, NE 68178

Series on Nursing Administration—Volume 6, 1994

Although policy, political, and economic implications exist in any rationing scenario, there is also a strong ethical context that deserves primary consideration. This chapter explores the ethics of health care rationing and the implications this poses for nursing. First, a basic overview of the various meanings of rationing and the specific contributions of ethics to the debate are presented. Second, the role of nursing in the allocation of resources, as distinct from other health care professionals, is examined on a macroallocation level, from the perspective of the nurse administrator and nursing staff. Finally, the principles and rules traditionally used to make rationing decisions are analyzed for their suitability for decisions in nursing practice.

OVERVIEW OF RATIONING

One can trace the concept of rationing throughout the history of formal health care delivery systems. Physicians have always rationed health care, for example, by decreased participation in Medicare, by participation in health maintenance organizations, or by denial of service to charity cases (Friedman, 1986). One model for rationing decisions that has been successfully applied in the past is triage. It is tempting to apply triage to the present situation in health care. Triage is an excellent method of distributing scarce resources but only for a very narrow set of circumstances. Triage presupposes an emergency situation, classically a war, in which evaluation of the wounded is based on their potential for return to battle followed by their potential for survival. Thus the most grievously injured are the last to be treated. The present situation in health care, though often deemed a crisis, is not the same as a raging battle and should not be confused as such. Generally, we are faced with rationing in situations in which the limits to resources are not absolute. In fact, one prominent health policy analyst goes even further to claim that in the United States individuals are denied health services in the face of abundant health care resources (Reinhardt, 1987). However, the entire argument about rationing depends on acceptance of the notion of *relative* scarcity of resources (Kapp, 1989). Whether scarcity of sufficient magnitude presently exists is still a question open to debate and one which is discussed again later.

It is important for the purposes of this discussion to describe the parameters of rationing. Health care rationing can be defined as "an action undertaken when there is (a) a recognition that resources are limited, and (b) when faced with a scarcity, a method that must be devised to allocate fairly and reasonably those resources. Rationing is the effort to distribute equitably scarce resources" (Callahan, 1992). Because rationing deals with distribution of resources, it is common to use the term *allocation* interchangeably with *rationing*. However, there is a distinction between the two terms: whereas allocation deals with the distribution of resources in general, rationing deals with distribution in situations of scarcity. Rationing presupposes insufficient resources to meet the needs of those who seek them.

Another relevant component of rationing is that it denies either some or all of the care that would be of benefit to an individual. The determination of said benefit poses its own ethical and policy problems and is now the subject of considerable research. It is clear, however, that defining health care benefit is central to the development of an ethically sound method of rationing. Ethical problems in rationing exist because one is contemplating denying a good to certain individuals who would benefit. For example, how is benefit defined in health care? Who is most qualified to determine benefit? The patient? Health care professionals? Third-party payors? Until an empirical definition of benefit is established, a normative description must suffice. The denied benefit in rationing might be large, even life-saving, or it might be very small but (qua benefit) is greater than zero (Baily, 1984).

Rationing can be understood also in terms of its relationship to market economies. First, market systems persistently deny goods to those who cannot afford them. All goods, including health care, are rationed in this manner. Second, the term *rationing* is used to refer to the denial of commodities to those who have the money to buy them. "The question now being raised is whether health care should be rationed in this sense, whether its availability should be limited, even to those who can pay for it" (Aaron & Schwartz, 1990).

The former assertion (that health care is the same as any other commodity) has been challenged. Health care may not be like other market commodities because it may be a natural monopoly—any service or product that is not economical to distribute on a competitive supply-and-demand basis. For example, the early telephone system was a monopoly until technology made it feasible for industrial competition. Further, consumers soon learned how to make reasonable judgments regarding one competitor over another. In the telephone scenario, society benefits from this competition; however, this is not the case in health care. When patients who are ill or injured present themselves in all their frailty to a health care professional, they are not prepared to negotiate the value or relative cost of the health care services offered.

The latter question of whether health care should be rationed even to those who can pay for it is beyond the scope of this chapter.

ETHICAL IMPLICATIONS

Ethical analysis can make several contributions to the examination of health care rationing. Ethics provides the tools (principles, such as justice and beneficence) and the framework (theories, such as utilitarianism) to answer both substantive and procedural questions. Rationing needs a clear and clearly defensible ethical basis if it is going to be fair and survive the pressures of the moment. To some, the pressures of the moment are sufficient to justify rationing.

Arguments for Rationing

Rationing has become a commonly prescribed remedy for the variety of ills affecting the U.S. health care system, such as (1) increased life expectancy that has resulted in the bittersweet outcome of an increase in the number of elderly in our society who naturally need chronic care services; (2) increased prevalence of disability that is a direct result of technological advances that have a tendency to extend life rather than cure or restore patients to functional status; and (3) increased cost of care and failure of regulatory efforts to control cost with no appreciable gains in terms of morbidity and mortality in comparison with other industrialized countries (Friedman, 1986; Kapp, 1989; Aaron & Schwartz, 1990). Further, others argue that health care presently is being covertly rationed based on ability to pay, age, insurance status, place of employment, and geographic location. An explicit rationing system would move the discussion into the public arena where specific proposals could be articulated and scrutinized (Morreim, 1988; Catholic Health Association, 1991).

Arguments Against Rationing

Others are not convinced that the situation is critical enough to justify an ethically suspect action like rationing. According to this view, the following measures should be tried to avoid or delay the need to ration:

- Eliminate waste (such as administrative cops and duplication of services)
- Eliminate ineffective services and increase efficiency
- Assess effectiveness of technology
- Emphasize prevention
- Provide more information about outcomes to patients
- Uncouple income from clinical decision-making
- Establish a "closed system" in which to make clinical decisions.

Each of these measures deserves individual examination regarding its merits and limitations in light of ethics.

Eliminate waste. The most commonly proposed measure to prevent the need for rationing is to eliminate waste in the health care system. The potential elimination of waste is proposed in all administrative and service in health care. This is not a novel recommendation. An early, though remarkably timely, nursing reference to the ethical implications of waste was addressed by Aikens as she answered the question "Is it wrong to be wasteful?" (Aikens, 1922):

> This question admits of little argument. Waste, as a general rule, indicates either ignorance or lack of conscience in the person responsible. Yet wilful (sic) extravagance on the part of nurses is not unusual. Many nurses have the mistaken idea that because property belongs to the city or to a corporation it makes little or no difference to anyone whether they are careless or extravagant or not in the way they handle supplies in their department. 'Use all you

want to, the city pays for it' or 'we don't have to pay for it' are remarks frequently heard that are indicative of the attitude of some nurses, especially in larger institutions.

The most salient point in Aikens' remarks is that there is a connection between the wastefulness of one nurse and society as a whole. The admonition to be frugal is especially pertinent today considering the disposable nature of supplies and equipment in the health care setting. Yet, even if every nurse was conscientious about the use of supplies and equipment, it would not greatly affect the overall problem of waste and duplication in the health care system.

Savings could be realized on a larger scale through the continuation of cost-containment measures, restriction of duplication of services, elimination of chronically empty beds, and development of managed care systems. "For a variety of reasons, not all providers could become as efficient as the best run HMOs, and economies would be realized over many years. As a result, savings would be achieved gradually and therefore would be hard to detect against the strongly rising trend in medical outlays" (Aaron & Schwartz, 1990). System-wide elimination of waste, although helpful, will not be sufficient to solve the problem of greater equity in light of increasing costs.

Eliminate ineffective services and increase efficiency. It is estimated that as much as 50% of the cost of health care services in the United States is medically unnecessary (Axene, Doyle, & Feren, 1991). If these ineffective services can be selectively eliminated, so the argument goes, enough resources would be available to provide beneficial care to all who need it (Brook & Lohr, 1986). Although this is an ethically worthy goal, increased efficiency may not do much better than elimination of waste in avoiding the possibility of rationing. In addition, most of the research in this area has focused on the evaluation of established *medical* procedures in certain classes of patients. What of the efficiency of *nursing* care? Is nursing service provided with greater efficiency than it was 30 years ago? The very nature of nursing care—labor intensive, hands-on service—has not appreciably changed even with the advent of sophisticated technology at the bedside. In fact, the introduction of more and more complex pieces of equipment at the bedside to monitor every possible body function may have had the opposite effect on efficiency in nursing practice. The recent recommendations for various types of nursing paraprofessionals to help overburdened nurses are signs that nursing is not immune from the push to greater levels of efficiency. The underlying ethical dilemma for nursing in this whole arena of efficiency is to protect those actions and interventions that produce *nursing* benefits and eliminate or defer to others those actions that do not.

Assess effectiveness of technology. As fast as efforts are made to contain costs in the U.S. health care system, expensive and questionably effective technology is added. New drugs, devices, diagnostic testing instruments, and therapies are all being developed at a pace that does not appear to have been affected appreciably by efforts to contain costs. Medical technology is introduced and disseminated before its effectiveness is tested. The recent wave of technologic assessment has been largely voluntary and focused on new technologies. Older technologies that are widely accepted, but possibly outmoded or ineffective, continue to be used because they remain eligible for reimbursement. A rigorous program of technology assessment could identify those that are safe and effective and eliminate useless or only marginally useful technology. Reimbursement policies could then be structured to promote the use of only those technologies that have established their safety and efficacy *and* those providers who can demonstrate their ability to use them safely and effectively (Priester & Caplan, 1989).

This will not be an advantage, however, with those types of technology that are truly helpful, on an individual or aggregate basis, but are inordinately expensive. As Callahan (1990) states:

> The great but rarely confronted failing of much of the faith in technology assessment might be called the *efficacy fallacy*—that if it works and is beneficial, it must be affordable, or at least ought to be so. That, of course, does not follow at all. Unless we are prepared to spend an unconscionable proportion of our resources on health care—letting schools, roads, housing, and manufacturing investments suffer in comparison—we cannot possibly afford every medical advance that might be of benefit.

Emphasize prevention. The citizens of the United States have had a long-standing infatuation with technology. To control the costs related to technology, "first dollar" rationing has been encouraged. First dollar rationing is evidenced in public programs (county, state, or federal) and private insurance programs that are more likely to limit an individual's access to basic services by nonpayment of the initial costs of care by the lack of coverage for basic services or by high deductibles and coinsurance (Merrill & Cohen, 1987). Thus patients may not receive basic, preventative services that would decrease the amount of chronic illness and disability that so burden the health care system. Clearly, the demonstration of preventative interventions and systematic evaluation of their effectiveness to reduce costs and conserve resources is needed.

Irrationally (though rational in light of the romance with technology), more expensive, tertiary care often is covered to "last dollar" coverage. The ethical implications of such a system are plain. In essence, a situation has been created in which the most vulnerable members of our society (e.g., children, the poor) are put at risk for future, predictably more disabling illness because first dollar coverage is not paid for. The benefits, both economically and ethically, of preventive care have been the subject of numerous proposals for health care reform, including *Nursing's Agenda for Health Care Reform* (ANA, 1991).

However, even if the focus can be shifted to preventative care and provide first dollar coverage, limitations will still exist regarding the extent of services that can be provided and for whom services can be provided. It is interesting to note that *Nursing's Agenda for Health Care Reform* (ANA, 1991) does not directly mention rationing. The closest the document comes to acknowledging that rationing might be part of the future of health care in the United States is the following recommendation for "Controlled growth of the health care system through planning and prudent resources allocation" (ANA, 1991). The document provides no guidance as to what constitutes prudent resource allocation.

Provide more information about outcomes to patients. Another strategy for promoting efficiency in the health care system is to provide accurate and adequate information to consumers of health care services so they can make wise decisions. This proposal is no more than a reaffirmation of the doctrine of informed consent. Informed consent requires that patients receive adequate information, understand the information presented, and are allowed to choose freely without coercion. Informed consent improves the care of patients by increasing the bond of trust between provider and patient and by facilitating patient autonomy through the provision of choice and the patient's participation in his or her own care (Cassell, 1978).

In light of the present discussion, the kind of information that patients must have to make prudent decisions must be expanded from that traditionally provided in informed consent discussions to include data regarding the safety and effectiveness of a specific treatment in comparison with other treatment options. Patients can make better decisions if they have access to information about the performance of hospitals and physicians regarding such data as morbidity and mortality rates. "But the availability of useful data for guiding consumers' purchases, either by patients or third parties, is still extremely limited" (Priester & Caplan, 1989). Finally, there is the persistent argument that patients may not be capable of appreciating information once it is provided. This argument does not eliminate the ethical duty to inform patients—it just makes it more challenging to provide the information in a way that is understandable and useful. One challenge is to provide information in advance of a crisis when persons are better able to process the information for rational decisions.

This strategy, though admirable, may not have any impact on reducing the use of expensive and questionably beneficial treatment. Patients may confuse what they want with what is good for them. Although individuals may get a profound sense of satisfaction in making their own choices from a staggering set of options, they may have to collectively limit those options for their overall benefit in the face of economic constraints.

Uncouple income from clinical decision making. There can be no doubt that financial incentives affect medical decisions. To uncouple physicians' incomes from clinical decision making thus allows a more feasible route to universal access to a basic minimum of care (Cassel, 1985). With few exceptions, nurses are not tied to any direct financial incentives in their relationship with patients. Therefore this conflict of interest generally is not a problem in nursing practice. When it is, it is interesting how nurses respond to the conflict between financial well-being and the patient's needs. For example, rationing is troubling to nurses in home care who are forced to refuse care to nonpaying patients or face the prospect of the home care agency going out of business (Reckling, 1989). Although nurses are aware that the financial health of the home care agency depends on patients who can pay, they still express concern regarding their ethical obligations to patients who need services but cannot afford to pay for them. Nurses often resolve problems such as this by visiting patients on their own time or "doctoring" the patient's record to make it appear that the patient is still eligible for services. These passive measures may take care of a few patients but do not address the broader problem of lack of reimbursable services for those who need them.

Establish a closed system. When resources are "saved" in one sector of the health care system, there is no guarantee that they will be better spent elsewhere. If a nurse says, "We can't have this patient in the intensive care unit because he will use up too many resources (i.e., equipment, supplies, nursing time and expertise) needed by other patients," the nurse may be standing on ethical ground if there actually is a patient who will indeed benefit more than the patient presently in the bed. This is predicated on the nurse's ability to recognize the subtleties of ethical analysis and the efficacy of the treatment the intensive care can provide. In the present system, nurses have little to no authority to divert resources from one area to another where the resources would be used to greater benefit.

In a closed system there is a fixed total resource within which trade-offs can occur. Discussions about what would be most beneficial to a community in comparison with the needs of an individual patient can take place only within a closed system. "Resources saved in one area can be directed elsewhere, and, conversely, if a need is identified, rational decisions can be made about where to cut back" (Cassel, 1985). This strategy would provide a framework for clinical and allocation decisions within organizations. Unlike the previous recommendations, the closed-system model seems to accept the necessity of rationing and proposes a system in which to implement it explicitly and ethically.

Because rationing can threaten the very lives of individuals, it requires strong ethical justification. Before any proposal for rationing can be taken seriously, those proposing rationing will have to demonstrate that the previously mentioned strategies and any other plausible proposals have been implemented and exhausted; that is, every reasonable attempt has been made to contain cost, improve efficiency, and eliminate waste.

Whether these strategies, individually or collectively, are capable of preventing the need for rationing is considered by some to be beside the point. According to this view, all of the previously mentioned measures are desirable but not sufficient to remedy the basic problem of providing access to health care. If a minimally basic level of health care is to be provided to all of the citizens in the United States, some degree of rationing cannot be avoided. A recognition of our limits and boundaries should be the point of departure for any plan for health care reform (Callahan, 1992).

Application of Ethical Principles

From this point on in the discussion, it is assumed that the need for rationing is demonstrable. The next step in ethical analysis is to explore the substantive nature of rationing. Regardless of the type of rationing proposal, additional basic, substantive questions should be addressed:

- Why is rationing ethically suspect?
- Is it ever ethically permissible to ration?
- Are there ethically legitimate reasons to withhold necessary treatment, limit it, or even withdraw it?

Rationing is ethically suspect because it runs counter to the assertions of several basic ethical principles.

Beneficence. The principle of beneficence requires that we do good and avoid harm. Of the two mandates, the duty to avoid harm is considered by some to be more binding. "The special training of health care workers—their *ability* to do good—is sometimes seen to impose upon them a responsibility or moral obligation to do good that is greater than that of others" (Mitchell & Achtenberg, 1984). It is a given in rationing that potentially beneficial services must be withheld from certain individuals. Those individuals who do not receive beneficial services are at best inconvenienced and at worst genuinely harmed. Thus rationing runs headlong into the duties of beneficence.

Respect for persons. The principle of respect for persons requires that individuals are treated with unconditional regard. The dignity of persons may be jeopardized when they are denied health care, especially if that health care is available to others. "People who experience rationing risk isolation from the community's general structures of mutual support and caring. They are thus separated from the majority of persons who do not experience similar rationing (Catholic Health Association, 1991).

Fidelity. The need to ration may run counter to the principle of fidelity. Fidelity has its roots in deontologic (from the Greek *deon*, or binding duty) theory. Deontologists argue that an act should be judged morally right or wrong because of qualities inherent in the act itself. Deontologists determine the rightness of an act insofar as it fulfills some principle of duty. Duties to others spring from relationships. Further, past actions or the history of relationships has moral worth. Fidelity is best understood as a "moral commitment to keep a promise or fulfill an action that creates an obligation beyond the usual respect due to persons and existing relationships" (Haddad & Kapp, 1991).

The potential conflict between fidelity and justice often becomes a clinical reality as is evidenced in the following case. It is acknowledged that this entire scenario could be subject to a variety of external factors beyond the ethical principles cited, such as economic considerations or the authority and power of the attending physicians. However, to highlight the ethical implications, these compounding variables have been deleted from the following case example:

> Steven Scott is the primary nurse for Mrs. Vottero, a 67-year-old with advanced cardiac decompensation, who is being maintained on intravenous amrinone therapy in the intensive care unit. Mr. Scott has been taking care of Mrs. Vottero for the past 5 days and has developed a warm and caring relationship with her. Mrs. Vottero is not expected to survive this episode of illness and has made it clear to her physician and nursing staff that she is ready to die. Though Mr. Scott has not explicitly stated so to Mrs. Vottero, he has made an implicit commitment to provide the best care possible to her until she dies.
>
> A new patient in cardiac shock must be admitted to the already full unit. The nursing and medical staff must choose which patient can be transferred to the general floor to make room for the new patient. Mrs. Vottero is a prime candidate for transfer because she is not expected to survive outside of the unit. However, Mr. Scott feels that he has a responsibility to Mrs. Vottero to provide the kind of care and attention that can be provided only in the intensive care unit. His sense of commitment may be heightened because he feels that his actions during Mrs. Vottero's hospitalization have encouraged her to trust him to provide comfort and be present during her last days of life.
>
> Yet this commitment must be weighed against the principle of justice (explained in greater detail in the following section), which requires that patients are to be treated equally unless there is a morally relevant reason not to do so. In this situation the new patient needs a higher level of nursing care and her prognosis is better than Mrs. Vottero's. Given these data, the principle of justice requires that Mrs. Vottero, who may have equal need but a grave prognosis, transfer from critical care to make room for the new patient. Mr. Scott cannot keep his promises to Mrs. Vottero and also meet the demands of justice. The principle of fidelity has deep roots in nursing practice and will be discussed again later.

Justice. In determining who will receive scarce resources and who will do without, one is relying on the principle of justice. The ideas of fairness, entitlement (who can legitimately claim what), and desert (who is worthy) are all central to our understanding of justice. The very heart of justice is fairness, which requires that every individual should be treated the same unless there is a morally relevant reason to treat him or her differently. Simply put, this principle of formal justice asserts that equals should be treated equally and unequals unequally. This is a good beginning but does not provide any information about what aspects of an individual should count when similarities and differences are being considered. What constitutes a relevant difference?

Entitlement pursues justice by giving everyone his or her due. "What persons are entitled to or can legitimately claim is based on certain morally relevant properties they possess, such as being productive or being in need" (Beauchamp & Childress, 1989).

Distributive justice deals with the allocation of burdens and benefits in society. The circumstances of distributive justice are the terms of cooperation of a society in which moderately self-interested individuals make claims against each other. The problems of distributive justice arise only in times of scarcity. Scarcity of important resources can lead to a breakdown in the ethical life of a community and require the adjudication of rights. Ethical principles, such as justice, function in this climate of competing claims and, at least on one level, provide guidance as to the right and good.

Material principles of justice identify relevant properties for distribution of scarce resources, such as nursing care. Ethically valid, material principles of distributive justice include giving each person an equal share, giving resources to those in need, and giving resources to those for whom they will do the most good. These material principles of justice can be used to help make rationing decisions. Criteria such as age, social worth, ability to pay, the absence of a disabling condition, gender, race, ethnic background, or religious belief should not be used to make rationing decisions. These criteria are morally irrelevant, according to deontological theory, when determining who will and will not receive beneficial health care resources.

The American Nurses Association Code for Nurses with Interpretive Statements states that prejudice is unacceptable under any circumstance. The Code states the following (ANA, 1985):

> The nurse provides services with respect for human dignity and the uniqueness of the client, unrestricted by considerations of social or economic status, personal attributes, or the nature of the health problem . . . The need for health care is universal, transcending all national, ethnic, racial, religious, cultural, political, educational, economic, developmental, personality, role, and sexual differences. Nursing care is delivered without prejudicial behavior.

Need is the most equitable criterion according to the Code. But need does not take care of the fact that often there are not enough health care resources to go around or enough to satisfy the wants of either patient or provider. A combination of ethically valid material principles might be more helpful, yet difficulties still are encountered when two principles conflict, such as need and prognosis. To determine which principle should take priority or how to decide when patients are equal in terms of the material principles that have been chosen, ethical theories must be considered.

Application of Ethical Theories

Because it has already been determined that there are situations in which rationing is ethically justifiable, the question of how to proceed fairly must be addressed. Of the numerous rationing procedures proposed, which is most fair? Most humane? In the discussion of material principles, fair screening criteria were established for selecting who will be eligible for receiving a scarce resource, such as an expert nurse's care in an intensive care unit. The most equitable criteria are need and prognosis or medical utility. Medical utility is understood as the "maximization of the welfare of patients in need of treatment" (Beauchamp & Childress, 1989). It is acknowledged that judgments about medical utility are subject to the values of the health care professionals involved and a great deal of uncertainty. Even with these limitations, medical utility criteria are still essential in determining fairly who will receive scarce resources and who will not.

If patients are equal in medical utility, how is choosing ethically to be accomplished? Before a discussion of the impersonal mechanisms of chance, such as lottery and queuing, the notion of social utility and its place in rationing deliberations is explored. "The ethical question is, then: 'Is it fair or just to employ criteria unrelated to the medical condition of patients in making allocation decisions and, if so, under what circumstances is it right to do so?'" (Macklin, 1985). A classic utilitarian would reply that all criteria that have an effect on outcome must be explored and included in the deliberation.

The theory of utilitarianism can take many forms, but basically it states that to choose the morally correct action, one must choose the action that produces the greatest possible good-to-evil ratio for all concerned. Any action is morally correct as long as it meets the rule of bringing about the greatest good for the greatest number. To arrive at a determination of what action will bring about the greatest good for the greatest number, utilitarianism requires that the possible outcomes of an action are predicted, both good and bad, to determine the one action that will bring about the most good (or in some cases, the least harm when no good can be achieved).

Thus a utilitarian would consider not only the criteria of medical utility, but also criteria that fall under the heading of social utility. The utilitarian perspective considers not only the needs and prognosis of a particular patient, but also the needs of society. From this perspective, institutions and health care professionals must consider the future contributions of a patient to society before investing valuable resources in him or her. Physicians have strongly contested the utilitarian perspective by arguing that they cannot serve two masters (i.e., society's needs and each patient's needs) in deciding what type and amount of medical care should be delivered (Levensky, 1984).

Numerous problems, both ethical and practical, exist regarding the application of a purely utilitarian model to rationing decisions. These problems include difficulty in developing acceptable criteria of social worth in a pluralistic society, violation of equal respect for persons, and denial of fair equality for opportunity (Beauchamp & Childress, 1989). Nurses have been specifically admonished not to consider the social worth of patients in their deliberations about who should receive what types of service. "Judgments as to the quality of life of individual patients are inappropriate and unsupportable (sic) and should never be used as a rationale for withholding and withdrawing essential care" (Levine, 1989). These sentiments are echoed in the Code for Nurses.

Even with these limitations and concerns, there are situations in which the social utility of patients may be the determining factor in rationing decisions. For example, of two liver transplant candidates who are in equal need and also equal in prognosis, one patient is a model citizen of the community and inherited the liver disease that led to the need for a transplant, whereas the other patient is a transient and a chronic alcoholic. The utilitarian would argue that the choice is clear: the greatest benefit to all concerned is to give the liver to the model citizen, in which case it will do the patient *and* society the most good.

Because a deontologist does not allow the inclusion of social utility criteria, the impersonal mechanisms of chance (e.g., a lottery) and queuing ("first come, first served") would come into play to resolve the conflict of choosing between the fictitious liver transplant candidates. If patients are truly equal in regard to medical utility, lottery and queuing are ethically viable options according to both deontological and utilitarian theories. However, utilitarians would see queuing or a lottery as rational only if it served to produce the greatest good for the greatest number.

In health care, it is more practical to use queuing as a rationing method. It is important to make certain that all individuals under consideration for a scarce resource have the same opportunity for "getting on line". The principle of justice requires that any roadblocks to access, such as lack of first dollar coverage, preventive care, or information about when to seek health care services, be corrected. Regardless of which theory is used to resolve rationing questions, it should not result in greater burdens falling on those who are least advantaged.

Dramatic examples, such as choosing who will and will not get a vital organ transplant, generally command more attention than those perceived as ordinary or routine. But the ethical concerns raised by the delivery of nursing care and the distribution of nursing staff in an institution are no less important than the life-and-death issues of determining organ transplant recipients. The ethical principles and theories presented in this section apply to rationing decisions at all levels.

DIFFERENCE BETWEEN RATIONING DECISIONS IN MEDICINE AND NURSING

The majority of the literature in health care rationing focuses on medical decisions and the dilemmas that physicians face. These dilemmas include the denial of treatments and procedures that run the gamut from life-saving to improving the quality of life (e.g., dialysis to chemotherapy). There is considerably less content in the nursing literature regarding rationing. The dilemmas identified in the literature are largely normative and include the following:

- Decisions about who should or should not be admitted to critical care units (Omery & Caswell, 1988; Fowler, 1989; Levine, 1989)
- Determination of patient assignments
- Safe delegation of responsibilities to support personnel
- Rationing equipment and supplies
- Patient placement (private room, proximity to nurses' station)
- Use of time (Botter & Dickey, 1989)

The dilemmas cited in the nursing literature show that it is not as much a matter of denying discrete, specific treatment to patients as it is a matter of reducing the amount and quality of care. Indeed, nurses may be involved in the literal denial of services to a particular patient or even a group of patients in a true triage situation. More often, nurses find themselves in the ethical quandary of diluting their services to patients—a sort of "soft" rationing—choosing between good care, necessary care, and potentially dangerous levels of care. This problem is compounded by insufficient knowledge of what nursing interventions are most effective.

In addition, nursing differs from medicine in that the scarce resource in question often is the nurse himself or herself, not a diagnostic test, medication, or surgical procedure. It is understood that physicians do have to decide how much time to spend with patients in the office or on rounds. But medicine has not identified as clearly and consistently as nursing that there is a therapeutic benefit, or healing, in the mere presence of the caregiver. Time spent with patients is not always functional or procedural for nurses. Time often is spent in providing comfort and presence.

The basic ethical question for nursing is: Is there harm in diluting what we know, at least implicitly, to be "good" nursing care? To answer this question, nursing must change the *implicit* to *explicit* to build a defensible argument against diluting nursing care. This question is explored further in the following discussion of rationing on a macroallocation and microallocation level in nursing practice.

MACROALLOCATION IN NURSING ADMINISTRATION

Society collectively decides how it will spend its resources in health care and other areas of mutual interest. An institution, whether an acute care facility or a home care agency, is a microcosm of society and thus undertakes allocation decisions that affect the institution as a whole. Macroallocation decisions are those that determine how much and what kind of services should be provided to what groups. Macroallocation decisions are considered to be distinct from microallocation or individual allocation decisions in two ways: the level at which the decision takes place and the amount of resources being considered.

Nurse administrators are responsible for many of the allocation and rationing decisions in health care institutions, such as dispersion of available nursing staff throughout a facility, limitation of admissions to specific units, and establishment of the desirable mix of professional (RN) and paraprofessional (LPN) nursing personnel. It is obvious from these few examples that the extent of a nurse administrator's ethical responsibility is broader than that of an individual nurse and thus has greater impact.

Nurse administrators must rely on numerous variables to predict and manage the need for nursing staff. Nurse administrators are ethically obligated to use sound methods to determine the best staffing levels for direct patient care. These methods, to be effective, must take into account workload, patient acuity, census, costs, staff preparation, staff mix, and even staff work preferences—just a few of the many variables that affect the nurse administrator's ability to safely and fairly distribute nursing staff (Philibert, 1986; Hashimoto, Bell, & Marshment, 1987; Parrinello, 1987; Shafer, Frauenthal, & Tower, 1987).

Even with the most sophisticated acuity system, the nurse administrator cannot completely plan for the staffing needs that often are identified by a seasoned nurse's "sixth sense" that a patient is about to "go bad" or that an entire psychiatric unit is about to "blow" (Benner & Tanner, 1987). The astute nurse administrator will heed the insights of expert clinicians to prevent the crisis situations that can lead to ethical quandaries.

In addition, nurse administrators have the ethical responsibility to see that nurses at the individual allocation level do not have to make decisions in a constant state of crisis. For example, if a critical care unit is filled to capacity and other patients need to be admitted, the nurse administrator, rather than the nurse at the bedside, is responsible for choosing from among the following alternatives:

- Transfer patients from the critical care unit to the general floor
- Raise the census of the critical care unit and thereby dilute nursing care
- Refuse admissions from the emergency department
- Cancel elective surgical procedures that could wait until the census declines
- Assign additional staff
- Implement a combination of these alternatives

Each of these options has ethical implications. The Von Stetina case is a tragic example of the consequences of raising the census and diluting nursing care (*Von Stetina v. Florida Medical Center*, 1982).

In this case, the plaintiff, Susan Von Stetina, a 27-year-old woman, was injured in an automobile accident and taken to an emergency room for trauma care. Posttrauma she developed respiratory distress syndrome and required intubation, mechanical ventilation, and pharmacologically induced paralysis for control of ventilation. Forty-eight hours posttrauma her condition improved but she remained ventilator dependent. At approximately 3 AM on the second day in the critical care unit, the patient was discovered to be severely bradycardic with an arterial carbon dioxide partial pressure of 85 mm Hg. Apparently the ventilator had been accidentally disconnected from the patient, the alarms were not functional, and the problem became apparent only when the electrocardiogram monitors picked up the bradycardia. Resuscitation was successful, but the patient remained permanently comatose.

What is important about the case for the purposes of the present discussion is that the intensive care nurses on duty that night were too busy taking care of newly admitted patients to provide safe care for Ms. Von Stetina and there is no indication that any administrator fulfilled his or her obligation to remedy this untenable situation. At the start of the shift, three registered nurses and one licensed practical nurse (who had been reassigned to the unit from a general floor) were in the unit to provide care for seven patients. Depending on the acuity of the patients in the unit, this ratio appears to approach the limits in which safe and adequate care can be provided. "Despite this situation, the hospital continued to admit patients (totaling five additional) to the ICU between the hours of midnight and 6 AM" (Englehardt & Rie, 1986). Evidence indicated that there were no administrative systems in place to deal rationally and ethically with just such a crisis situation. The ultimate tragedy in this case was that there were two patients in the critical care unit who were to be discharged voluntarily the next day and one who met the criteria of brain death.

It was not evident from the transcripts of the preceding case whether this was a common staffing pattern in the critical care unit at this particular hospital. It is possible that an emergency situation such as this could arise in any health care setting, which would ethically require the use of triage principles to resolve rationing dilemmas, but this should not be a daily occurrence. This last point highlights the fact that nurse administrators have ethical obligations not only to patients but to their employees.

A participative management process is essential if nurse administrators and staff nurses are to fulfill their separate but entwined ethical obligations. Although individual nurses have a responsibility to carry out their practice and to participate with their peers, nurse administrators as integrators and controllers of resources and as facilitators of outcomes must have the skills to bring together all of the processes previously described to implement ethical allocation decisions.

To ensure the involvement of nurse administrators and staff nurses in rationing decisions, there must be an ethical framework for decision making that takes into account the traditional principles and theories and the everyday practical knowledge of both groups. Nurses do not have to become experts in ethics but do need to do the following:

- Become familiar with the unique language and fundamental concepts of ethics

- Recognize the various sources of values in a pluralistic society
- Develop a coherent strategy for the analysis of an ethical problem
- Understand their own set of values—its cultural and psychological sources—and the influence of these values in the professional role
- Implement the principle of respect for persons so nurses can share control in decisions that affect their lives.

In addition, nurse administrators and staff nurses alike need to develop the ability to articulate their knowledge of ethics and approaches to resolving ethical problems so they can communicate with others involved in or affected by their decisions. The nurse must be able to present coherent justification for rationing decisions regardless of the level of responsibility within the health care organization. External support for dealing with ethical problems and developing justification for decisions also can be provided by an ethics consultant or an ethics committee when appropriate. The most valuable support in making these difficult decisions, however, often comes from peers who understand best the context of the problem. Thus continuing education in ethics for all staff members is highly beneficial.

REFERENCES

Aaron, H., & Schwartz, W.B. (1990). Rationing health care: The choice before us. *Science, 247*(4941), 418-422.

Aikens, L. (1922). *Studies in ethics for nurses*. Philadelphia: W.B. Saunders.

American Nurses Association (ANA). (1985). *Code for nurses with interpretive statements*. Kansas City, MO: Author.

American Nurses Association (ANA). (1991). *Nursing's agenda for health care reform*. Kansas City, MO: Author.

Axene, D.V., Doyle, R.L., & Feren, A.P. (October 4, 1991). *Analysis of medically unnecessary health care consumption*. Seattle: Milliman & Robertson.

Baily, M.A. (1984). "Rationing" and American health policy. *Journal of Health Policy and Law, 9*(3), 489-499.

Beauchamp, T.L., & Childress, J.F. (1989). *Principles of biomedical ethics* (3rd ed.). New York: Oxford University Press.

Benner, P., & Tanner, C. (1987). Clinical judgment: How expert nurses use intuition. *American Journal of Nursing, 87*(1), 23-31.

Botter, M.L., & Dickey, S.B. (1989). Allocation of resources: Nurses, the key decision makers. *Holistic Nursing Practice, 4*(1), 44-51.

Brook, R.H., & Lohr, K.N. (1986). Will we need to ration effective health care? *Issues in Science and Technology, 3*(1), 68-77.

Callahan, D. (1990). Rationing medical progress: The way to affordable health care. *New England Journal of Medicine, 322*(25), 1810-1813.

Callahan, D. (1992). Symbols, rationality, and justice: Rationing health care. *American Journal of Law and Medicine, 18*(1&2), 1-13.

Cassel, C.K. (1985). Doctors and allocation decisions: A new role in Medicare. *Journal of Health Policy and Law, 10*(3), 549-564.

Cassell, E.J. (1978). Informed consent in the therapeutic relationship: Clinical aspects. In W.T. Reich (Ed.), *Encyclopedia of bioethics*. New York: Macmillan.

Catholic Health Association. (1991). *With justice for all?*, St. Louis: Author.

Englehardt, H.T., & Rie, M.A. (1986). Intensive care units, scarce resources, and conflicting principles of justice. *Journal of the American Medical Association, 255*(9), 1159-1164.

Fowler, M.D.M. (1989). Biographic limits to life-extending technology. *Heart and Lung, 18*(2), 203-205.

Friedman, E. (1986). Doctors and rationing: The end of the honor system. *Primary Care, 13*(2), 349-364.

Haddad, A.M., & Kapp, M.B. (1991). Theoretical bases for ethics and law. In A.M. Haddad and M.B. Kapp (Eds.), *Ethical and legal issues in home health care*, East Norwalk, CT: Appleton & Lange.

Hashimoto, F., Bell, S., & Marshment, S. (1987). A computer simulation program to facilitate budgeting and staffing decisions in an intensive care unit. *Critical Care Medicine, 15*(3), 256-259.

Kapp, M.B. (1989). Health care tradeoffs based on age: Ethically confronting the "R" word. *The Pharos of Alpha Omega Alpha, 52*(3), 2-7.

Levensky, N.G. (1984). The doctor's master. *New England Journal of Medicine, 311*(24), 1573-1575.

Levine, M.E. (1989). Ration or rescue: The elderly patient in critical care. *Critical Care Quarterly, 12*(1), 82-89.

Macklin, R. (1985). Are we in the lifeboat yet? Allocation and rationing of medical resources. *Social Research, 52*(3), 607-613.

Merrill, J.C., & Cohen, A.B. (1987). The emperor's new clothes: Unraveling the myths about rationing. *Inquiry, 24*(2), 105-109.

Mitchell, C., & Achtenberg, B. (1984). Study guide: Code gray, Boston: Fanlight Productions.

Morreim, E.H. (1988). Cost containment: Challenging fidelity and justice. *Hastings Center Report, 18*(6), 20-25.

Omery, A., & Caswell, D. (1988). A nursing perspective of the ethical issues surrounding liver transplanation. *Heart and Lung, 17*(6 pt. 1), 626-631.

Parrinello, K.M. (1987). Accounting for patient acuity in an ambulatory surgery center. *Nursing Economic$, 5*(4), 167-172.

Philibert, M.B. (1986). Patient acuity systems: Taking the measure of nursing care. *Nursing Management, 17*(11), 60-61.

Priester, R., & Caplan, A.L. (1989). Ethics, cost containment, and the allocation of scarce resources. *Investigative Radiology, 24*(11), 918-926.

Reckling, J.B. (1989). Abandonment of patients by home health nursing agencies. *Advances in Nursing Science, 11*(3), 70-81.

Reinhardt, U.E. (1987). Rationing despite surplus: A paradox as American as apple pie? *HealthSpan, 4*(2), 13-18.

Shafer, P.L., Frauenthal, B.J., & Tower, C. (1987). Measuring nursing costs with patient acuity data. *Topics in Health Care Financing, 13*(4), 20-31.

Von Stetina v. Florida Medical Center, 2 Fla. Supp. 2d 55 (Fla. 17th Cir 1982), 436 So. Rptr. 2d 1022 (1983), *Florida Law Weekly, 10* (May 24, 1985), 286.

Wiener, J.M. (1992). Oregon's plan for health care rationing. *The Brookings Review, 10*(1), 26-31.

CHAPTER 3

Cost Versus Quality of Health Care

Bobbie Berkowitz

This chapter addresses the dilemma of controlling cost while maintaining quality of health care. The assumptions of universal access and cost control are the basis for a review of how quality is defined, the factors that influence a definition of quality, and what can be anticipated in a rationed-care marketplace. The potential for contribution of nurse administrators to achieving quality at a reasonable cost is included.

As we begin the discussion of cost versus quality of health care and its relationship to rationing, let us assume that we are striving for universal access to health care. We will assume that universal access is sound public policy because without it we cannot control the costs of health care nor guarantee an acceptable level of quality. Universal access to health care for the entire population will, of course, have a price tag. Managing that price tag introduces the subject of rationing.

The debate over health policy, including rationing, occurs every day in the public and political arenas. The public debate tells us that the increased cost of health care driven by an exaggerated entrepreneurial spirit may lead to decreased quality as priorities are skewed. On the other hand, haphazard decreased spending on health care leads to decreased quality of services

Chief of Nursing Services, Seattle-King County Department of Public Health, 110 Prefontaine Place South—Suite 600, Seattle, WA 98104-4600

Series on Nursing Administration—Volume 6, 1994

and products and, in some cases, total lack of health care. These scenarios have led to rationing, either both deliberate and planned, as in the case of Oregon, or as a consequence of system failure, as in the case of the 36 million Americans who have no health care coverage.

The public's eye is on rationing, and the public debate is setting the stage for health care policy. Several examples can be found in three recent news stories. Cost versus quality was explored by Wilson (1992a) in a *Seattle Times* story, "Prescription for Profit," in which he described the decreased quality and increased costs of physician referrals to self-owned diagnostic centers and laboratories. This same decline in quality as a result of joint ventures was reported by Ahern and Scott (1992). The ability to balance quality and cost was reported by Marmor and Godfrey (1992) in a *New York Times* OP-ED about the successes of Canada's model of health care. A *Seattle Times* editorial (Wilson, 1992b) reported that cost control requires rationing. This editorial suggested that the only way to ensure affordable access to health services for the uninsured is to limit medical services. These somewhat contradictory public opinions, along with policy themes generated from Oregon's experience with rationing, are explored in this chapter on cost versus quality of health care rationing.

The story of rationing has unfolded in Oregon over the past several years. The Oregon Health Services Commission was charged with the mission of increasing access to health care for approximately 400,000 of its population with limited or no access to health care. The initial activity focused on Oregon's Medicaid population. The strategy set forth by the Oregon legislature was to provide the governor of Oregon with a prioritized list of health services with accompanying actuarial data determining the cost of providing these services (Executive Summary, 1990).

Hadorn (1991a,b) examined the Oregon Health Services Commission's draft priority list of health services with an eye to what he calls the "rule of rescue." This rule, which propels the system toward a perceived duty to save a threatened life, could work against a priority list developed by a cost-effectiveness strategy. The pressure to provide a service to save a life may far outweigh its ranking on a priority list.

The cost and quality outcomes of Oregon's plan are yet to be experienced, although speculation of those outcomes exists. Outcomes were a consideration when the Oregon plan was developed. The outcomes of the various condition/treatment pairs were considered in relation to health status, cost effectiveness, and quality of life. Hadorn (1991a,b) was critical of the use of quality of life indicators to develop public policy, such as the Oregon plan, because measures of quality of life do not necessarily correlate with individuals' perceived quality of life. Public policy based on the judgments of one set of individuals about the quality of life of others can lead to discrimination. Eddy (1991a) proposed that a disturbing outcome of the Oregon plan will be continued escalating costs of health care as a result of a lack of system-wide cost controls and a continued lack of access for a large percentage or Oregon's poor who do not qualify for Medicaid. He did state that despite these drawbacks, Oregon has focused our attention as a nation on both the health care crisis and the problems associated with the Medicaid system.

For nurse administrators to join the debate and participate in and guide the development of solutions for controlling the costs of health care while assuring quality, they need to become familiar with four current issues related to the cost and quality of rationing:

- The financial impact of rationing health care
- The affordability and cost of quality
- Who or what is rationed
- The marketplace variables that influence cost and quality outcomes of the health system.

Each of these issues is examined for what it can tell nursing administration about strategies and rationale for future decisions about health care cost and quality.

FINANCIAL IMPACT OF RATIONING

Rationing policies may be structured in multiple ways with varying outcomes. For example, if policy is structured so that rationing is at the benefit level, it is the comprehensiveness of the benefit that is rationed. According to Grogan (1992) this tends to be the type of rationing policy found in the United States today. This type of policy can lead to two strategies. One strategy is to ration by setting a minimum benefit package for a specific group of individuals. Another strategy is to shift resources from low-priority services for covered individuals to high-priority services for uncovered individuals. This is basically what Oregon has proposed (Eddy, 1991b). A second structure limits certain services, such as medical technology and devices or organ transplants, through reimbursement payments that restrict the supply of these services or procedures. An alternate to a policy of benefit rationing is to provide comprehensive benefits and universal access that are managed through institutional and governmental policy (Grogan, 1992). This is closer to the type of policy that the Washington State Health Care Commission (1992) has pursued. It is also the type of policy proposed by the Physicians for a National Health Program (Grumbach, Bodenheimer, Himmelstein, & Woolhandler, 1991).

Setting minimum benefits for health services has a number of impacts on the cost and quality of health care and, potentially, on nursing practice. Three examples of potential financial risks associated with rationing are explored:

- Inability to manage total health care expenditures

- Limiting access to a range of providers
- Supplemental benefits

There seems to be agreement about at least two issues related to the costs of our health care system. The first issue is that too much money is spent on health care. Recent statistics from the U.S. General Accounting Office (1992a) stated that in 1991 more than $700 billion was spent on health care, or 13% of the gross national product. In 1975 $125 billion was spent. One can see that the cost has been rising steadily. The second issue is that the costs are not equally distributed nor are services equally received by those who need them. The number of uninsured individuals increased from approximately 27 million in 1982 to 36 million in 1992. It is imperative that the strategies for health care reform have sound cost control policies. With this in mind, consider how much of the total health care expenditures could potentially be controlled with a rationed minimum benefit package.

Experience with various models of health system design and health reform proposals suggests that piecemeal reform neither assures universal access nor accomplishes significant cost control. Controls on costs must be applied to as much of the system as possible to achieve savings that will not be spent immediately in another part of the system. This is the danger of applying the principles of rationing to only a segment of the population or a portion of health services. The costs of those services not rationed will continue unchecked, and those groups of individuals not subjected to rationing will continue utilization rates that add to health care costs. Given these potential financial impacts of rationing, proposals that provide access to a comprehensive set of personal health services plus access to a range of public health services with significant cost controls at the premium and point of service level and regulation at the system and insurance plan level stand a much better chance of controlling total health care expenditures.

Nurses are cost-effective providers of care. The incentives in nursing do not motivate the profession toward unnecessary or inappropriate care. Quality does motivate nurses to provide some interventions over others, especially when the interventions are less invasive. The cost effectiveness of nurse practitioners with prescriptive authority is a good example.

The exquisite combination of medical and nursing knowledge that nurse practitioners possess, their unique contribution to the health care system, and their distinctive approach to health care for individuals and families make them highly valuable resources. The important contribution nurse practitioners bring to their clients' health care is what they bring as nurses—the commitment to approaching human beings holistically, recognizing that they are diverse and dynamic individuals. The cost effectiveness of nurse practitioners comes from the fact that they can deliver a full range of services, including providing prescriptions for medications, as well as the consumer education necessary for clients to use resources effectively. The health conditions of those who use primary care have become increasingly acute over the past 10 years. Their health care problems and lack of financial resources put them at high risk of facing long-term individual and family crises. The addition of prescriptive authority to the scope of the nurse prac- titioner in a number of states in recent years has enabled nurse practitioners to offer primary care services to high-risk populations who, because of their socioeconomic situation and dysfunctional family patterns, are not always welcome in the private provider's office. This trend is growing, and although entitlement programs are beginning to increase the eligibility limits for low-income families, finding primary care continues to be difficult for them. Despite the effectiveness of nurse practitioners, their services often are excluded from insurance plans and hospital privileges often are denied. Restrictive nurse practice acts can work to limit nurse practitioners' ability to provide a full range of services. The restrictions in nurse practice acts fre- quently are the result of pressure from our colleagues in medicine. If these types of restrictions were placed within a benefit package because of rationing, access would be limited to more costly providers and reduce the opportunities for individuals to experience the comprehensive, quality, and cost-effective care of nurse practitioners.

There is evidence that nurses are able to perform many procedures that, if billed properly, could cost the system less. Griffith, Thomas, and Griffith (1991) found that a significant number of the procedures coded for physi- cian payments are performed by registered nurses. Another issue immedi- ately surfaces from this finding—namely that nurses clearly are not being paid equal rates for equal services.

The third financial outcome of rationing has to do with the offering of supplemental benefits packages. The challenge to design a package of health services that is perceived as affordable in the marketplace necessitat- ed the exclusion of services heretofore deemed essential. Two primary actions follow: supplemental insurance packages that fill the service "gap" are offered; and the public system develops a series of categorical programs that provide specific services to specific groups of people. Classic exam- ples of supplemental benefit packages include vision, dental, medigap, and long-term care coverage. The proliferation of supplemental and categorical programs can lead to increased complexity and expense in the system. Instead, a universal comprehensive package that offers all essential services with cost-sharing mechanisms based on ability to pay is an approach that can reduce the number of separate programs that must be managed and marketed.

The notion of affordability must embrace quality as well as the scope of the benefits package. This is the content of the next section on affordability of quality.

AFFORDABILITY AND COST OF QUALITY

The quality of a health care system can be judged in part by the health of its people and the price of its services. The quality of our own system must be questioned. Does a quality system deny a poor woman access to prenatal care and then spend hundreds of thousands of dollars to save her low-birth-weight premature infant? Is a quality system one that does not guarantee health care access to all of its citizens? South Africa and the United States are the only developed countries that share this distinction (Woolhandler & Himmelstein, 1989). Does a quality system have the finest health care technology available in the world but rank twenty-first in infant mortality, seventeenth in male life expectancy, and sixteenth in female life expectancy? These U.S. statistics taken from a *Consumer Reports* article were part of the prediction that of the $817 billion the United States would spend on health care in 1992, $200 billion would be wasted on unnecessary administrative and medical procedures ("Health Care Dollars," 1992.) Does this sound like a quality system?

The quality of a system's health is affected by many factors: health status of the population, life-style choices, environmental status, socioeconomic status of individuals, and financial resources available for health-related research are just a few (Graig, 1991). The cost of our system is also a reflection of its quality. The relationship between cost and quality, as pointed out by Lundberg (1992), may actually be a negative one—as costs go up, quality goes down. Or, in the case of the high-volume provision of specialized technology, lower costs can lead to higher quality. Examples of this in relation to high volumes of radiologic services like mammography and magnetic resonance imaging were described by the U.S. General Accounting Office (1992b). They found that concentrated high-volume utilization of these technologies contributed to increased quality as providers became experts through experience and costs decreased as a result of concentrating the volume. A reformed health care system must use quality as a factor more powerful in competition than risk aversion. Risk avoidance by insurance companies who shift high-risk individuals out of their plans and into risk pools capitalize on their young and healthy enrollees, but the high-risk individual faces very costly premiums or cancellation of policies. Quality along with effectiveness of health care should enhance the price sensitivity of health insurance.

Quality as a factor of the system and not just of the service takes into account whether individuals, once assured access through an insurance plan or some other payment mechanism, can actually obtain the health service. Guaranteed access does not necessarily ensure that the individual receives the health care. Take, for example, the non-English-speaking family whose child is suffering with chronic otitis media. The family may walk through the door of the clinic and into the examination room, but if a translator is not present, the quality of care may be compromised simply because the provider cannot understand all of the information about the patient and the family cannot understand the health care teaching. This is an example of what is known as *nonfinancial barriers to care*. These barriers are nonfinancial because they are independent of financial access to care but they cost the system in terms of inappropriate or inadequate care as a result of an individual's inability to access the care needed because of demographic, geographic, transportation, language, cultural, or racial barriers. Ginzberg and Ostow (1991) described specific barriers to access that can lead to poor quality outcomes. They stated that the preference physicians show for patients who are not poor, minorities, or geographically isolated is an indicator that physicians themselves can block access. They point to the already overstressed public system of hospitals, community clinics, and public health centers as evidence that increasing access will place additional burdens on these programs without relief from the private sector.

A quality system considers the cost effectiveness of a variety of provider types, not just the traditional medical model. Access should be to the health service itself, leaving the individual to choose which qualified provider he or she wants to visit. Incentives can be built into the system for the individual to pair cost effectiveness with provider type and quality of expected outcomes. An example of cost effectiveness, quality, and provider type is nicely illustrated in a recent report from Washington State's First Steps Program. The First Steps Program was developed to ensure both access and quality outcomes to low-income women in need of prenatal care. Cawthon (1992) reported that in Medicaid births from July 1989 to December 1990, women who received prenatal care from certified nurse or licensed midwives had the lowest rates of low-birth-weight infants and low percentages of both social and medical risk factors. Normal birth weight and low social and medical risk factors naturally correlate. However, if this group of women chose prenatal care from nurse midwives, this data would suggest they not only would have positive birth outcomes, but also would have chosen cost-effective care.

Nurse administrators are experts at establishing quality health programs. It has been only recently that nurse administrators also have been equally concerned about the cost effectiveness of services. This is not to say that nurse administrators have not always been concerned about costs. The financial viability of the institutions in which nurse administrators work has always been part of their management expectations. However, nurse administrators have not consistently documented nursing outcomes in relation to cost (Holzemer, 1990). Cost effectiveness now implies that costs and quality must be part of the same equation, and cost savings that sacrifice quality or spending increases that do not improve quality should no longer be tolerated. This applies to the principles of rationing as well. Rationing policies that determine what or who is rationed must be viewed in light of their relationship to quality.

WHO OR WHAT IS RATIONED?

Rationing at its most basic means equally distributing a scarce resource. When rationing is applied to health care, this meaning must be examined carefully. This section examines the issues involved in the question of who or what is rationed.

The initial question becomes, Must we ration at all? Let us assume that because the United States has always either intentionally or unintentionally rationed health care in one form or another, it probably will continue to do so. This assumption allows us to examine the underlying principles of rationing. One underlying principle is that a scarcity exists for a resource, which must then be apportioned among individuals. In the case of health care, what is the scarce resource? Are the services, providers of health care, or the means to pay for health care scarce? The answer is all three. The largest deficit in this equation has become the financial resources to pay for health care, or, as was pointed out earlier, the distribution of financial resources. The most significant fiscal hardship has occurred in the public sector, which attempts to cover the uninsured and underinsured. In many parts of the country, especially in rural America, health care providers also are scarce. For example, the Washington State Health Personnel Resource Planning Committee (1992) studied eight health care professions (including nursing) that were in short supply. The short supply was thought to contribute to problems associated with access to health care.

Health care that is provided but not compensated for is becoming scarce. This uncompensated care or charity care has become a major burden, especially to hospitals (Washington State Department of Health, 1992). This phenomenon has led to major cost shifting between the nonpayors and the payors. As the payors in the system balk at supporting uncompensated care through the costs of the premiums they pay to insurance companies, providers and hospitals are less willing to provide care for nonpaying patients (Perkins & Perkins, 1992). Scarce health services also exist relative to some of the high technology medical devices and services. Organs for transplant often are in short supply. Experimental drugs usually are limited and therefore are perceived to be a scarce resource.

Not all of these scarce resources are amenable to fluctuations in the health industry marketplace nor can they be increased by health care reform. For example, the availability of organs for transplant will not necessarily be improved by decreasing the cost of transplants. Decreasing the cost of transplants would, however, have an effect on the equal distribution of this particular scarce resource. If all individuals had equal financial access to organ transplants, rationing decisions could be made on the basis of appropriateness and effectiveness of the transplant for the particular individual.

A second underlying principle of rationing has to do with the ethical considerations of equal distribution. Equal distribution requires that consensus has been achieved regarding the equality of the distribution; otherwise "equal" is a perception of either the distributor or the receiver of the resource. Under equal distribution, the additional consideration exists that not all may actually receive the resource. This can lead to the perception that some are more equal than others. The ethics principle by virtue of its importance to our American social norms becomes part of the policy driving health care reform and rationing. Dougherty (1991) related the ethics of access to health care to three values. The first he described as the requirement for a minimum level of care for all because we believe that health is a prerequisite to the enjoyment of life and liberty. The second value is that of solidarity—a sense that access to health care is a benefit of citizenship in an advanced society. The third value is for a productive society and the social utility of providing health care as a way of ensuring this value. These values frame the ethical decisions leading to what and how much health care will meet our societal needs.

Given these two principles, we can approach the question of who or what gets rationed in several ways. We examine two methods in particular. Each method emphasizes the scarcity of financial resources, but the focal points of equal distribution are different.

Method one uses the *minimum set of health services for all* approach. Each individual is assured a basic set of services either through a public-sponsored system for low-income individuals or through private- or employer-purchased plans. In this method, basic health services are distributed equally to all. To manage fiscal scarcity, we could propose to increase taxes. To avoid cost shifting to private plans, we could set a cap on the price of the basic set of services. This would control some of the costs associated with providing a basic set of health services to all. Two parts of this plan are rationed. Financial resources are rationed—insurers may charge only a set price for the plan; and services that fall outside the basic set are rationed to those who can afford to purchase supplemental plans. Individuals requiring those supplemental services will either (1) be denied the services, (2) be provided the services free of charge, or (3) purchase them. The overwhelming challenge here is to decide what services are included in a basic plan. Traditionally, many of these basic plans leave out preventive care, prescription drugs, medical equipment and supplies, mental health, chemical dependency treatment, long-term care, prenatal care, and organ transplants. Many argue that these are basic and essential services if you happen to require them.

Method two sets up a comprehensive set of services for all, including preventative and public health services. Individuals are assured access through a health plan financed by individuals, employers, and a public tax structure. To control costs a capitated budget is set on insurance premiums, managed care is required, and a regulatory structure controls administrative costs, assures service quality, and sets the benefit levels. In this system all health services are distributed equally, but those individuals who can afford it will pay a larger portion of the financial burden through premium share, deductibles, and point-of-service cost sharing. Critics of this approach argue that this system is not affordable and regulatory control is unacceptable. An advantage to this method is that by covering all services, the majority of costs in the health care system can be controlled.

In each of the scenarios just described, nurse administrators will have a part. "Basic" services may imply a set of services in which the primary skills of nurses will not be used. Nurses are highly skilled in prevention strategies, health promotion activities, occupational health programs, patient and community education, and long-term and prenatal care. Many nurses function as independent practitioners in mental health and chemical dependency treatment programs. Nurses are certainly central in acute and emergency medical care but can be very influential on quality when they are allowed to practice nursing independent of the medical model structure. A basic plan that limits access to prevention services, education, and chronic and long-term care also limits the opportunities for access to nurses. A comprehensive plan, although allowing access to a variety of services, must be managed to control costs. Here again, nurses are skilled providers of consumer education, case management, utilization review, quality improvement, and numerous other strategies to promote quality, efficiently utilize resources, and ensure access.

The marketplace is a primary factor in deciding which of these methods could become public policy. In the next section we review the marketplace variables that can help or hinder access to services and quality.

MARKETPLACE VARIABLES

As shown in the previous section, the supply of health care services and certain provider types is limited and there is an unlimited demand for health services. This should provide the perfect environment for the marketplace. The marketplace has not been the perfect environment for health care, however. This section examines some of the reasons and potential solutions.

Who and what dominates the health industry? Grace (1990) named at least four groups: (1) hospitals, (2) physicians, (3) private insurance companies, and (4) consumers. She pointed to the overcapacity of hospitals, the surplus and salaries of highly specialized providers, the perverse incentives of insurance reimbursement policies, and the limited information and decision-making power given to consumers by health care providers as the major contributors to the escalation of health care costs. Within this framework the marketplace has not worked as it should to balance supply and demand, introduce price sensitivity, and promote quality and efficiency. As Enthoven (1992) said, "The U.S. medical care system was not organized for quality and economy. It was organized to meet the conflicting professional and financial interests of doctors, hospitals, and insurance companies. . . ." Depending on these dynamics to fix the health care industry should leave us skeptical. Are there variables in the marketplace that can assist the health industry in controlling costs? The answer depends on why we turn to the market. Let us explore the strategies of supply and demand and competition.

Although physician fees make up only 20% of health expenditures, their decisions drive approximately 80% of the costs (Grace, 1990). The salaries of physicians are 2 to 3 times those of professionals with comparable educational requirements. If the supply of physicians increases, the reduction in demand should reduce these system costs. The same should hold true for medical technology. In reality, the opposite has occurred. The increase in the supply of physicians has occurred in the high-cost specialties instead of in cost-effective primary care (Grace, 1990). The services and referrals supplied by these specialists tend to be the higher-technology variety, thereby driving the demand for technology. Consumers have come to expect such life-extending services (Booth, 1985).

Competition usually serves to increase the price sensitivity of consumers and the quality and efficiency of the product of services. In health care, however, insurance companies serving as third-party payors have all but removed price sensitivity from consumers. The majority of consumers have relatively limited knowledge of the costs of services. There is no incentive to choose health services based on cost and therefore no incentive to hold down costs. Fees for services based on charges rather than costs drive up prices even further. Lawrence (1991) proposed that the only way to readjust these disincentives for cost and quality is to promote organized, integrated care systems that incorporate financial incentives for providers, insurers, and consumers. Rabkin (1991) envisioned a system in which negotiated agreements among payors, providers, and consumers would control the extent and quality of care, capitated payments, and controls on risk. Matula (1991) suggested that to control costs, consumers must reduce their dependency on high-cost, high-technology medical interventions and increase their demand for cost-effective prevention services. Can the marketplace assist us in moving toward the goals cited by these three authors?

Enthoven (1992) challenges us with a proposal worth reviewing. Our ability to act on his proposal may depend on how much faith we have in the marketplace. He proposed a system of health care organizations that integrate the functions of providing care and insurance. In this way providers share the risk of inefficient and costly care. He proposed a regulatory structure that sets the standards by which medical practice and technology is deemed effective and sets a standard uniform benefit package. He also proposed managed competition. Enthoven recommended a health insurance purchasing corporation that (1) qualifies competitors through their ability to provide high-quality, cost-effective care, (2) runs open enrollments, (3) integrates price-conscious incentives for consumers, (4) standardizes benefits, and (5) compensates plans that enroll a disproportional share of high-risk individuals. Through this system, Enthoven hopes to bring market forces to bear on incentives for high-quality economic care, favorable health outcomes, an emphasis on prevention, total quality management, selection of providers based on quality and efficient practice patterns, concentrated complex procedures in high-volume centers, and decision making about interventions based on maximum benefit to the patient.

Evaluating plans like Enthoven's requires sophisticated knowledge about the economics of health care. Gaining this knowledge is a good place for nurse administrators to begin in addressing strategies for managing cost and quality.

STRATEGIES FOR NURSE ADMINISTRATORS

As the United States moves toward health care reform, the systems that provide the health services will be consulted for strategies to manage reform. Nurse administrators will be called on to offer their leadership in areas that require the delicate balance of cost and quality. Quality programming that assumes cost as a factor will be required. As Beyers (1986) pointed out, in the past, quality assurance expertise was rarely recognized in the health care hierarchy. Now quality assurance systems affect governance, administration and management, patient response data, and strategic planning. Decision making among technologies that weighs patient outcomes with the cost of the service will become the norm. Assisting the system and the individual in making cost-conscious choices about health care will become a skill nurses provide. The likelihood that nursing will be ready for this challenge is good. The amount of nursing literature on quality is vast, and the amount of literature on balancing cost and quality is growing. This section reviews strategies for managing cost and quality by nurse administrators. Within the past 3 years the literature in nursing, medicine, public health, public policy, economics, and management has been flooded with articles, books, reports, and proposals on health care reform. Nursing will be wise to combine its wisdom with that of its colleagues as nurses position themselves to provide a significant contribution to health care reform.

Creating and managing change is what we face as health care reform becomes an attainable reality. In addition, we should prepare ourselves for a large investment in consumer education. We must break our bonds with the traditional systems that have promoted and profited from the health care industry and create systems that promote cost-effective services and quality outcomes in a managed environment. Mitchell, Krueger, and Moody (1990) cited three themes that point to nursing as the change agents of reform: (1) more nurses than any other type of provider are working within the health care industry; (2) nursing has traditionally been a voice for the moral and ethical issues of equal access; and (3) nursing has extensive experience in coordinating disparate segments of the health system to benefit individuals and society. Let us turn to some examples in the literature in which nurse administrators, as change agents, have made significant impact on cost and quality of health care.

Designing systems that lead to efficiency and quality is the future of nursing administration. Curran and Smeltzer (1991) described a process of improving the operations of an institution. This process analyzed external and internal comparisons of efficiency based on financial data. The process set goals for improvement in costs and quality. Implementation relied heavily on monitoring and evaluation of cost and quality indicators. According to the authors, this process led to a business-like organizational culture with defined goals and decentralized authority. It streamlined the work of nursing staff with resultant improved job satisfaction.

The successes of managed care cited by Wood, Bailey, and Tilkemeier (1992) as quality and efficient resource utilization are compatible with the goals of nursing management. These authors cited the example of Memorial Hospital of Rhode Island's "care map." The success of this system, which integrated managed care and quality improvement, was measured in quality, resource utilization, and length of stay.

Masters and Schmele (1991) point to total quality management (TQM) as a premium method for improving quality and decreasing costs in health care. They predict that with TQM in place, an institution can significantly reduce system waste. The authors cited 11 advantages of TQM:

- Increased quality
- Increased productivity
- Increased savings in time and money
- Increased teamwork
- Increased employee morale
- Employee ownership of the improvement process
- Compliance with accreditation standards
- Decreased rework
- Decreased employee turnover
- Decreased recruitment costs
- Decreased overall costs

Two methods for integrating cost variables into quality assurance activities were described by Larson and Peters (1986). They supported using cost-benefit and cost-effectiveness analyses, depending on the purpose of the analysis, to make decisions about alternatives in quality improvements, evaluate the consequences of each alternative, and evaluate the final decision.

Each of these examples requires nurse administrators to be informed, strategically placed in positions of power within institutions, visionary, and challenged by change. There is no substitute in the cost-quality balance for quality. Nurse administrators are masters at quality, and this is the opportunity of our future.

SUMMARY

As we move toward the twenty-first century our society no longer should tolerate a health system that is biased, sexist, racist, and homophobic. If this seems a harsh criticism, review the way we promote, package, sell, and pay for our health system. Review the incentives in the current system to shift individuals who are in the most need out of the private system. Review the business strategies used by insurance companies to avoid risk and increase profits. Addressing the costs and quality of our system in a sensitive, ethical, and equal way can promote the underlying principle of rationing—equal distribution of a scarce resource—in a way that ensures universal access.

Nurse administrators need to rally their courage to promote the kind of quality that leads to a fair and just health system. They need to justify quality that uses the cost effectiveness and efficiency of nursing services. They need to become experts at quality systems that manage utilization, not exclusion. When nurse administrators are asked if this type of quality is affordable, let us hope they answer a resounding *absolutely*!

REFERENCES

Ahern, M., & Scott, E. (1992). Effects of physician joint ventures on health care costs, access, and quality: Exploring some issues. *Nursing Economics, 10,* 101-109.

Beyers, M. (1986). Cost and quality: Balancing the issues through management. *Journal of Nursing Quality Assurance, 1,* 47-54.

Booth, R. (1985). Financing mechanisms for health care: Impact on nursing services. *Journal of Professional Nursing, 1*(1), 34-40.

Cawthon, L. (1992). Specialty of prenatal care providers. II. *First Steps Database, 3*(2). Olympia, WA: Washington State Department of Health.

Curran, C., & Smeltzer, C. (1991). Operation improvement: Efficiencies and quality. *Journal of Nursing Quality Assurance, 5,* 1-6.

Dougherty, C. (1991). Setting health care priorities. *Hastings Center Report, 21*(3), 1-10.

Eddy, D. (1991a). What's going on in Oregon? *Journal of the American Medical Association, 266,* 417-420.

Eddy, D. (1991b). Oregon's plan: Should it be approved? *Journal of the American Medical Association, 266,* 2439-2445.

Enthoven, A. (1992). Can health care costs be contained? *World Monitor, 5,* 34-39.

Executive summary. (1990). *Oregon Health Services Commission Preliminary Report,* Salem, Oregon.

Ginzberg, E., & Ostow, M. (1991). Beyond universal health insurance to effective health care. *Journal of the American Medical Association, 265,* 2559-2562.

Griffith, H., Thomas, N., & Griffith, L. (1991). MDs bill for these routine nursing tasks. *American Journal of Nursing, 91,* 22-27.

Grace, H. (1990). Can health care costs be contained? *Nursing and Health Care, 11,* 125-129.

Graig, L. (1991). U.S. health care crisis: Moving towards a national solution? In *Health of nations: An international perspective on U.S. health care reform* (pp. 17-54). Washington, D.C.: Wyatt.

Grogan, C. (1992). Deciding on access and levels of care: A comparison of Canada, Britain, Germany, and the United States. *Journal of Health Politics, Policy, and Law, 17,* 213-232.

Grumbach, K., Bodenheimer, T., Himmelstein, D., & Woolhandler, S. (1991). Liberal benefits, conservative spending. *Journal of the American Medical Association, 265,* 2549-2553.

Hadorn, D. (1991a). Setting health care priorities in Oregon: Cost effectiveness meets the rule of rescue. *Journal of the American Medical Association, 265,* 2218-2225.

Hadorn, D. (1991b). The Oregon priority-setting exercise: Quality of life and public policy. *Hastings Center Report, 21*(3), 11-16.

Health care dollars. (1992). *Consumer Reports, July*, 435-448.

Holzemer, W. (1990). Quality and cost of nursing care: Is anybody out there listening? *Nursing and Health Care, 11*, 412-415.

Larson, E., & Peters, D. (1986). Integrating cost analyses in quality assurance. *Journal of Nursing Quality Assurance, 1*, 1-7.

Lawrence, D. (1991). In The high cost of health. *GAO Journal, 13*, 14-15.

Lundberg, G. (1992). National health care reform: The aura of inevitability intensifies. *Journal of the American Medical Association, 267*, 2521-2524.

Marmor, T., & Godfrey, J. (1992, July 23). Canada's medical system is a model. That's a fact. *New York Times*, OP-ED.

Masters, F., & Schmele, J. (1991). Total quality management: An idea whose time has come. *Journal of Nursing Quality Assurance, 5*, 7-16.

Matula, B. (1991). In The high cost of health. *The GAO Journal, 13*, 19-20.

Mitchell, P., Krueger, J., & Moody, L. (1990). The crisis of the health care nonsystem. *Nursing Outlook, 38*, 214-217.

Perkins, C., & Perkins, D. (1992). Uncompensated care: The millstone around the neck of U.S. health care. *Nursing and Health Care, 13*, 20-23.

Rabkin, M. (1991). In The high cost of health. *The GAO Journal, 13*, 16-17.

U.S. General Accounting Office. (1992a). *Access to health care: States respond to growing crisis*. (GAO/HRD-92-70) Washington, D.C.

U.S. General Accounting Office (1992b). *Excessive payments support the proliferation of costly technology*. (GAO/HRD-92-59), Washington, D.C.

Washington State Health Care Commission. (1992). *Draft final recommendations*, Olympia, WA.

Washington State Department of Health. (1992). *1990 annual financial report for Washington hospitals*, Olympia, WA.

Washington State Health Personnel Resource Planning Committee. (1992). *Health personnel resource plan*, Washington State Department of Health, Olympia, WA.

Wilson, D. (1992a, July 6). Prescription for profit. *Seattle Times*.

Wilson, D. (1992b, July 26). Ethics: Kickbacks banned, but issues are muddy. *Seattle Times*.

Wood, R., Bailey, N., & Tilkemeier, D. (1992). Managed care: The missing link in quality improvement. *Journal of Nursing Care Quality, 6*, 55-65.

Woolhandler, S., & Himmelstein, D. (1989). Resolving the cost/access conflict: The case for a national health program. *Journal of General Internal Medicine, 4*, 54-60.

CHAPTER 4

Politics, Power, and Vested Interests: Washington at Work

Nancy J. Sharp

Understanding the dynamics of the process of public policy formation is critical if nurses are to influence health care policy. The politics and power of vested interest groups are central to this process. This chapter discusses the role of vested interests in the Washington lobby, including the resources and strategies of professional nursing associations and members and the effectiveness of the nursing lobby. Politics, political support, and the power of individuals are analyzed with recommendations for how nursing and nurses can have greater influence in shaping health policy.

VESTED INTERESTS AND THE WASHINGTON LOBBY

The number one premise of Norman Ornstein and Shirley Elder's classic reference on lobbying is as follows (Ornstein & Elder, 1978):

Americans are, on the whole, a society of joiners and of groups. From childhood—through the Girl Scouts, Campfire Girls, Cub Scouts, Boy Scouts; the

President, Sharp Legislative Resources, Bethesda, MD 20817

Series on Nursing Administration—Volume 6, 1994

YM and YWCA; Little League, church, and synagogue youth groups, and so on—Americans are encouraged to join and to identify with organizations and associations. It is not surprising, then, that American politics would have a significant group dimension.

"Groups are the raw material of politics." So stated Arthur F. Bentley in his classic reference on political groups in 1908, *The Process of Government*. Groups with "special interests" or "vested interests" have been an important part of the American policy process since the beginning of our political nation. Over the more recent years as our health care system has grown more complex, we have seen a growth in the number of health groups that lobby for their special interests. Further, in Washington, the special interest groups are heavily relied on to provide technical and complex information to the harried and overburdened legislators and their staffs.

From Alaska lands to zero population growth, every conceivable issue has attracted the attention of competing interest groups, and across the country they and their lobbyists have become a potent force in the political process. Their ranks include the traditional rich and powerful Capitol Hill lobbies, as well as the many grass roots coalitions that derive power from sheer numbers and fierce determination.

Groups are, of course, diverse. In the health care field there are (1) voluntary health organizations, such as the March of Dimes, the Cystic Fibrosis Foundation, and the American Diabetes Association; (2) professional practitioner organizations, such as the American Nurses Association (ANA), the American Medical Association (AMA), and the National Association for Pediatric Nurse Associates and Practitioners (NAPNAP); and (3) the industry or trade groups, such as the American Hospital Association (AHA) and the Health Industry Manufacturers Association (HIMA). All of these groups and many others have Washington representatives lobbying on behalf of their special interests on Capitol Hill.

Some groups have very organized and active grass roots components. As we all have seen in our hometown newspapers, as well as on the evening television network news, grass roots lobbying—either for or against a specific issue—can be very effective. When grass roots members are called on to send letters or call their Washington representatives, they have been known to jam the U.S. Capitol's switchboard. Some day maybe we will hear that so many nurses (hundreds? thousands?) called in on an issue that the Capitol switchboard was closed down for the day.

Interest Group Resources and Strategies

Group resources fall into several categories: *physical* resources, particularly money and membership size; *organizational* resources, including membership skills and unity, leadership skills, and substantive expertise; *political* resources, such as campaign expertise, political process knowledge, political strategy expertise, and political reputation; *motivational* resources, such as ideological commitment; and *intangibles*, such as over-all prestige or status. Each group has a special mix of these resources. How the group combines its goals, focus of activity, motivation, mix of resources, and skill at using them determines that group's political influence (Ornstein & Elder, 1978).

Discussion Question: Which of these resources do our professional nursing associations have and use effectively?

Of the physical resources, money is perhaps the most important resource available to a group in influencing public policy, because it can be used to attract many other resources, including substantive, political, and leadership expertise, as well as public relations talent. At the least, if a group is denied access to decision makers through the regular channels, it can buy space in newspapers or time on radio and television to make its case. Many interest groups maintain offices in downtown Washington staffed with lobbyists, public relations officials, and experts in the field to supply information to Congress and the Executive Branch, to monitor relevant government activity, and to finance magazine and newspaper advertisements giving the views of the particular group. On the other hand, groups with fewer monetary resources may rely heavily on volunteers, have storefront offices, obtain public attention through press releases, and give no campaign contributions to legislators, *and they can still make a difference with an organized effort.*

In his farewell address to the nation delivered on January 14, 1981, President Jimmy Carter expressed concern about the proliferation of single-interest groups, which he said was "a disturbing factor" that "tends to distort our purposes, because the national interest is not always the sum of all our single or special interests." But comments like these have produced little in the way of restrictions on lobbies or the way they operate. The dilemma for would-be reformers is that lobbying derives from basic American rights, such as freedom of speech, and any efforts to control it must avoid any denial of those rights.

Lobbying has been recognized as a legitimate, protected activity from the earliest years of the United States. The First Amendment to the Constitution provided that "Congress shall make no law...abridging the freedom of speech or of the press; or the right of the people peaceably to assemble and to petition the Government for redress of grievances."

Discussion Question: Are you or your nursing association using your Constitutional rights to lobby for the health care reforms that are needed now in the 1990s?

Health Care Political Action Committees

The medical and insurance industries, positioning themselves for a prolonged political fight over national health care legislation, contributed about $10 million to the 1992 fall campaigns of House and Senate candidates. Donations from the political action committees (PACs) of individual companies and trade coalitions, most of whom oppose a government-administered "single-payer" system that theoretically would guarantee all Americans some health care, rose 22% compared with the same period during the 1990 election season.

PAC contributions to members of the three key committees where initial legislation dies or thrives—House Ways and Means, House Energy and Commerce, and Senate Finance—rose an average of 45% according to an analysis of Federal Election Commission records compiled in September 1992 by Citizen Action, a Washington-based consumer advocacy group.

For the $800 billion-a-year health care industry, which includes hospitals, insurers, pharmaceutical companies, equipment manufacturers, business owners, physicians, and others in every community in the country, what Congress or the Executive Branch does or does not do to overhaul the health care system may spell prosperity or extinction to some firms and entire industries.

Most PAC officials argue that their money buys access, not votes, and with so much indecision in Congress over various health care proposals, access is key. Meetings with members and their staffs are where an organization can hope to convince a lawmaker that the organization's position is worth backing. The PAC contributions give the association a better chance of being "a player" in the eventual debate over how to change a system that many believe is broken. Association presidents say that it is extremely important that they are seen as "players" and get high visibility so that the candidates will know where the associations stand on issues. The candidates do care about money to help their reelection efforts, and the PAC money is a conduit for the organization to get a message across and educate legislators on issues.

Because of the unspecific lobby registration laws, it is impossible to determine an exact number of lobbyists in Washington. But whether they refer to themselves as political consultants, lawyers, foreign representatives, legislative specialists, consumer advocates, trade association representatives, or government affairs specialists, there are approximately 100,000 people working directly or indirectly as lobbyists in Washington. Only about 7300 are registered under federal law (Peters, 1992).

Actually, there are millions of lobbyists. When you write your congressperson, you are lobbying: broadly speaking, lobbying is any attempt to influence the action of a public official. This is a basic right of every American citizen.

Discussion Question: Who lobbies for nursing in Washington?

The Nursing Lobby

There are approximately 40 nurse-lobbyists (both paid staff and volunteer members) listed in *The Nurses' Directory to Capitol Connections*

(Sharp, 1993) representing both the Nursing Tri-Council and the specialty nursing organizations. Over the years more and more specialty nursing associations have become involved in lobbying in Washington. Some of the groups' national headquarters are located in Washington, D.C., and some have a government relations office there. When there is an issue of common concern to all the groups, a coalition is formed, such as the "Nurses' Coalition for Legislative Action," which worked very hard and very well for the passage of the legislation that created the National Center for Nursing Research as part of the National Institutes of Health. The co-directors of this coalition were from four specialty nursing organizations: American College of Nurse Midwives (ACNM); Organization for Obstetric, Gynecologic, and Neonatal Nurses (NAACOG)—(new name: Association of Women's Health, Obstetrics, and Neonatal Nurses [AWHONN]); National Association of Pediatric Nurse Associates and Practitioners (NAPNAP); and the National Organization of Neonatal Nurses (NAON).

The Nursing Tri-Council consists of the four groups listed below. The presidents and the executive directors of these groups meet periodically to determine priorities for nursing's issues.

- American Association of Colleges of Nursing (AACN)
- American Nurses Association (ANA)
- American Organization of Nurse Executives (AONE)
- National League for Nursing (NLN)

The nursing organizations with either headquarters offices or government relations (GR) offices in Washington are listed in the box on p. 49.

Is the nursing lobby effective? What legislation has the nursing lobby, either as the total group or as a single nursing specialty, succeeded in getting enacted that benefited either a particular patient population or a particular nurse population? It may be easier to enumerate what the certified nurse midwives, the nurse anesthetists, and certain groups of nurse practitioners have accomplished legislatively. As far as we can tell, no one is really keeping a tab, so it is not easy to keep track of the legislative victories of the separate nursing groups. Further, it not considered to be in good form for the lobbyists of the various groups to toot their own horn. The ownership of certain legislative victories is best kept low key. The good that comes to the whole group (even the actual lobbying work) was strategically orchestrated by a very small group of politically savvy individuals.

Further, it is far easier to keep track of those areas in which the nursing associations defeated some pending legislative proposal. Unfortunately, it is easier to raise the ire to rally *against* something than to rally *for* something. Grass roots constituents almost always will rise to the occasion when some legislation is pending that will cut their autonomy, their income, or their practice.

Nursing Organizations with Offices in Washington, D.C.

American Academy of Nurse Practitioners (GR office)

American Association of Colleges of Nursing

American Association of Nurse Anesthetists (GR office)

American College of Nurse Midwives

American Nephrology Nurses Association (GR office)

American Nurses Association (with GR office for American Association of Critical Care Nurses, Association of Operating Room Nurses, Emergency Nurses Association, and International Association of Enterostomal Therapy)

American Organization of Nurse Executives (GR office)

Association for Practitioners in Infection Control (GR office)

NAACOG, the Organization for Obstetric, Gynecologic, and Neonatal Nurses

National Association of Nurse Practitioners in Reproductive Health

National Association of Orthopaedic Nurses (GR office)

National Association of Pediatric Nurse Associates and Practitioners (GR office)

National Association of School Nurses (NASN)

National League for Nursing (GR office)

North American Transplant Coordinators Organization (GR office)

Nurses Organization of Veterans Affairs

From *The Nurses' Directory of Capitol Connections* by N.J. Sharp, 1993, Washington, D.C.: Capitol Associates.

POLITICS AND POLITICAL SUPPORT

As the late Illinois Senator Everett Dirksen is reputed to have said, "The first law of politics is to get elected. The second is to be reelected." Further, to be reelected requires political support.

When legislators have to decide which legislation to support and which to oppose, they base their decisions on which legislative positions provide the greatest amount of political support. Like other participants in the political process, legislators also make implicit cost-benefit calculations. The benefits to legislators from providing legislation to an organized group is the political support received from that group. The cost to the legislators of providing those legislative benefits is not the dollar cost of legislation, since they do not bear it, but instead is the loss in potential political support from their actions. As long as legislators receive net positive benefits from providing legislation, they are expected to do so (Feldstein, 1988).

The Committee System

Because the legislature as a whole cannot deal with all the issues that come before it, it delegates part of the legislative functions to committees. Committees were established with jurisdiction over different policy areas. The committee structure enables the legislature to divide up work, develop expertise in complex areas, and provide for a more efficient size for group discussion. However, this process provides each of the relevant committees with near monopoly power over their area of jurisdiction. Any legislation proposed has to be approved by the relevant subcommittee and consequently the parent committee to be initiated and then funds appropriated.

The committee system also provides the link between the interest groups seeking benefits and the provision of benefits by the legislature. Membership on committees generally is based on self-selection. Legislators with strong special interest constituencies have an equally strong incentive to be a member of those committees that deal with that special interest legislation. Legislators whose constituents are farmers seek membership on the agricultural committees, and legislators from urban areas select committees whose jurisdiction deals with urban affairs. Interest groups desiring special legislation for their group seek out legislators on the relevant committees and subcommittees dealing with their problems. In this manner legislators are able to provide legislative rewards in return for political support (Feldstein, 1988).

The cost of producing legislation is the legislator's time (Feldstein, 1988). Further, the time spent on any one bill means there is less time to spend on others. That is the real cost of legislation. Legislators could receive political support by enacting other legislation, or they could provide constituent services—also a source of political support. Even the way that the legislature is organized affects the time and ease of passing legislation. For example, the committee structure, the rules provided, whether filibusters are permitted, and the type of voting procedures in place are all considerations that affect the time—hence the cost—of producing legislation.

POWER AND THE INDIVIDUAL

Washington's main product—what people in Washington create, organize, manipulate, and respond to—is words: for example, legislation, floor statements, resolutions, proclamations, speeches, legal briefs, court decisions, newsletters, reports, and press releases. The network news from Washington is really what was said that day; when Congress or the President does something, it is with words (Feldstein, 1988).

Health interest groups demand legislation that is in the member's interest. Going beyond that statement, however, it is said that many health associations, such as the American Medical Association, have claimed that they are educational organizations, not trade associations representing the narrow economic interests of their members. Further, such associations claim that the legislation they favor is in the public's interest and that they are concerned with quality rather than economic interests. Thus it is important to be specific about the types of legislation on which a health association takes a position (Feldstein, 1988).

"Legislation redistributes wealth" (Feldstein, 1988). According to Feldstein, the legislative goal of associations with individuals as members—physicians, dentists, nurses, optometrists—is assumed to be to maximize the incomes of its current members. Health professionals are no different from other individuals; they will say that they have many goals, of which income is only one. However, income is the only goal that all members have in common. Further, Feldstein states that goals such as increased autonomy and control over their practice are highly correlated with incomes. Income is thus a more general goal.

Discussion Question: Do nurses support legislation that increases their income?

Nurse Power: Does It Exist? Yes and No

At present the nursing community as a whole is not a major player in the world of Washington politics. Unfortunately, when the Washington insiders need help on a health care issue, they do not think of and call in the nursing community representatives as the first contact. The nursing community representatives are definitely "second string" players and maybe thought of when someone says, "Hey, what about the nurses?" This is true especially as the nursing community waits to be sked to participate in the political process. Fortunately, now in the '90s we see much of this waiting transformed into taking action.

What do we need to be a power? We need to learn to "be there" when general discussions are held. We need to encourage our "street savvy" nurse colleagues to collect intelligence about an issue. We need to get better at "schmoozing." We need to get some "fire in the belly" about issues we care about. And, we need the courage to "take the lead" on some issues that are especially important to the nursing community. And finally, we need to provide information to help make decisions, do research, and collect data. These "people skills" are a necessary part of the process, in addition to the obvious skills of organizing and leading an organization or legislature to make decisions.

Nurses should adopt a "be there" strategy to increase their power. With a "be there, in your face" strategy, an organized nursing organization could send an official representative to every meeting, briefing, press conference, hearing, coalition meeting, and strategy session, even without an invitation, politely showing that nurses care about the issue being discussed. This would make the nursing presence so accepted, so expected, and so visible that no meeting would start without the nursing representative there. We are not there yet in Washington. Maybe this nursing presence is much stronger in some state capitols.

Having street savvy is knowing "what's happening" and requires that nurses have keenly developed radar sources and resources who are part of an intelligence-gathering team. Street savvy individuals will hear what is happening first through the many intricate informal networks and be able to pass on information to each other at all times, day and night. It is critical that nurses encourage their nurse colleagues to develop and fine-tune this skill.

"Schmoozing"—some people have it and some people do not. Some people are very skilled at paving the way to good relationships with many people at the same time. A particularly politically savvy person "works a room," smiling and greeting everyone in a room with a bit of news from intelligence gathering, a bit of gossip, or a comment predicting how a situation is going to come out. Shaking hands, smiling, and moving through a crowd can be learned.

Developing "fire in the belly" about some issue means that a person becomes so focused on a issue that all of his or her energy, organizing talent, concentration, and strategy-building skills are geared toward the ultimate outcome on an issue.

"Taking the lead" or offering to be the "lead agency" on an issue means having the personal resources to organize the effort, make phone calls, prepare agendas, find meeting rooms, notify all interested parties, provide photocopying and faxing, and offer stationery, taxi money, and parking facilities. It means delegating tasks and keeping lists so that details don't fall through the cracks. It means following through on all details—large and small.

To "provide meaningful information" means to have the adequate access and resources to get information and, further, to pass the information on to appropriate parties. It must be understood, however, that all the correct information in the world does not necessarily lead to a good decision; politics usually intervenes on the final decision. As Feldstein said, politics and political support superimpose themselves on the most efficient data information and determine the outcome on an issue.

Clearly, we have two million nurses in this country who have inside information on how our current health care system works or does not work. These two million voices with years of clinical nursing experience could indeed be a mighty force if organized to rate our health care system's strong points and defects. The only skill the grass roots nurses lack is how to impact the process, since this skill is not necessarily taught in basic nursing education.

Walker and Choate (1984) stated that "an absence of socialization of the nurse in the educational process as a participant in policymaking or as a policymaker may partly account for nurses' lack of impact." Although we stated earlier that things have improved in the 1990s, nursing education could still use additional resources and opportunities for nurses to learn these skills. The full process of learning to become a statesperson includes having an understanding of law, legislation, lobbying, policy, politics, power, and regulation. Practicums including direct hands-on experiences in the unique Washington, D.C. laboratory would add immensely to the students' preparation for further involvement.

Not every nurse will be interested in sharing his or her clinical nursing expertise to impact federal health policy. However, for those nurses who are interested in learning more, *The Nurses' Directory of Capitol Connections* (Sharp, 1993) can be a starting point for your networking. This directory lists approximately 400 nurses who are involved with policy positions in Washington-based associations and federal agencies. The directory further describes internships and fellowships for nurses to participate in to learn more about the process. Finally, for those master's level programs that have a health policy competent to the nursing administration program, Sharp Legislative Resources in Bethesda, Md. can be contacted to plan a 1-week to 6-month educational program with opportunities for hands-on experience and input to the Washington policy-makers. For assistance in finding an internship placement in Washington, call the author in Bethesda, Md. at (301) 469-4997.

CONCLUSION

A quote from Aburdene and Naisbitt (1992) illustrates the potential for nursing's and nurses' influence in the political process.

> After two decades of grassroots politicking from the school board to the statehouse, U.S. women are winning the offices that will catapult them into top leadership. With the backing of female voters—now the majority of the American electorate—as well as men seeking new leadership, a new generation of women, today about 40 years of age, will take office as governors and in the House and Senate over the next two decades. By 2008 U.S. women will hold at least 35% of governorships. A woman will be electable, or already elected, as U.S. president. (p. 3)

Perhaps that first female U.S. president will be a nurse. Why not?

REFERENCES

Aburdene, P., & Naisbitt, J. (1992). *Megatrends for women*. New York: Villard Books.

Feldstein, P.J. (1988). *The politics of health legislation: An economic perspective*. Ann Arbor, MI: Foundation of the American College of Healthcare Executives.

Ornstein, N., & Elder, S. (1978). *Interest groups, lobbying, and policy making*. Washington, D.C.: Congressional Quarterly.

Peters, C. (1992). *How Washington really works*. Reading, MA: Addison-Wesley.

Sharp, N.J. (1993). *The nurses' directory of capitol connections*. Washington, D.C.: Capitol Associates.

Walker, M., & Choate, K. (1984). Nurses as policymakers: Curriculum implications. *Nurse Educator, 9*(1), 39-42.

READING LIST

Cohen, R.E. (1992). *Washington at work*. New York: Macmillan.

Congressional Quarterly. (1982). *The Washington lobby*. Washington, D.C.: Author.

Gray, R.K. (1992). *The power house: The selling of access and influence in Washington*. New York: St. Martins Press.

Lierman, T. (1992). *Building a healthy America*. New York: Maryann Liebert.

Pertschuk, M. (1986). *Giant killers*. New York: W.W. Norton.

Smith, H. (1989). *The power game*. New York: Random House.

Smucker, B. (1991). *The nonprofit lobbying guide: Advocating your cause and getting results*. San Francisco: Jossey-Bass.

Toffler, A. (1990). *Powershift: Knowledge, wealth and violence at the edge of the 21st century*. New York: Bantam Books.

Wolpe, B.C. (1990). *Lobbying Congress: How the system works*. Washington, D.C.: Congressional Quarterly.

Zorack, J.L. (1990). *The lobbying handbook*. Washington, D.C.: Professional Lobbying and Consulting Center.

CHAPTER 5

Accountability for Allocation of Health Care Resources: Is the Fox Guarding the Henhouse?

Elizabeth I. Merwin

"Providers of health services may be considered accountable when those who use them and those who pay the bills can hold them responsible for meeting their objectives or needs" (Brown, 1988). Health care providers must develop strategies to meet this challenge. This chapter focuses on the implications of this challenge for nurse administrators.

Public debate is brewing. During the twentieth century the United States has been willing to continually increase its resource allocation for health care. But what has the collective public received for its contribution? Unfortunately, the resounding answer is that no one really knows. Ever-increasing health care expenditures may have created the proverbial *greatest health care system on earth* (as it is commonly referred to in the

Associate Professor of Nursing, Virginia Commonwealth University/Medical College of Virginia; Fellow, Thomas Jefferson Health Policy Institute, Charlottesville, VA 22903

Series on Nursing Administration—Volume 6, 1994

United States), or it may be just the most costly system. Although the public has been willing to expend large sums to provide better health care, it is clear that it is no longer willing to do so without the health care community assuming responsibility for evaluating the results of the expenditures.

An overwhelming concern of the public and the provider community is that cost-containment efforts may reduce quality of care. But no one can define quality of care. What is it? How is it measured? What is an acceptable level of quality care? What are the relationships among resource use and various levels of quality of care? If resources have to be limited, how should those decisions be made? What roles should health care professionals play in allocation decisions? These are all questions raised repeatedly in the literature, with different opinions offered as answers. They will be the most significant questions that must be answered in the debate on how to contain health care costs while providing quality care.

This chapter reviews the use of microstrategies and macrostrategies to promote accountability for health care resource use in today's health care system. Several proposals for changing the health care system from the perspective of accountability are reviewed also. The need for greater consumer involvement in all phases of the policy-making and implementation processes within the health care system is described. Finally, strategies that practicing nurse administrators can use to increase accountability for both quality of care and resource utilization within their institutions are proposed.

ACCOUNTABILITY IN TODAY'S HEALTH CARE SYSTEM

Historical Perspective

The problems faced by today's health care system are a response to rapid growth during this century. O.W. Anderson (1991) classified the period from 1875 to 1930 as time spent creating the "infrastructure" for today's health care system. He pointed out that this country first responded to expanded medical technology—related to the principles of antisepsis and the availability of anesthesia—by expanding the number of hospitals from a minimal number in 1875 to 4000 in 1900. He characterized the period from 1930 to 1965 as time spent expanding third-party reimbursement for health care. He noted that from 1965 the overriding concern has been cost-containment efforts. The health care industry has experienced tremendous growth in a relatively short time; however, voluntary and mandatory cost-containment mechanisms have failed to make significant impacts on cost containment. Only recently has there been pressure to determine results of health care expenditures. Accountability for outcomes or results of expenditures of health care dollars may well become Anderson's fourth stage in the evolution of the health care system.

The increase in government's involvement in promoting the growth of the health care system is apparent when reviewing major legislative actions

TABLE 5-1 Comparison of Health Care Expenditures from 1929 to 1990

Year	Expenditures * (in billions)	% GNP*	% Public funds†
1929	3.6	3.5	13.6
1965	41.6	5.9	26.2
1970	74.4	7.3	37.0
1980	250.1	9.2	42.4
1990	666.2*	12.2	42.4

*From National Center for Health Statistics. (1992). *Health, United States, 1991.* Hyattsville, MD: Public Health Service.
†National Center for Health Statistics, 1989. (1990). Hyattsville, MD: Public Health Service; U.S. Department of Health and Human Services, Health Care Financing Administration, Office of the Actuary. In Health Insurance Association of America. (1991). *Source book of health insurance data.* Author.
Note: The 1992 reported figures of expenditures are slightly different from the figures used in 1990 and 1991 data sources, which were the basis for % public fund computations.

of this century. Whereas many health care–related laws early in the decade increased government's funding of communicable disease programs, the 1946 Hill-Burton Act allowed for additional hospitals to be built, as well as for expansion of the services of existing hospitals (Litman, 1991). Medicare and Medicaid legislation was passed in 1965, followed by the Health Maintenance Organization (HMO) Act of 1973, which provided low-cost loans to establish new HMOs (Litman, 1991). All of these legislative efforts served to promote growth in the health care system, presumably with the effect of improving health care services to the public.

The effect of these legislative changes on the health of the public is difficult to judge. Indeed all such judgments are somewhat subjective and limited in scope. What is possible to measure is the effect on health care expenditures. In 1929 the United States spent $3.6 billion on health care; by 1965, when Medicare and Medicaid were enacted, $41.6 billion went to health care. In 1990, $666.2 billion was allocated to health care (Table 5-1).

COST OF CARE

There has been a steady increase in the percentage of both the gross national product spent on health care and the public versus private dollars allocated for health care (see Table 5-1). Even with the tremendous increase in health care expenditures and the availability of public programs, 34.7 million people remained uninsured in 1990 (Himmelstein, Woolhandler, & Wolfe, 1992). It may be naive to place too much importance on the increase in public funding for health care because, as stated by McCarthy and Thorpe (1986), when discussing the source of health care dollars, it is important to recognize that "dollars take different routes on their way from consumers to providers." This statement recognizes that government-sponsored programs are funded by taxpayers. Although there have been attempts by the private sector (particularly businesses and insurance companies) to contain health care costs, Schwartz and Mendelson (1991) estimate that although the rate of increase of Medicare expenditures declined after implementation of the prospective payment system, the non-Medicare expenditures continued to increase "almost 9% per year." They believe that their findings suggest that some of the success of containing costs within a large public program is at the expense of the private sector. Another interpretation is that the public programs have found successful mechanisms to control costs, whereas the private sector has not.

The continual increase in health care expenditures has prompted society to call for cost-containment efforts ranging from retrenching, to rationing care, to evaluating the outcomes of care in order, ultimately, to fund care that makes a difference. How these allocation decisions are made will affect society's access to health care and its quality in the future. Although society has been willing to continue to increase its commitment to health care, it is recognized that growth cannot continue, particularly in light of our aging society. Taeuber (1983) estimated that in 1990, 12.7% of the population will be 65 years old or older, with 1.4% 85 or older, but by the year 2050, 21.7% of the population will be 65 or older, with 5.2% 85 or older. Because of the increased health care needs of elderly persons, these statistics are frightening and suggest that more radical actions are needed to control health care costs in the United States.

IMPORTANCE OF ALLOCATION DECISIONS

The need for hard decisions to control resource utilization is clear. Fuchs (1974) pointed out that choices are always necessary regarding the use of resources, that all resources have different potential uses, and that people may be biased in their perceptions of society's desire for resource allocation decisions. Fuchs argues that some people have a "romantic" perspective of the unlimited availability of resources. Callahan (1988) believes that the time has come to develop a plan to ration health care, since the gains made in improving the efficiency of the system will not compensate for the continual expansion of technology, which is a large factor in escalating health costs. He believes the public's value systems must be changed and the current focus on individual needs overshadows a broader view of the community's needs. On the surface there is general agreement among all elements of the health care system that something must be done to contain health care costs. Agreement ends, however, when applied to any specific solution or patient. The interests of society as a whole, as represented through public decision making, often are in direct conflict with individual patients' needs. This conflict consistently is addressed in the literature. Attempts to control costs through limiting access to major procedures may achieve the goal of reducing health care costs but also may result in patients not receiving procedures necessary to live. This conflict can be expected to be at the forefront of health policy decision making as different cost-containment or resource-allocation decisions are made or considered. The fact that a large percentage of health care dollars is spent on a small number of people will continue to pressure policy makers to deal with this conflict. Berk, Monheit, and Hagan (1988) show that "during 1980 the top 1% of persons ranked by health care expenditures accounted for almost 30% of total health expenditures, and the top 5% incurred 55% of all health expenditures."

Role of Health Professionals

The role of health care professionals is simultaneously unclear, crucial, and uncharted in the resource allocation process. Traditionally, nurses and physicians have been educated to provide the best care possible to individual patients. With few exceptions, such as public health and group counseling or teaching, professionals have not been taught to apply their knowledge for the welfare of the common good of a population of patients; nurses often struggle with the reality of having too few staff members to provide the comprehensive quality of health care they are taught in nursing school. As Reigle (1988) pointed out, nurses ration nursing care when there are too few nurses to meet patients' needs and they set priorities to decide which patients' needs will be met and which will not be met. Nurses face these types of rationing decisions daily but have little information to use in evaluating the consequences of different patient priorities. Likewise, physicians are called on increasingly to make resource allocation decisions. Welch (1991) points up two difficulties faced by physicians in making these decisions: "physicians find it painful to deny service to patients and fear that doing so will destroy the physician-patient relationship, and they are often concerned that patients will be underserved and may not receive the services they need." Physicians often are reimbursed on a fee-for-service basis and thus have a built-in economic incentive to provide services.

In the recent literature there is a consistent call for greater involvement of the public in resource allocation decisions and some expressed desire to avoid placing individual practitioners in the position of making resource allocation decisions. For example, Jecker (1990) stated, "We don't want individual physicians deciding willy nilly how to ration the medical care at their disposal. Achieving social justice requires instituting global policies and calls for public debate, not backstage bartering."

POLICY ANALYSIS AND OUTCOMES RESEARCH

To assist in resource allocation decisions, greater effort is being placed on the use of policy analysis and outcomes research. Policy analysis can be thought of as "who gets what, why, (and) what difference it makes" (Dye,

1987). Outcomes research has been defined as research that "studies the end results of medical care—the effect of the health care process on the health and well-being of patients and populations" (Lohr, 1990). These related strategies are used to bring the issue of health care effectiveness into the cost-containment debate. Increasingly, an economic evaluation methodology, cost-effectiveness analysis (Thompson, 1980; Drummond, Stoddart, & Torrance, 1987), is used to relate the cost of an intervention to its clinical outcome. The focus on outcomes research was strengthened by the creation of the Agency for Health Care Policy and Research (AHCPR), established by Congress in 1989. As stated in the law, its purpose "is to enhance the quality, appropriateness, and effectiveness of health care services, and access to such services, through the establishment of a broad base of scientific research and through the promotion of improvements in clinical practice and in the organization, financing, and delivery of health care services" (AHCPR, 1989a). Major initial activities of this organization include the development of "clinical practice guidelines and quality standards," and "extramural research on medical treatment effectiveness and patient outcomes" (AHCPR, 1989b). The Health Care Financing Agency is also increasing its focus on outcome evaluation in its peer review activity. Peer review organizations will be required to refocus their objectives from review of quality problems in individual cases to placing more emphasis on identifying "patterns" of quality-of-care problems using large data bases to identify organizational, systems-level quality-of-care problems (Jencks & Wilensky, 1992).

HEALTH CARE REFORM

The need for major health care reform is consistently documented in the literature; many authors debate the necessity, advantages, and disadvantages of and the potential for the establishment of a national health plan (Ginzberg, 1990; R.J. Anderson, 1991; Thier, 1991; Hodge, 1991). However, the lack of agreement as to how such reform should take place is recognized. The debate is whether this country wants a "national health program" or a "national medical care system" (Anonymous, 1988) for it has been argued that "medical care is the least important of the three basic elements; much more important are prevention and the standard of living within a national health program."

Issues such as the scope of health services, right to care, and consumer responsibility for health behaviors remain to be clarified. There is no indication that the country agrees even on a definition of health. Keller (1981) pointed out that "accountability to society by consumers for preserving their health may be impossible until a workable, precise, clear definition of health is developed. Consumers at present are unable to identify what their ultimate goal for health might be and for what they should hold health care professionals accountable." There also is disagreement about the extent to which health care is a right versus the individual's responsibility for his or her own health care (Rodgers, 1981). The influence of clients' choice of health behaviors on their need for health care and the system's desire to hold clients responsible for their health behavior (Rodgers, 1981) remains a pressing issue. As Crawford (1977) pointed out, it may be erroneous to expect that life-style risk behaviors are under an individual's control without considering the environment in which the individual lives. Nevertheless, enhancing individual responsibility for health care is an element in many plans to reform the health care system. Weick (1984) warned that "a final effect of the emphasis on individual responsibility for health is the erosion of the notion that people have a right to medical care. . . With a shift from social to individual responsibility for health, self-care becomes a sad substitute for access to the medical system, especially for the poor, who have the fewest resources for altering their life-style in the recommended ways."

Local Reform

The push for community involvement through local efforts is a current trend in this country, as well as internationally. Mahler (1986), in a speech as Director-General of the World Health Organization, stated, "It has become clear that district health systems can provide a good opportunity for people to become genuinely involved in shaping their own health care, the size of the system places it within their grasp, they can see for themselves what is going well and what is not, and they are close enough to those who manage the system to be able to influence their decisions." But for it to work, he believes several actions must first occur: (1) there must be a "sound national policy framework"; (2) there must be a central authority to oversee the national plan; and (3) district plans must be accountable to the central authority, as well as locally.

The need for locally developed organizations is supported by Shortell and McNerney (1990), who promote identifying, through research, a geographic area's health care needs, "matching resources with needs," reimbursing providers based on outcome measures, and placing "caps on expenditures." These strategies of "clinical and fiscal accountability would be linked and based on an epidemiologic assessment of the health needs of the population."

The focus on local strategies is also supported by the American Hospital Association's (AHA) plan for health care reform (Davidson, 1992). The plan calls for the development of "community care networks," which would change the system from focusing on "individual patient encounters" to meeting the needs of communities, based on collaboration among multiple provider groups. The networks "would be responsible for an enrolled population and would be paid a fixed annual payment per enrollee." The AHA sees this plan as financially and clinically advantageous. Further, AHA argues that reporting to the community results of satisfaction surveys and information on the cost and quality of care provided would promote accountability to the public (Davidson, 1992).

Oregon Initiative

State governments already are making attempts at health care reform (Sorian, 1992). A prominent example of an organized effort on the state level to reform health care is the proposed revisions to the Medicaid program in Oregon. Legislators enacted a law that develops a system to dramatically revise eligibility for Medicaid, as well as alter reimbursable services. The Oregon Basic Health Services Act expands coverage by Medicaid to all individuals earning less than the federal poverty level (Fox & Leichter, 1991). It is expected that core services provided to Medicaid recipients will influence core services ultimately defined in private plans (Fox & Leichter, 1991). To define and prioritize a list of services that will be reimbursed in the Medicaid plan, the state used consumer input through public hearings, community meetings, and a telephone survey (Fox & Leichter, 1991; Kitzhaber, 1990).

Initially, a cost-effectiveness methodology was used to prioritize services; the results of this methodology have been severely criticized, and additional prioritization focusing on the potential benefit of services has been used (Fox & Leichter, 1991; Hadorn, 1991). The resulting revised priority ranking of services will provide the basis for financial allocation decisions based on how much money is available to fund services. The amount of money allocated for Medicaid each year will determine how far down the priority list Oregon can go in funding services. The rationing of health care dollars in this way attempts to ensure that dollars are spent on highest priority services (Fox & Leichter, 1991; Hadorn, 1991; Kitzhaber, 1990).

Criticisms of the plan include that (1) it rations care only for the poor and not for the rich; (2) it does not eliminate current inefficiencies; and (3) it is a plan to ration health care (Kitzhaber, 1990). The Oregon plan has spurred much national public debate, although it has yet to become operational because the federal government waiver allowing it to modify its Medicaid plan in this manner is still pending (Fox & Leichter, 1991). In August 1992 the federal government denied approval of the waiver, stating that it would violate the Americans with Disabilities Act (Firshein, 1992). However, Oregon is expected to resubmit a revised plan that might be better received in light of the national health reform efforts.

National Reform

Numerous different proposals for health care reform have been made. Unfortunately, there is no consensus about how reforms should be made. Enthoven and Kronick (1989; 1991) support mandated employer insurance, a pooled public insurance plan, subsidies for the poor, managed care, and "managed competition." Himmelstein and Woolhandler (1989) propose drastically overhauling the system by creating an entirely government-owned and government-operated system. The Pepper Commission (1990), made up of members of the House of Representatives and the Senate, held hearings in cities across the country, met with top health care leaders, and met in numerous working sessions to study the health care system. They recommended in their task force report a national plan to provide "universal coverage," which would require individuals to be covered by either a private or public insurance plan. The commission supported replacing the state-run Medicaid program with a federal plan that covers "the unemployed and the poor," mandating large employer provision of health insurance benefits, and providing tax incentives and assistance to employers who have only a few employees, to assist them in providing health insurance to employees. The commission also recommended the establishment of "a federally specified minimum benefit package that includes preventive and primary care as well as other physician and hospital care." Requiring employers to provide health insurance to their employees is referred to as a *play or pay* type of plan. This plan is in contrast to The President's Comprehensive Health Reform Program (1992), which attempts to increase "access to affordable insurance" by offering tax credits "large enough to purchase a basic health package" for the poor, and allowing for tax deductions for the middle class, reducing costs of insurance through "pooling" of small companies and individuals, increasing health services provided in underserved areas, reducing costs of paperwork, and reducing malpractice costs. It avoids placing increased burdens on employers, does not provide for universal coverage, and states that it does not ration health care.

Numerous national nursing organizations formed a coalition and offer support for "Nursing's Agenda for Health Care Reform" (ANA, 1991). It incorporates the "play or pay" principle, managed care, mandated basic services, a focus on prevention, and a call to ensure quality care for "vulnerable" populations. This agenda calls for increasing consumers' involvement in their health care. Consumers also support health care reform. Most want to maintain a mixed public and private system rather than a government-controlled system, but 41% of the public think that significant changes are needed and 26% think that the system is "beyond repair" (HIAA, 1992).

ACCOUNTABILITY CRITERIA WITHIN HEALTH CARE REFORM

Accountability is a broad concept that has different interpretations at microlevels versus macrolevels of the health care system. It can be viewed as the responsibility an individual provider has for the outcomes of care provided to an individual client (microperspective), or it can be viewed as society's ability to meet the health care needs of its people (macroperspective). Some criteria for evaluating current and future allocation strategies are helpful in thinking about accountability in health care decision making. Shortell and McNerney (1990) suggest that two themes for evaluating health care reforms should include responsibility and accountability. Any changes should meet the responsibility of caring for the presently uninsured, and they should also ensure "both clinical and fiscal accountability." To meet these criteria, the following actions are recommended (Shortell & McNerney, 1990):

- The establishment of a set of benefits mandated for all
- The allocation of resources on the basis of defined needs
- The payment of providers on the basis of performance
- The establishment of clinical and fiscal accountability at the level closest to that of care delivery
- The establishment of a global cap on expenditures based on the needs of the population and capabilities of providers in the area

Brown (1988) also identified the need for criteria to use in the evaluation of different national health programs. Of seven principles he identifies and uses to compare several proposed national health programs, three are directly related to accountability. They include the following (Brown, 1988):

- Efficiency of resource usage
- Planning and market allocation of resources
- Accountability of health services

He recognizes that reimbursement policies influence provider behaviors—and particularly practitioner autonomy. He calls for an integration of planning and market strategies, believing that a system based only on planning would be too bureaucratic and when one relies only on the market, providers' needs may reduce their acting to best meet the health care needs of society. However, he points out that the market approach allows consumers to express their satisfaction with care through their choice of provider. It should be recognized that consumers are becoming less able to freely choose their provider as different types of reimbursement policies, such as HMOs and PPOs, are implemented. The limited number of specialist providers in the community, as well as the presence of single hospitals in some smaller communities, may eliminate or substantially reduce consumers' ability to choose a provider.

Regulations requiring providers to submit health care data allowing for evaluation of care also are suggested as a strategy to increase accountability (Enthoven & Kronick, 1989; Brown, 1988). Formal reporting procedures, approval mechanisms for services, and review of quality assurance mechanisms and financial aspects of programs are other strategies recommended for accountability (Brown, 1988). As another strategy to increase consumer involvement in policy making and decision making throughout the health care system, Brown (1988) discusses how one prior proposal to develop a national health care system outlined a plan to have consumers elect a board of directors to govern the local health care center; however, he cites examples from the literature of how difficult it is to ensure consumer participation.

Other strategies for accountability Brown (1988) suggests include having standards for quality assurance and financial performance, involving the community in accreditation of plans, and promoting local ownership of plans. He notes the lack of accountability for meeting a community's health needs when there is for-profit multihospital system ownership of a hospital. He argues that decisions for these hospitals are made by administrators within the corporate structure far away from the local community, resulting in decisions that promote offering services that are profitable as opposed to meeting the community's needs.

So, is "the fox guarding the hen house?" On a microlevel—yes. Physicians and nurses have the responsibility to make decisions on behalf of patients. However, there are built-in conflicts in the current health care system for both physicians and nurses. Regardless of type of health insurance policy and even in the absence of health care insurance, physicians control access to treatment, most treatment decisions, and referral to additional health care providers. Insurance companies are left to pay for care provided or to challenge a physician's clinical judgment regarding the need for care. Hospitals employ all types of professionals and nonprofessionals to carry on their work. But physicians are not employees and are not under the direct supervision of administrators. Instead, they typically are members of an autonomous medical staff with its own bylaws, organization, and communication system. Administrators must develop relationships with the medical staff that allow for their influence on quality assurance and risk management matters; at the same time, they must balance their need to keep physicians happy, because physicians are their source of referral of patients and thus their pathway to financial success.

Nurses must serve as patient advocates. This may require confronting physicians and hospitals while representing the patient's desires or needs. But like the patient, they may be powerless to modify physician or hospital behavior. Unlike physicians and hospitals, nurses tend to receive fixed incomes regardless of their stand on issues or clinical decision making. However, there are two ways that nurses may be influenced to act in ways other than a patient's best interest. Because a nurse is an employee, usually of a hospital or physician, the nurse's need to keep his or her job may reduce the risks he or she is willing to take on behalf of a patient in challenging a physician or hospital employer. Such challenges take personal energy and motivation, and some nurses may adopt an attitude of just fulfilling the necessary tasks for patients and not fulfilling their responsibilities as a patient advocate.

On the macrolevel, health professionals influence legislators' views on health care issues through lobbying and campaign donations, as well as through membership on policy-making boards. Because health professionals will gain or lose financially as a result of changes in health policy, they can never be completely unbiased when evaluating and promoting the effect of certain policies on patients.

It might be postulated that there is a linear relationship between the amount of income one receives from the health care system and the potential for accusations of conflicts of interest when one enters into decision making regarding health systems changes proposed to improve the system. Changes that have the potential for changing patient care also may change the income of providers.

As Feldstein (1988) points out in his self-interest theory, all professions choose to support legislation that is in their best economic interest. Nursing has not been as effective as medicine either in promoting its economic welfare or in influencing health policy formulation. Nursing may be making progress in this regard through the proposal "Nursing's Agenda for Health Care Reform" (ANA, 1991). Although the goal of this plan to increase access to care for vulnerable populations is in society's best interest, one method to accomplish it is to promote the use of advanced practice nurses—nurse practitioners and clinical nurse specialists. Doing so should, over time, create more jobs for higher-paid, better-educated nurses, thus enhancing the economic welfare of the profession. This is a good example of a policy that can be expected to affect patients, as well as providers.

There should be recognition of the intrinsic conflict of providers who are motivated by (1) economic incentives because of the need to work as a means of livelihood and (2) the need to be a patient advocate, representing only a patient's best interest. Even when a health professional makes a decision based only on his or her perspective of a patient's best interest, the motivation often is suspect. This is unfortunate but reflects the conflict inherent in a career in which one derives his or her income from providing clinical care.

To prevent conflicts of interest, third-party review and involvement, particularly by educated consumers, are necessary. There needs to be a certain amount of tension in the policy-making process so that options are fully explored. Community leaders, organized consumer groups, and individual consumers must become more involved in changing the health care system.

IMPLICATIONS FOR NURSING ADMINISTRATION

The increasing focus on accountability in the emerging public debate regarding methods of health care reform poses challenges for nursing administration. The education of our students, from RN preparation programs through doctoral education in nursing, must change to allow practitioners to become more accountable to the public. Likewise, educational programs must increase students' abilities to participate in policy-making debates that will stimulate reform. The reforms that are made can be expected to continue to drastically change the practice environment. Students must be educated to be proactive in shaping future changes.

Nursing education programs must increase students' in-depth understanding of the cost of health care in relation to outcomes of health care. This will require a greater emphasis at all levels of programs on quality assurance and outcome evaluation, cost analysis, and methodologies such as cost-effectiveness analysis. Whereas we have tended to focus on the clinical aspects of the practice of nursing within most of our educational programs, we now need to recognize that the best clinical knowledge is obsolete if it cannot be applied in the practice arena. As many of the proposed changes in the health care system are calling for local reform, it is more important than ever for nurses to be able to participate in the policy-making arena. Increased focus on leadership skills, communication skills, and political action is a must if students are to be competent in these endeavors. A major task facing nursing administrators is convincing nurses who want to practice nursing in the clinical setting that it is worthwhile for them to learn and become competent in the administrative and policy-making aspects of nursing. Likewise, as Hinshaw (1988) suggested, nurse researchers need to identify policy implications of their studies.

Another major implication is the need to incorporate computer skills in all levels of nursing education and staff development programs. Undergraduate programs need to require statistics courses and computer courses in their curriculum to allow students the experience of doing small quality assurance and cost-effectiveness studies at that level. Likewise, staff development programs need to be available to nurses who need additional competencies in these areas. To teach computer and statistical skills only at the master's or even doctoral level within nursing will fail our profession and will prohibit nurses from fully participating in quality and cost evaluations expected to influence the health care systems of the future. Accrediting agencies should ensure that nursing programs at both the undergraduate and the master's level have appropriately integrated computer and statistical courses to ensure students have the basic skills necessary to evaluate quality of care. Likewise, certification and accreditation agencies should continue to increase their expectations of quality evaluations within all types of health care settings.

Nursing practice perhaps has the most to gain from upcoming changes in health care reform. Nursing often has wanted the opportunity to prove its worth. Often the ability to substantiate the worth of nursing care has been impaired by the lack of data. All evidence indicates that more and more data will become available to evaluate the quality of nursing care within health care settings. The challenge to leaders of nursing practice is to ensure that the right questions are posed, the right problems are studied, and data are used to answer the most important questions. Although nursing services have been used to report incidence types of information, less emphasis has been placed on using complex research techniques in program evaluations. Continual acceleration of standards by accrediting and certification agencies in the area of quality assurance will motivate nursing services to improve their ability to conduct complex program evaluations. The trend has been to hire clinical nurses (nurses with clinical expertise) as researchers in practice settings, particularly in academic medical centers. However, it is expected that the need will increase to hire nurse researchers who have administrative experience. The timing for this is excellent, following the increase of doctoral programs in nursing in this country over the past decade. The risk to nursing service is that in the uproar that is sure to ensue after major reform, the struggle for day-to-day provision of quality care may overshadow the opportunity to determine data-base methods of quality evaluation. Such evaluation can lead to major system improvement. If nurses are not employed who have the ability to study cost, as well as quality of care problems, it is unlikely that nursing will maintain and gain influence in the whole health care arena.

Another implication of the changes is the need to provide nurses with additional skills to facilitate consumer involvement in health care decision making. Nurses traditionally have included consumers in planning for their own individual nursing care. Only recently has there been an increased focus on including consumers in policy-making decisions in health care. We need to recognize that bonafide consumers (e.g., not just a spouse of a very important person) bring different perspectives to the debate on health care issues. Sometimes health professionals are reluctant to involve consumers, fearing that consumers will not have the technical knowledge to understand the issues. Personal experience in working with mental health consumers on policy-making boards has shown that they have valuable input and perspectives that often are overlooked by professionals. As nurses we should support the appointment of consumers to all policy-making boards within the health care system. We also need to treat consumers equally and develop ways to support their involvement in decision making. Consumers should become as influential at health policy decision making as physicians and hospital administrators.

CONCLUSION

Although the previous decade has proved to be quite challenging for nurse administrators, all indications show that the next decade will be even more challenging. The public is no longer willing to accept at face value the expectation that health care providers are providing quality care in a cost-effective manner. It will be our challenge to demonstrate to consumers and therefore to society as a whole that we are using their health care dollars to their best benefit and that the outcomes of care reflect the large economic contribution that society makes to health care.

There is much uncertainty about how the health care system will change in the future; however, certain trends are evident. The literature is consistent in identifying an obsessive concern with both the cost and quality of care. Standards for health care can be expected to continue to evolve to ensure accountability for both quality and cost-of-care outcomes. Another trend that is evident is the increased emphasis on consumer participation and responsibility within the health care system. Debate regarding preferred strategies to reform the health care system will continue. It is important that professionals continue to engage in that debate with representatives of all segments of society. Collectively, we will be able to continue to improve the health care provided in this country.

REFERENCES

Agency for Health Care Policy and Research (AHCPR) as established by Section 6103 of Omnibus Budget Reconciliation Act of 1989 (P.L. 101-239, December 19, 1989a). *Agency for Health Care Policy and Research (AHCPR)*. Department of Health and Human Services Highlight Summary, 1-16.

AHCPR Program Note. *Agency for Health Care Policy and Research (AHCPR)* (1989b). Department of Health and Human Services, 1-2.

American Nurses Association (ANA). (1991). Nursing's agenda for health care reform. *American Nurse* (Suppl. PR-3 22OM).

Anderson, O.W. (1991). Health services in the United States: A growth enterprise for a hundred years. In T.J. Litman & L.S. Robins (Eds.), *Health politics and policy* (2nd ed.) (pp. 38-52). New York: Delmar.

Anderson, R.J. (1991). Is it time for universal health care in America? *Respiratory Care, 36*(2), 110-114.

Anonymous. How important is medical care in a national health program? (1988). *Journal of Public Health Policy, 9*(1), 7-10.

Berk, M.L., Monheit, A.C., & Hagan, M.M. (1988, Fall). National health expenditure data. *Health Affairs, 7*(9), 49-60.

Brown, E.R. (1988). Principles for a national health program: A framework for analysis and development. *The Milbank Quarterly, 66*(4), 573-617.

Callahan, D. (1988). Allocating health resources. *Hastings Center Report, 18*(2), 14-20.

Crawford, R. (1977). You are dangerous to your health: The ideology and politics of victim blaming. *International Journal of Health Services, 7*(4), 663-680.

Davidson, R.J. (1992, May/June). Community care networks: Cornerstone of health care reform. *Journal of American Health Policy, 2*(3), 12-15.

Division of National Cost Estimates. (1991). Office of the Actuary: National health expenditures, 1986-2000. In R.E. Curtis, *Source book of health insurance data*. Washington, DC: Health Insurance Association of America.

Drummond, M.F., Stoddart, G.L., & Torrance, G.W. (1987). *Methods for the economic evaluation of health care programs*. New York: Oxford University Press.

Dye, T.R. (1987). *Understanding public policy* (6th ed.). Englewood Cliffs, NJ: Prentice Hall.

Enthoven, A., & Kronick, R. (1989). A consumer-choice health plan for the 1990s: Universal health insurance in a system designed to promote quality and economy (First of two parts). *Universal Health Insurance, 320*(1), 29-37.

Enthoven, A.C., & Kronick, R. (1991). Universal health insurance through incentives reform. *Journal of the American Medical Association, 265*(19), 2532-2536.

Feldstein, P.J. (1988). *The politics of health legislation: An economic perspective*. Ann Arbor, MI: Health Administration Perspectives.

Firshein, J. (1992). Anatomy of a waiver: Oregon Plan stumbles. In R. Sorian (Ed.), *Medicine and Health, Perspectives: supplement to Medicine & Health*. New York: Faulkner & Gray.

Fox, D.M., & Leichter, H.M. (1991). Rationing care in Oregon: The new accountability. *Health Affairs, 10*(2), 7-27.

Fuchs, V. (1974). *Who shall live?* New York: Basic Books.

Ginzberg, E. (1990). Sounding board: Health care reform—why so slow? *New England Journal of Medicine, 322*(20), 1464-1466.

Hadorn, D.C. (1991). Setting health care priorities in Oregon: Cost effectiveness meets the rule of rescue. *Journal of the American Medical Association, 265*(17), 2218-2225.

Health Insurance Association of America (HIAA). (1992, January). *Timely attitudes: A summary of two recent public opinion surveys on health care reform*. Washington, D.C.: Author.

Himmelstein, D.U., & Woolhandler, S. (1989). A national health program for the United States. *New England Journal of Medicine, 320*(2), 102-108.

Himmelstein, D.U., Woolhandler, S., & Wolfe, S.M. (1992). The vanishing health care safety net: New data on uninsured Americans. *International Journal of Health Services, 22*(3), 381-396.

Hinshaw, A.S. (1988). Using research to shape health policy: Nursing research findings are powerful instruments for influencing those who make health care policy. *Nursing Outlook, 36*(1), 21-24.

Hodge, M.H. (1991). New perspectives on our national health care dilemma. *Health Care Management Review, 16*(3), 63-71.

Jecker, N.S. (1990). Integrating medical ethics with normative theory: Patient advocacy and social responsibility. *Theoretical Medicine, 11*(2), 125-139.

Jencks, S.F., & Wilensky, G.R. (1992). The health care quality improvement initiative: A new approach to quality assurance in medicare. *Journal of the American Medical Association, 268*(7), 900-903.

Keller, M.J. (1981). Toward a definition of health. *Advances in Nursing Science, 4*(1), 43-64.

Kitzhaber, J.A. (1990). Oregon act to allocate resources more efficiently. *Health Progress, 71*(9), 20-27.

Litman, T.J. (1991). Appendix: Chronology and capsule highlights of the major historical and political milestones in the evolutionary involvement of government in health and health care in the United States. In T.J. Litman & L.S. Robins (Eds.), *Health Politics and Policy* (2nd ed.) (pp. 395-411). New York: Delmar.

Lohr, K. (Ed.). (1990). Medicare: A strategy for quality assurance, Volume 1 (Washington: National Academy Press), p. 56, quoted in *Health outcomes research: A primer* (1992) (p. 2). Washington, D.C.: Foundation for Health Services Research. Author.

Mahler, H. (1986). Accountability for health for all. *WHO Chronicle, 40*(6), 211-215.

McCarthy, C.M., & Thorpe, K.E. (1986). Financing for health care. In S. Jones (Ed.), *Health Care Delivery in the United States* (3rd ed.) (p. 305). New York: Springs.

Office of the President of the United States. (1992). *The President's Comprehensive Health Reform Program* (pp. 1-94). (1992, February 6).

Reigle, N. (1988). *Presentation at The Sixth Annual Conference on Ethics and Health Care*, Medical College of Virginia, Richmond, VA.

Rodgers, J.A. (1981). Health is not a right. *Nursing Outlook, 29*(10), 590-591.

Schwartz, W.B., & Mendelson, D.N. (1991). Hospital cost containment in the 1980s: Hard lessons learned and prospects for the 1990s. *New England Journal of Medicine, 324*(15), 1037-1042.

Shortell, S.M., & McNerney, W.J. (1990). Criteria and guidelines for reforming the U.S. health care system. *New England Journal of Medicine, 322*(7), 463-466.

Sorian, R. (1992). Stepping up to bat: States take the lead on health policy. *Journal of American Health Policy, 2*(3), 14a-16a.

Taeuber, C. (1983). America in transition: An aging society. *Current Population Reports*, Special Studies Series P-23, No. 128 (Bureau of the Census, Washington, D.C.: U.S. Department of Commerce). In *The Aging population in the twenty-first century: Statistics for health policy* (National Research Council, 1988). Washington, D.C.: National Academy Press.

The Pepper Commission: U.S. Bipartisan Commission on Comprehensive Health Care (Final Report). (1990). *A call for action* (pp.7-8). Washington, D.C.: U.S. Government Printing Office.

Thier, S.O. (1991). Health care reform: Who will lead? *Annals of Internal Medicine, 115*(1), 54-58.

Thompson, M.S. (1980). *Benefit-cost analysis for program evaluation.* Beverly Hills: Sage.

Weick, A. (1984). The concept of responsibility in a health model of social work. *Social Work in Health Care, 10*(2), 13-25.

Welch, H.G. (1991). Should the health care forest be selectively thinned by physicians or clear cut by payers? *Annals of Internal Medicine, 115*(3), 223-226.

Paradoxical Effects of Rationing Health Care

Section Two comprises only three chapters and is brief for good reason. The reality of rationing health care has just begun to be internalized among providers. Therefore little is to be written to date that is based on research, experience, or wisdom.

In Chapter 6 Capuzzi shares insights into the rationing initiative in process in Oregon. A clear picture of the three major players—consumers, payors, and providers—is offered, along with the conflicting perspective and priorities among the three constituencies.

In Chapter 7 Simmons highlights the paradox that our society espouses the value of a healthy life-style, yet most health care funding has sickness or injury as a prerequisite to covered service. The irony and cost implications for such a philosophy and practice is not a new concern, particularly in public health, but it does need to be revisited during any health care reform that seeks both cost and quality improvements.

The discussion of healthy life-style is followed by Chapter 8, in which Feather presents continuity of care systems as more beneficial to consumer and payors than is our current episodic care system. He suggests an honest appraisal of providers' current preparation for and delivery of health care.

This section triggers a critical analysis of health care as it is currently delivered in the United States. It also highlights some of the inherent points of conflict in any effort to reallocate the use of available health care resources.

CHAPTER 6

Consumer, Provider, and Third-Party Payor Perspectives of Health Care Rationing

Cecelia Capuzzi

The paradoxical effects of rationing are presented within the framework of the initiative in Oregon. The perspectives of consumer, provider, and payor are explored. The points of agreement and disagreement among their concerns and priorities are outlined. A case is made for rationing of care as both an opportunity for and a risk to nursing.

ONE STATE'S EXPERIENCE

In 1989 the Oregon Basic Health Services Act was passed by the state legislature. The Act encompassed three bills aimed at increasing access to health care for most Oregonians; at that time approximately 400,000 individuals were without health insurance (Oregon Health Services Commission, 1991). The first bill, Senate Bill (SB) 27, proposed to increase Medicaid coverage for all citizens who were at or below the federal poverty level (FPL) The second bill, SB 935, contained legislation to phase in small business insurance reform and mandated small businesses to offer health

Associate Professor, School of Nursing, Community Health Care Systems Department, Oregon Health Sciences University, Portland, OR 97201

Series on Nursing Administration—Volume 6, 1994

insurance for their employees and their dependents by 1994. The last bill, SB 534, created a high-risk health insurance pool for those currently unable to get insurance because of preexisting health conditions.

To provide state-financed health coverage to an increased number of citizens, the legislature had to decide how to finance the additional costs. Because states must maintain a balanced budget, the legislature had to either seek additional state monies or redistribute current dollars. The political climate in Oregon disallowed the first option because citizens were irate with the current high property taxes. The second option of reallocating state dollars could be accomplished in two ways: either take monies from nonhealth programs (e.g., education) and add these for health services; or redistribute the monies within the health program. Again, the first option was not popular because most state programs were operating at reduced budgets since the recession in the early 1980s. In addition, many believed that the monies for the current health programs were not being spent cost-effectively. Therefore the legislature decided to publicly finance health care for an increased number of citizens by offering a package of "basic health services"; likewise the health insurance offered by small businesses or through the high-risk insurance pool would be this same basic package.

SB 27 specified the process for developing the basic health services package. First a health service commission (HSC) composed of five physicians, one public health nurse, one social service worker, and four consumers was appointed to develop a list of health services ranked from the most to the least in importance, representing comparative benefits. These health services were to include outpatient services, health promotion and preventive services, and inpatient and provider services. SB 27 directed the commission to conduct public hearings soliciting input from patient advocates and health providers; the HSC also was to collect data about the values of the community toward health care (Sixty-fifth Oregon Legislative Assembly, 1989).

Implementing

After nearly 2 years of work, the HSC published a ranked list of 709 health services that incorporated the above-mentioned data. This list, along with an actuarial report that gave rates for each service, was presented to the 1991 Ways and Means Subcommittee on Health of the Oregon Legislature.

Another intent of SB 27 was to change the allocation process for publicly financed health care in the state. Until this time, blocks of money were allocated biennially for state-funded health programs, with the largest portion going to Medicaid. When allocating monies for Medicaid, the legislature determined what the costs were of mandated services and then debated which optional services to provide. During these deliberations, advocacy groups lobbied for their constituencies and often presented emotional testimony. Rarely did the legislature consider the effectiveness of the optional service or the impact on the number of citizens. If dollars fell short of expected revenues, one of several strategies was employed to balance the budget: eligibility criteria were altered to decrease the number of persons enrolled in Medicaid; reimbursement to health providers was decreased and consequently some providers refused to care for Medicaid patients; or select optional health services were no longer reimbursed. Again, advocacy groups lobbied legislators for protection of their favorite services with varying success; the actual effects of the ultimate decisions were never known. Allocation of health services was an implicit process (Capuzzi, in press).

This situation became uncomfortable when the legislature decided not to fund soft tissue organ transplants and subsequently a child died needing a bone marrow transplant. In 1989 the Oregon legislature decided that the health allocation process needed to be changed; decisions needed to be made explicitly (Kitzhaber, 1991). SB 27 stated that the legislature could not alter the order of the ranked health services presented by the HSC; instead they first were to decide how much money was available per person and then determine how many services could be purchased. This would be the package of "basic health services." For example, if the legislature determined that $127 was available for each person whose income was at or below the FPL, 587 of the 709 health services could be purchased.

Legislators now could evaluate the effects of their allocation decisions; the nonreimbursable services could be examined to determine the fairness and equity of such decisions. If some nonfunded services were deemed essential, additional dollars could be allocated. In fact, this situation occurred during the 1991 legislative session when the Ways and Means Committee increased the initial allocation by $33 million because it was decided that the package of health services was not adequate as defined by the originally proposed dollars. SB 27 also stated that if monies fell short of expectation during the biennium, individuals no longer would lose their health insurance coverage (i.e, eligibility criteria could not be altered) nor would health providers be paid less; instead, fewer services would be reimbursed. Services to be eliminated would be those having the lowest rankings; that is, services would be eliminated by proceeding up the list, first eliminating those that were rated as being less effective.

Although the intent of the Oregon Basic Health Services Act was to increase access to health care for additional numbers of people, many focused on the specifics contained in SB 27 and framed the issue around health care rationing. Proponents of the Oregon plan responded that there already was rationing of health care; that SB 27 was changing the "rationing of people" to the "rationing of services" through priority setting.

What is health care rationing? What is the difference between rationing and allocation of resources? Between rationing and priority setting? Other critics berate the concept of rationing; instead they tout the need to exercise cost containment. What is the difference between rationing and cost containment? Still others say that we need to manage health care. Again, what are the differences between the rationing of health care and managing care? The differing perspectives of consumers, health providers, and third-party payors depend on which definition of rationing is used. Moreover, their perspectives vary according to what is to be rationed (e.g., patients, providers, services) and how the rationing is implemented. Last, their views depend on their perceptions of the need for rationing.

The Oregon plan provides a case for discussing the issues of health care rationing and the paradoxical views of consumers, health providers, and third-party payors. The remainder of the chapter examines these differing perspectives using Oregon's plan to compare and contrast the issues.

CONSUMER PERSPECTIVES

Who Are the Consumers?

When discussing the perspectives of consumers, first it is necessary to identify who is being considered. Consumers are individuals who use the health care system: the general public, patients, clients.

Consumers also are groups of people having similar characteristics, such as age, or having like health problems, such as diabetes. These latter consumers often are organized as special interest or advocacy groups, such as the AARP or the American Diabetes Association. Some consumer groups are composed of representatives for specific individuals, for example, parents of disabled children. These consumer groups frequently are represented by lobbyists or special spokespersons and express a common perspective on an issue. Their perspectives on rationing depend on their analysis of a particular rationing plan's effect on their population of interest.

Other consumers whose views can be explored are those of the unions or trade groups. Like advocacy or special interest groups, unions are represented by spokespersons or lobbyists and are particularly interested in the potential limitations in health care for their constituents.

Perspectives on Health Care Rationing

Most social and political issues in the United States are examined in terms of the concept of autonomy—will there be a limit on freedom of choice? Most Americans oppose any restrictions on their freedom, including the idea that their choices on health care might be hindered. National health insurance has been opposed successfully to date in this country because of the belief that other countries that have national health care limit consumer choice. As the public begins to consider the need for rationing, autonomy continues to be an important factor for acceptance of any plan.

The belief that health care is a right is another factor that influences consumers' views about health care rationing. In a study conducted by Gabel,

Cohen and Fink (1989), 72% of those surveyed thought that citizens had a constitutional right to health care. Even though the legality of this right is erroneous, any discussion about rationing is examined in terms of limitations of those rights.

Similarly, unions have fought hard for health care benefits for their workers, and these benefits are seen as "rights." Discussions of rationing that reduce what workers currently receive usually are opposed. In fact, as SB 935 was being implemented in Oregon, industries with unions who currently provided health insurance were able to use existing federal legislation to temporarily prevent the prioritized list of health services from governing their employee's health benefits.

Last, consumers' perspectives on rationing are affected by their knowledge of health care issues. For example, a Harris poll was conducted for the Harvard Community Health Plan, Brookline Village, Massachusetts. At the beginning of the survey, only 37% thought that it was reasonable for insurance companies to cover some treatments and not others; by the end of the survey, this number had increased to 56%. The author attributed this change to increased knowledge about the issue (Larkin, 1988). The Health Insurance Association of America (HIAA) yearly surveys 1500 households. Gabel et al. (1989) analyzed several years of data, and the results were contradictory. For example, although the majority supported more spending on health care and federal expansion of health care coverage to the uninsured, they did not want higher taxes. In addition, although more than two thirds of those surveyed were dissatisfied with the cost of care, they resisted approving means to control costs. These results suggest that consumers have different levels of understanding about health care financing.

Data support the tenet that consumers prefer implicit rationing as compared with explicit rationing. When there is explicit rationing, decisions are made at the macrolevel and thus the consumer has less control (Fry, 1990). As long as the public trusts that physicians make health care decisions fairly and based on clinical factors, patients favor rationing decisions being made at this level. When there is discussion of health care decisions being made at the macrolevel using patient criteria such as financial resources or life-style characteristics, the public is less supportive (Lee & Miller, 1990). The results of a 1985 study by the American Board of Family Practice also support this contention. Given six circumstances for rationing health care, the largest percentage (37%) supported rationing services if the decisions were made by the patient's personal physician (Potter & Porter, 1989).

When rationing concerned health services, consumers' opinions varied. In the HIAA study, 71% agreed with the statement that "health insurance should pay for any treatments that will save lives even if it costs one million dollars to save a life" (Gabel et al., 1989). This is consistent with the initial results previously cited by the Harris poll. On the other hand, when Oregon made the decision to not fund organ transplants in 1988, letters ran

4:1 in support of the policy. Subsequent media polls also indicated a majority of support (Larkin, 1988). This support could have been affected by the fact that this rationing related to a publicly funded program and did not affect those with private health insurance. On the other hand, many private health insurance policies also do not reimburse for certain organ transplants.

The public is reluctant to ration high technology to limit costs. Only 5% of those surveyed accepted that technology should be rationed according to ability to pay. Yet when responding to subsequent questions on choosing among technologies, many came to accept that there were economic limits (Gabel et al., 1989). Conversely, the majority of respondents supported the substitution of inexpensive care for expensive care, possibly not realizing that expensive care often included high technology.

Many consumers supported measures that could limit their access, such as outpatient preadmission testing, mandatory second surgical opinions, and managed care (Gabel et al., 1989). Moreover, a majority of respondents rejected nonprice rationing strategies that produce inconvenience (e.g., longer waits, use of clinics, care by paraprofessionals) and opposed any rationing strategies that lower the quality of care (Gabel et al., 1989).

When the discussion centers on the rationing of individuals, consumers again have differing opinions on what patient criteria are acceptable. Callahan (1987) suggested that age be a criterion; that most costs occurred during the last days of life. Gabel et al. (1989) found that if age was a criterion, respondents favored caring for premature infants before the elderly. Input from citizens meetings in Oregon gave similar results, although the age criterion was moderated by type of health care. Nearly 600 citizens at 19 meetings revealed that the top five priorities for care were (1) preventive care for infants, (2) preventive care for children, (3) preventive care for adults, (4) long-term care of the elderly, and (5) critical care for children (Crawshaw, Garland, Hines, & Anderson, 1990).

Alternatively, the Public Policy Committee of the American Geriatrics Society endorsed the position that chronological age should not be a criterion for exclusion of individuals from medical care (Jecker & Pearlman, 1989). Also, age (patient over 65 years of age) as a criterion for rationing was the fifth of six options (13%) of the respondents in the American Board of Family Practice study (Potter & Porter, 1989).

Consumers seem to agree that ability to pay or economic status should not be used as a rationing criterion (McGregor, 1989). If rationing is needed, all should be affected by it. This has been a major criticism of the Oregon plan—that SB 27 focused on the Medicaid population, which includes particularly women and children.

On the other hand, those who currently do not have access to health care in Oregon (those above the 58% of FPL; single individuals below 58% FPL, those employed by small businesses that do not provide health insurance, and the medically uninsurable) perceived the Oregon plan positively;

they would rather have access to limited services rather than nothing. Also, there is a positive response to the prioritized list of health services by those who already receive Medicaid because this list includes needed services that previously were not provided (e.g., dental care).

Social worth and severity of illness also were criteria evaluated by consumers. In the HIAA household surveys, there was a higher priority for curing cancer and helping people with disabilities than for rehabilitating alcoholics or treating infertility (Gabel et al., 1989).

In addition, quality of life and length of life were considered as rationing criteria. Sixty-six percent would commit resources to making life better for one hundred patients with arthritis than to a surgical procedure that would give one person 5 years more of life (Gabel et al., 1989). The second highest circumstance for rationing health care (34%) in the American Board of Family Practice study mentioned the presence of a terminal illness (Potter & Porter, 1989).

Conversely, others have questioned the use of quality of life as a criterion. What may be poor quality of life to some can be perceived differently by others (Ferrans, 1987). Furthermore, some individuals charge that this criterion discriminates against the disabled. The federal waiver needed to implement the Oregon plan recently was denied because it was believed that the use of quality of life in determining the priority of health services violated the Americans With Disabilities Act.

Although there were several studies about consumers' views on health care rationing, there still is not a clear indication of the number who support the concept in some form and the number who totally oppose rationing under any circumstances. It is known that many believe that other factors contribute to the rising cost. Of those questioned in the HIAA household survey, more than 70% blamed hospitals and physicians for the increasing costs; another 50% blamed insurance and drug companies; and 35% laid the problem on the federal government (Gabel et al, 1989). These consumers think that if there was a focus on the providers, the number of tests ordered, and their profits, rationing would not be necessary (Etzioni, 1991).

In summary, consumers' perspectives on rationing vary greatly. In addition, studies that have focused on rationing do not provide a clear consumer mandate on how to provide access to health care or to control costs. Researchers found that as consumers learn more about the issues, their views change. It is known that many consumers who have good private health insurance or Medicare are satisfied with the status quo. These individuals also fear the loss of benefits when rationing is discussed (Ginzberg, 1991). Those individuals without health care perceive any rationing plan that increases their access differently from those who do have access to health care. There appears to be a consensus that any rationing plan should affect all consumers, and the public prefers certain patient criteria above others. There also seems to be some acceptance for limiting third-party reimbursement for some health services. What is clear is that consumers need more information about the issues of access to health care and about health care financing. Moreover, consumers need to be involved in discussions that solicit their views on all aspects of rationing. The process used by the Oregon Health Decisions provides a useful model to facilitate these discussions (Crawshaw et al., 1990).

PROVIDER PERSPECTIVES

Who Are the Providers?

As with consumers, the term *provider* needs to be defined. There are many different health providers (e.g., physicians, nurses, dentists), each with similar and differing concerns on rationing. In addition, most health providers have professional organizations who represent them collectively and develop position statements on health care issues. Providers also can be administrators of health care institutions, such as hospitals. Like consumers, how rationing is defined and the methods for implementation are proposed affect providers' views. This section examines the perspectives of three major health providers—physicians, nurses, and hospital administrators.

Physicians' Perspectives

Physicians have a long history of resisting outside control by either the government (Ginzberg, 1991) or private third-party payors (Consumer Reports, 1990b). Physicians, like consumers, are concerned with autonomy. There are several aspects of a loss of autonomy about which they are concerned.

First, physicians fear the effects of rationing on their freedom to make individual clinical decisions. They do not want to be put in the position of being prevented, because of outside restrictions, from doing something that their professional judgment deems necessary. Physicians believe that rationing will interfere with their ability to act in the patient's best interest as an advocate (Daniels, 1989). This introduces another related concept, the ethic of agency that "requires that physician decisions be 'pure' in the following sense: they must be free from consideration of the physician's interests and they must be uninfluenced by judgments about the patient's worth" (Daniels, 1989). Physicians assert that rationing interferes with this ethic.

Both Daniels (1989) and Agich (1990) refuted the physicians' assertion, saying that rationing can be compatible with the ethic of agency. As Daniels (1989) described his ideas, this compatibility depends on what is rationed (e.g., individuals vs. services) and the methods of rationing (e.g., needs of society vs. individuals, access for all). Daniels further argued that the present cost-containment measures that reward institutions and providers for providing care at a lower cost are more detrimental to the ethic of agency than is rationing.

Agich (1990) questioned whether this claim for autonomy is valid as "professional autonomy involves possession of authoritative knowledge, yet what is technically or medically appropriate and effective is frequently not a settled matter." Thus the autonomy to use "clinical judgment" does not necessarily result in the scientifically best treatment of the patient.

Physicians believe also that they are losing autonomy in performing their physician role. They argue that their duty is to the patient—not to society—and that instead of using their clinical expertise, they are placed in the role of administrator (Lee & Miller, 1990). They are uncomfortable with having to consider the relative need for services of one patient versus others.

Opponents to this position argue that social responsibility is part of the physicians' role because their decisions can limit others. "Does clinical freedom include the freedom of the renal physician to deny 10 heart patients their bypass grafts...?" (Williams, 1988).

Third, physicians fear a loss in autonomy to generate an income (Ginzberg, 1991). Any rationing plan that limits a physician's access to patients, particularly those with conditions that give high reimbursements, or includes a cap on reimbursements is opposed (Hill, 1990; "Cut Competition," 1991).

Physicians also are concerned about the effects of rationing on quality of care. They are caught between a legal dilemma of standard of care and economics (Morreim, 1992). There are three aspects of this standard of care. First, physicians are to deliver the same care as other physicians in their communities. Second, although doctors can refuse to accept a patient, once they do accept a patient, they must continue the care regardless of ability to pay and at an acceptable standard or be charged with abandonment. Third, the community standards of care now incorporate expensive technologies. It is unclear what the legal outcomes to physicians are if they do not provide all care they believe is necessary despite rationing policies. The decision of the *Wickline v. State of California* case judged that the health provider "who complies without protest with the limitations imposed by a third party payer, when his medical judgement dictates otherwise, cannot avoid his ultimate responsibility for his patient's care. . ." (Bellocq, 1989). On the other hand, Oregon's health plan specifically provides protection against "criminal prosecution, civil liability or professional disciplinary action for failing to provide a service which the Legislative Assembly has not funded or has eliminated from its funding.." (Sixty-fifth Oregon Legislative Assembly, 1989), but as yet this has not been tested in the legal system. Abrams (1987) asserted that all that is required is for the physician to inform the patient of such needed treatment; then the consumer can decide whether to purchase the service or forego the treatment.

One author indicated that physicians have supported rationing in the past and thus any arguments against rationing are invalid. Agich (1990) said that under the current system, physicians are not obligated to accept every patient except in emergencies; they are free to choose whom to serve, when, and where. This is evident by specialty and practice site choices of practitioners. Being free to make these choices, the medical ethic is silent on distributional problems and thus implicitly supports rationing. "Rationing health care is certainly a moral concern, but we need to be wary of appeals to professional autonomy that disguise economic and political self-interest" (Agich, 1990).

If rationing is necessary, physicians have mixed views on how it should be implemented. Many do not like being put in the role of rationer of care and would prefer that these decisions be made at the macrolevel, whereas others would rather make these decisions at the individual patient level so that there is less restriction on their clinical autonomy.

As mentioned, acceptance of rationing depends on how physicians view the impact of the rationing plan. The Oregon Medical Association supported the Oregon Health Plan (Larkin, 1990). They favored the expanded eligibility, the coverage for prevention and ancillary services, and the improved reimbursement rates. They were less accepting of the prioritized list and may use methods to "beat the system" (Steinbrook & Lo, 1992). In other words, physicians supported those aspects of the plan that improved access of care and benefited them economically but disapproved those factors that limited their clinical decision making and potential quality of care.

Nurses' Perspectives

Nurses' perspectives, like those of consumers and physicians, vary on the issue of health care rationing (Davidson & Huckabay, 1986). Some oppose rationing, as indicated by one nurse's letter to the editor that stated rationing violates nursing's ethical code and to condone it would require a different professional ethic of social welfare and societal good (Finkelstein, 1989). Others indicated that there are other solutions to rising health care costs (Wood, 1991). Alternatively, others say we already ration health care and that we need to determine what the best methods are (Rooks, 1990). The major professional nursing organizations have remained silent on the issue of rationing but have come out in support of a national health care plan that would provide universal access to a basic set of health services (ANA, 1991). In addition, managed care is supported by Huey (1988), although this is defined as a form of rationing by some.

Nurses have concerns about health care rationing similar to those of other providers—autonomy, quality of care, and liability. Furthermore, nurses' perspectives are influenced by their nursing roles. Nurse clinicians, like most physicians, frequently believe that their duty is toward the individual patients, whereas nurse managers must consider the good for aggregates of people. For each, the effects of rationing bring different issues.

Nurses have the same concerns about rationing's effect on their autonomy. Nurses only recently have gained the recognition that they have legitimate spheres for independent decision making and resist any new limitations on their clinical judgments. Nurses also identify advocacy as a component of their role and, when their decisions about specific interventions are limited, believe that their duty toward their patients is seriously compromised.

Nurses have some unique perspectives about health care rationing, particularly provider rationing through governmental policies, nonreimbursement, and limited training monies. Unlike physicians who fear an encroachment on autonomy, nurses who have experienced provider rationing are watchful that any proposed rationing plan does not reduce the gains that have been made in the past decade or stymie future expansion.

On the other hand, when rationing is part of health care reform, it can be an opportunity for increased autonomy. For example, several implications of the Oregon health plan seemed positive and the Oregon Nurses' Association supported the legislation. First, the Oregon Basic Health Act changed the allocative decision-making process to include the expertise of health providers. In addition, SB 27 gave nurses a legitimate place in health policy decision making by mandating that one of the health service commissioners be a nurse (Capuzzi, in press). Second, the emphasis on preventive services also was seen as an opportunity, because this is the primary role of nurse clinicians and practitioners. Third, the rapidly expanded access to more than 400,000 citizens raised the question of who could provide this care. Because nurse practitioners and clinicians can be educated more quickly and at a lower cost, expansion of nursing was viewed favorably. Ward (1990) wrote that nurses need to be asking the following questions: Who will pay? What services are provided? Who will be reimbursed? Who will make the decisions about what services are offered? Will nurses have direct access to patients? Will nurses be primary caregivers and case managers? Will nursing services be included in the mandated benefits? In summary, the definition of rationing and how rationing is implemented again affect nurses' perspectives. If the rationing plan limits access to health services that are provided by nurses, the plan will be seen negatively; likewise, if the rationing plan limits or denies reimbursement to nurses, the plan will be opposed.

Nurses also value autonomy in their professional roles and do not want outside regulations altering their practices. Some nurses resist making allocation decisions. Like their physician counterparts, they question whether their obligations are to the individual patient or to society as a whole. Conversely, many new nursing roles place nurses in the position of rationing care—discharge planning, utilization review, case management, and administration (Consumer Reports, 1992). In these situations, nurses are confronted with decisions about what is best for the patient versus what is best for the organization or the community. How long should the patient stay? What services does the patient need?

Last, nurses are watchful that any rationing plan does not hurt them economically. Unlike physicians, who have been unfettered by reimbursement controls until recently, nurses need to ensure that any rationing plan compensates them at a reasonable rate for their services.

Quality of care likewise is an issue when rationing is proposed. Any limits on resources, services, or personnel can place the nurse in the situation of not upholding a standard of care for his or her patients. Unlike many other health providers, nurses have dealt with limited resources most of their professional lives. Institutions never have been generous with nursing resources, and now to contain costs, institutions are reducing the number of nurses and support personnel, increasing case loads, and reducing the availability of supplies and equipment (Collins, 1990; LaRochelle, 1989; Lindeman & McAthie, 1990). Any further rationing that involves a decrease in health care resources and personnel that compromises quality of patient care will not be accepted by nurses. On the other hand, if the rationing plan is actually a reallocation of resources with an increase for nursing care, that rationing might be a welcomed strategy.

Liability issues stemming from rationing also are a concern for nurses. As with physicians, it is unclear what the legal outcomes for nurses are who do not provide an accepted standard of care because of rationing. For example, will case managers be liable for not providing services that are deemed necessary for a client because the services are not reimbursable? Conversely, is there a liability if nurses fail to tell clients about community services without first adequately informing them about the financial consequences? Although Kapp (1989) says that except for a few specific programs, such as Women, Infants, and Children (WIC), consumers have no legal right to health care in the United States and provider liability can be negated merely by informing the client of the service and the costs, many of these situations have not been tested in the legal system.

Another issue of rationing is that of abandonment of patients—specifically abandonment of nonpaying patients. This is a significant problem in home health care and for community agencies that rely on patient reimbursement. Often it becomes a choice of refusing care or going out of business and depriving others of care. The legal status is unclear, particularly in the chronic care arena when no emergency exists. Moreover, the ANA Code of Ethics is unclear on the duty of professional nurses to provide health care without reimbursement (Reckling, 1989).

Health care rationing has several implications for nurses. First, in reviewing the literature for this chapter, this author was struck by the disparity in writings between nurses and physicians on the issue—more physicians are knowledgeable about the issues of health care costs and rationing. Like consumers, nurses need to be educated about the topic so that they can enter into a meaningful dialogue on the issue and assess the effects of differing rationing plans on nursing. Second, nurse administrators are in key positions (and sometimes "hotseat" positions) when developing and implementing strategies for cost containment. Many argue that there are other means of decreasing cost. Nurse managers are in a position to identify means of cost control that protect nursing resources. On the other hand, nurse managers must have data to support reasons for not reducing nursing resources that further compromise patient quality. Third, in this climate of scarce resources and discussions of rationing, nursing must conduct effectiveness and outcome research.

Hospital Administrators' Perspectives

Hospital administrators are just one example of institutional providers, but because the majority of the literature about institutional providers' perspectives on rationing focuses on hospital administrators, this section will address solely their views. Hospital administrators are concerned about the number of uninsured and the increasing cost of health care. They report that they provided more than $8 billion in uncompensated care in 1988; this was a 10% increase over the previous year (Consumer Reports, 1990a). In addition, hospital administrators also can be "consumers" when they purchase health care for their employees. In this role, they again are concerned with increasing health care costs, reporting that 40% of the increasing hospital costs in the past 10 years was the result of increases in salaries and benefits for employees ("Cut Competition," 1991).

On the other hand, certain types of hospital care generate large amounts of money and hospital administrators do not want limitations on services that bring a profit or enable them to remain competitive (Daniels, 1989). Furthermore, hospital administrators are not willing to limit purchases of technology, and they oppose the certificate of need regulations ("Cut Competition," 1991). As with consumers, physicians, and nurses, hospital administrators' perspectives on rationing depend on their definition of rationing and the methods of implementation.

Administrators of hospitals also are grappling with questions of costs, allocation of services, and rationing. In a 1990 survey of 250 hospital CEOs, 53% responded that they did not favor the development of an organized health care rationing mechanism such as the Oregon plan. Despite this response, others who were polled thought that it was a plan that was needed to deal with many of the health care problems (Larkin, 1990). In a later study, more than 85% of hospital CEOs responded negatively when asked whether patients have the right to receive the best technology available for treatment, regardless of their ability to pay. Conversely, these CEOs also believed that a patient's medical needs, not ability to pay, should determine what treatment was received (Johnsson, 1991).

The Oregon Association of Hospitals supported the Oregon Basic Health Act, saying that "Once people become aware of the intention of the legislation, opposition melts away" (Larkin, 1990). Jean Thorne, Oregon's Medicaid director, pointed out that hospitals have much to gain under the Oregon plan because it adds 120,000 people with insurance—a guaranteed paying population (Burke, 1991). The legislation also guaranteed that reimbursement would be at cost and not altered during contract periods. On the other hand, several hospitals that provided expensive tertiary care that might no longer be reimbursable were concerned as the legislation was being written.

Another study by the American College of Health Care Executives surveyed 995 randomly sampled health care executives on the topic of allocating resources, and again the majority (62%) said all persons were entitled to health services regardless of ability to pay (Kelly, 1990). If priority were given to some individuals, it would be for the working poor, all below poverty line, Medicaid and Medicare recipients, and all persons except drug abusers, in that order. This group also favored explicit rationing using such criteria as effectiveness, the quality of life, costs to society, and costs of service. Infants, children, and youth, isolated and frail elderly, high-risk obstetrical patients, minorities with limited access because of language or ethnicity, and minority AIDS patients were thought to be the most needy.

The responses of hospital administrators were not unlike those of consumers; there were contradictory responses, and the criteria favored for rationing were similar. Hospital administrators responded to different rationing plans similarly to the way consumers and other providers did—if the rationing was viewed as beneficial or the positives outweighed the negatives, the proposals were approved. If the proposals were viewed as economically detrimental, they were opposed.

THIRD-PARTY PAYOR PERSPECTIVES

Who Are the Third-Party Payors?

The several categories of third-party payors include private insurance companies, such as Blue Cross/Blue Shield, and government-sponsored insurance programs at the federal, state, and local levels, such as Medicare and Medicaid. Also there are health providers who provide third-party reimbursement (e.g,. health maintenance organizations) and employers who self-insure their employees.

The following illustrates that third-party payors will have differing perspectives on rationing (Etzioni, 1991):

> The argument that society should interfere in people's decisions to purchase more health services has to be assessed differently according to which resources people are using to make these purchases: personal funds, insurance pools, or taxpayers' monies. As long as a person uses his or her own dollars, our society abides by the code of "consumer sovereignty," which dictates that we should not as a society seek to influence people's choices unless there is a compelling social need.

Private Health Insurance Perspectives

Most agree that private insurance companies already ration health care; for example, every policy that has limits on what it will cover is in fact rationing health services (Veatch, 1992). In addition, private insurance companies can limit who purchases their policies (e.g., those with preexisting conditions). As health care costs increase, private insurance plans accept fewer clients (Consumer Reports, 1990a). Other rationing strategies used by all third-party payors are increasing premiums, copayments, and deductibles.

Private insurance companies are businesses that want to make profits, and it behooves them to insure the healthy and deny services to those with high-cost illnesses (Consumer Reports, 1990a). Private insurance companies have increased their odds of having healthier customers by switching from community ratings to risk management strategies (Consumer Reports, 1990a). Furthermore, insurance companies have little incentive at this time to control costs; they are more interested in attracting new business (Hill, 1990).

The issue for private insurance companies is not rationing per se but a major change in the payment system. The Health Insurance Association of America (HIAA) has been a major lobbyer against a national health insurance system (Consumer Reports, 1990b). Alternatively, if a rationing plan included private insurance payors as intermediaries as has occurred with Medicare, there would be less opposition—particularly if this were seen as the lesser of the two evils. Private insurance companies also would be opposed to rationing policies that affected them adversely by mandating that they cover all individuals and all health services while capping their premiums. But if the rationing plan increases the numbers that are mandated to be insured, as with the Oregon plan, private insurance companies will approve.

Government Health Insurance Perspectives

The issues of rationing are totally different for public third-party payors. Currently they contribute about 40% of the monies for health care (Ginzberg, 1991). Moreover, the amount of monies for payments is limited by taxpayers' willingness to spend dollars for health care. Because the two major publicly sponsored health insurance programs, Medicare and Medicaid, are being hurt by the spiraling costs of health care, rationing as a means for controlling costs is being given even more consideration. A prime example is the Oregon plan, which was a response to increasing costs that made public programs insolvent. Likewise, there is less opposition to the concept of regulation from public programs as compared with private entities. Any rationing strategy that encourages the private sector to provide private insurance is welcomed by the public insurance sector because it means that fewer individuals have to be insured by the public dollars.

Health Maintenance Organizations' (HMOs) Perspectives

HMOs are in the dual role of being providers of care and third-party payors and thus have some perspectives on rationing from each group. HMOs traditionally have controlled costs by using rationing strategies such as managed care, limiting services through second opinions, and referrals. As providers who have attempted to give the least amount of care without creating iatrogenic problems, HMOs are less concerned if rationing of services means that fewer non-cost-effective services are provided. Furthermore, health providers working for an HMO are less concerned with autonomy as they have chosen to work under conditions that limit total freedom in clinical decision making. Conversely, HMOs are finding that their costs are also rising (Hill, 1990). Moreover, HMOs are concerned about having too many clients with costly health problems.

Employers' Perspectives

There are three groups of employers: those who offer private health insurance plans; those who self-insure; and those who do not offer health insurance as a benefit. Large businesses usually fit the first two categories and are very concerned about rising costs of health care. Between 1984 and 1989, the average portion of the payroll that went toward health insurance rose from 7.9% to 13.6% (Hill, 1990). If a business offers private health insurance, its perspectives are similar to those of consumers.

Some businesses have elected to pay directly for their employees' health bills, are self-insured, and take on the concerns of third-party payors. Their concerns are similar to those of government-sponsored health insurance because paying for health care is not their prime business and they also are limited in the amount of money to spend.

Small businesses are the employers who are more likely not to provide any health insurance to their employees and dependents; the costs of health insurance are so high that these companies often cannot afford this and still stay in business. As the number of small businesses increased over the past decade, more individuals are without health insurance. When these consumers become ill, their costs are shifted to those who do pay (i.e., those with private or public health insurance).

Because of this situation, employers who offer good benefits would like those who do not to be forced to provide health care even if it involves some form of rationing. This has been a major change in attitude regarding the government's role; big businesses now want more government regulations to control the cost of health care (Hill, 1990). Small employers still do not want to be mandated to provide coverage because they continue to fear negative economic consequences (Ginzberg, 1991).

In Oregon, the business community's reactions to the Oregon plan was generally positive (Brown, 1990; Eddy, 1991). The Associated Oregon Industries, which represents large businesses, hopes it will decrease the cost shifting. On the other hand, the National Federation of Independent Business representing smaller businesses was less supportive because of mandating coverage (Brown, 1990). Alternatively, these small businesses were positive about limiting services so as to make an insurance premium more affordable ("Cut Competition," 1991). Mehlman (1991) also agreed that the winners might be businesses, because this plan is aimed at stopping the increasing costs and does not discuss additional taxation.

In conclusion, rationing of health care is a complex issue. There are some aspects on which consumers, providers, and third-party payors agree, but there are many other points on which they differ. Beliefs about autonomy, rights, and professional roles affect viewpoints. In addition, economics is a major consideration on whether any one rationing strategy is favored or rejected. Each of these three major constituencies with equal and opposing viewpoints on rationing has at its core an economic self-interest. In the past, of the three groups, the perspectives of the physician providers and the third-party payors have predominated. But in the past decade there has been a shift in the balance of influence among these groups as each has diversified. It is likely that the traditional physician groups and private third-party payors will continue to have a strong influence on the shape of the future health care system. Primary evidence of their influence is seen with the number of health care reform proposals that continue to support a public-private partnership in financing the health care system. On the other hand, many physicians have formed alternative groups that now oppose the views of the American Medical Association; they are speaking with a strong voice for more radical changes in the health care system. Also, as mentioned earlier, government third-party payors, HMOs, and self-insured businesses have different concerns about access and cost of health care as compared with private health insurance companies, and some of these concerns are more congruent with the other constituencies. In addition, the public's image of private third-party payors is tarnished, and the public is beginning to question the social salience of this group to society as more citizens become uninsured. The public has become more vocal about a need for change in the health care system. Their influence will rest on whether they can become more knowledgeable about the health care problems and solutions and issue a clear mandate. Likewise, although nurses' influence also has increased politically, it remains to be seen whether the number of nurses who are knowledgeable about the issues increases and whether they can exert a united influence on health care reform. The *Nursing Agenda for Health Care Reform* is one positive step in this direction.

Resolving the differing perspectives on health care rationing requires a balance of each group's views and interests. Nurses need to ensure that their perspectives are heard; likewise, nurses and others need to promote the public's understanding of the issues and guarantee that their views are considered. Although economic considerations are important to each group, there should be equal weight given to the social and ethical elements of the different rationing strategies. In this way the best reconciliation of conflicting perspectives can be achieved to strike a public policy course.

REFERENCES

Abrams, F. R. (1987). Access to health care. In G. R. Anderson & V. A. Glesnes-Anderson (Eds.), *Health Care Ethics* (pp. 49-68). Rockville, MD: Aspen.

Agich, G. L. (1990). Rationing and professional autonomy. *Law, Medicine & Health Care, 18*(1-2), 77-84.

American Nurses Association (ANA). (1991). *Nursing's agenda for health care reform.* Kansas City, MO: Author.

Bellocq, J. A. (1989). Liability for cost containment. *Journal of Professional Nursing, 5*(2), 63, 113.

Brown, C. (1990). Dr. Kitzhaber goes to Washington, *Oregon Business, 13*, 23-25.

Burke, M. (1991). Hospitals gain from Oregon plan, says Medicaid director. *Hospitals, 65*(1), 44.

Callahan, D. (1987). *Setting limits: Medical goals in an aging society.* New York: Simon & Schuster.

Capuzzi, C. (in press). Oregon model of decision-making and its implications for nursing practice. In J.C. McCloskey & H.K. Grace (Eds.), *Current Issues in Nursing*, 4th ed. St. Louis: Mosby-Year Book.

Collins, H. L. (1990). When the profit motive threatens patient care. In C.A. Lindeman & M. McAthie (Eds.), *Nursing Trends and Issues* (pp. 432-438). Springhouse, PA: Springhouse.

Consumer Reports. (1990a, August). *The crisis in health insurance, part 1.* Mount Vernon, NY: Consumers Union of United States.

Consumer Reports. (1990b, September). *The crisis in health insurance, part 2.* Mount Vernon, NY: Consumers Union of United States.

Consumer Reports. (1992, August). *Are HMOs the answer?* Mount Vernon, NY: Consumers Union of United States.

Crawshaw, R., Garland, M, Hines, B., & Anderson, B. (1990). Developing principles for prudent health care allocation, the continuing Oregon experiment. *Western Journal of Medicine, 152*, 441-446.

Cut Competition to cut costs. *Oregon Business, 14*(7), 23-34.

Daniels, N. (1989). Cost containment and justice. *Mt. Sinai Journal of Medicine, 56*(3), 180-184.

Davidson, L. A., & Huckabay, L. M. D. (1986). Health care rationing: Ethical reflections. *Nursing Administrative Quarterly, 10*(3), 59-67.

Eddy, D. M. (1991). Oregon's plan, should it be approved? *Journal of the American Medical Association, 266*(17), 2439-2445.

Etzioni, A. (1991). Health care rationing: A critical evaluation. *Health Affairs, 10*(2), 88-95.

Ferrans, C. E. (1987). Quality of life as a criterion for allocation of life-sustaining treatment: The case of hemodialysis. In G. R. Anderson & V. A. Glesnes-Anderson (Eds.), *Health Care Ethics* (pp. 109-124). Rockville, MD: Aspen.

Finkelstein, L. E. (1989). Rationing health care violates our ethical code. *Nursing Outlook, 31*(1), 8.

Fry, S. T. (1990). Rationing health care services, ethical issues for nursing. In J. C. McCloskey & H. K. Grace (Eds.). *Current Issues in Nursing*, 3rd ed. (pp. 582-586). St. Louis: Mosby-Year Book.

Gabel, J., Cohen, H., & Fink, S. (1989). Americans' views on health care: Foolish inconsistencies? *Health Affairs, 8*(1), 103-118.

Ginzberg, E. (1991). Interest groups and health reform. *Transactions & Studies of the College of Physicians of Philadelphia, 13*(3), 235-247.

Hill, R. L. (1990). Running out of choices. *Oregon Business, 13*, 19-22.

Huey, F. (1988). To the president and congress: Nurses know that U.S. citizens can get better access to better health care at affordable costs. Are you ready to change the system? *American Journal of Nursing, 88*, 1483-1493.

Jecker, N. S., & Pearlman, R. A. (1989). Ethical constraints on rationing medical care by age. *Journal of the American Geriatrics Society, 37*, 1067-1075.

Johnsson, J. (1991). High-tech health care: How much can we afford? *Hospitals, 65*(16), 80.

Kapp, M. B. (1989). Legal concerns affecting nonprofit community agencies that serve the elderly. *Quality Review Bulletin, 15*, 86-91.

Kelly, L. S. (1990). Survey of health care executives reveals priorities for allocation of care. *Nursing Outlook, 38*(3), 110.

Kitzhaber, J. (1991). A healthier approach to health care. *Issues in Science and Technology, 7*(2), 59-65.

Larkin, H. (1988). Will the public support health care rationing? *Hospitals, 62(9)*, 79.

Larkin, H. (1990). CEOs split over Oregon Medicaid reform. *Hospitals, 64*(2), 75.

LaRochelle, D. (1989). The moral dilemma of rationing nursing resources. *Journal of Professional Nursing, 5*(4), 173, 236.

Lee, R. G., & Miller, F. H. (1990). The doctor's changing role in allocating U.S. and British medical services. *Law, Medicine & Health Care, 18*(1-2), 69-76.

Lindeman, C. A., & McAthie, M. (1990). *Nursing Trends and Issues*. Springhouse, PA: Springhouse.

McGregor, M. (1989). Technology and the allocation of resources. *New England Journal of Medicine, 320*(2), 118-120.

Mehlman, M. J. (1991). The Oregon Medicaid program: Is it just? *Health Matrix, 1*, 175-199.

Morreim, E. H. (1992). Rationing and the law. In M. A. Strosberg, J. M. Wiener, R. Baker, & I. A. Fein (Eds.), *Rationing America's Medical Care: The Oregon Plan and Beyond* (pp. 159-184). Washington, DC: Brookings.

Oregon Health Services Commission (1991). *Prioritization of Health Services, A Report to the Governor and Legislature*. Salem, OR: Oregon Health Services Commission.

Potter, C., & Porter, J. (1989). American perceptions of the British national health service: Five myths. *Journal of Health Politics, Policy and Law, 14*(2), 341-365.

Reckling, J. B. (1989). Abandonment of patients by home health nursing agencies: An ethical analysis of the dilemma. *Advances in Nursing Science, 11*(3), 70-81.

Rooks, J. (1990). Let's admit we ration health care—then set priorities. *American Journal of Nursing, 90*(6), 39-43.

Sixty-fifth Oregon Legislative Assembly (1989). *Senate Bill 27*. Salem, OR: 65th Oregon Legislative Assembly.

Steinbrook R., & Lo, B. (1992). The Oregon Medicaid demonstration project—Will it provide adequate medical care? *New England Journal of Medicine, 326*(5), 340-344.

Veatch, R. M. (1992). The Oregon experiment: Needless and real worries. In M. A. Strosberg, J. M. Wiener, R. Baker, & I. A. Fein (Eds.), *Rationing America's medical care: The Oregon plan and beyond* (pp. 78-90). Washington, DC: Brookings.

Ward, D. (1990). National health insurance: Where do nurses fit in? *Nursing Outlook, 38*(5), 206-207.

Wiener, J. M. (1992). Rationing in America: Overt and covert. In M. A. Strosberg, J. M. Wiener, R. Baker, & I. A. Fein (Eds.), *Rationing America's Medical Care: The Oregon Plan and Beyond* (pp. 12-23). Washington, DC: Brookings.

Williams, A. (1988). Health economics: The end of clinical freedom? *British Medical Journal, 297,* 1183-1186.

Wood, C. (1991). Health care rationing: The Oregon experiment. *Nursing Economics, 9*(4), 239-243.

CHAPTER 7

Preventive Health Care for America's Underserved: From Policies to Payoffs

Susan J. Simmons

Health objectives for the year 2000 provide a blueprint for achieving quality of health and life while reducing disparity in access to care. The economic impact of pursuing the national health objectives is explored. Recognizing the lack of "fit" between a prevention orientation to health care and the traditional sick-care focus of contemporary health care in the United States, strategies are offered to address access, cost, and quality through allocation of resources to prevention services. Examples of such efforts are provided.

Nursing's focus on health-related experiences across the life span is reflected in its growing data base on the characteristics, outcomes, and interventions associated with health promotion. Such a focus, along with similar efforts from other disciplines, inspired the development of public policy guidelines, such as those contained in *Healthy People 2000: National Health Promotion and Disease Prevention Objectives* (U.S. Public Health Service, 1990). The year 2000 objectives provide a comprehensive blueprint for improving healthy life, reducing health disparities, and achieving access to preventive services for all Americans. In fact, mobilizing the creativity and commitment of the nation in the interest of health promotion is now recognized as both a health and economic imperative.

Policy Coordinator, Office on Women's Health, Office of the Assistant Secretary for Health, Department of Health and Human Services, Washington, D.C. 20201

Series on Nursing Administration—Volume 6, 1994

To understand the dynamics of health promotion, health status and preventive care patterns must be analyzed. The concept of equitable access to preventive care for all Americans has been nourished in recent years by the demonstrated effectiveness of clinical preventive services in reducing premature morbidity and mortality (U.S. Preventive Services Task Force, 1989). Yet an equal opportunity for health promotion through preventive care remains unrealized for a growing percentage of citizens. According to the National Association of Community Health Centers (Hawkins & Rosenbaum, 1992), approximately 50 million Americans were underserved in 1990. Given that an estimated 35 million citizens are without health insurance (Friedman, 1991) and 20 million more have insufficient coverage in the event of serious illness (Pepper Commission, 1990), it is not unreasonable to suggest that access to preventive care has become one of the pivotal health priorities of the 1990s. Nursing's long-standing awareness and support of health promotion for underserved groups can and should serve as a touchstone for realizing equitable access to preventive health care.

This chapter addresses four issues pertaining to health promotion for the underserved:

1. Clinical and cost effectiveness of preventive health care
2. Health status and preventive care profiles of the underserved
3. Policy and programmatic initiatives targeting preventive care access
4. Strategies for strengthening nursing's leadership and participation in health promotion for America's underserved

In this context, the term *underserved*—known also as *medically indigent* or *socioeconomically disadvantaged*—applies to persons who because of age, gender, ethnicity, income, education, residence, or insurance status have seriously limited access to clinical preventive services. Given the overwhelming significance of income as a determinant of primary and preventive care access, this report includes the status of both the poor (those below the federal poverty level) and the near-poor (those below or just above the federal level yet without public or private health insurance coverage). Preventive health care is broadly defined here as any health care provider/client interaction that promotes health and prevents illness, disability, and premature death. More specifically, preventive health care consists of counseling, screening, and immunization services designed either to inhibit the occurrence of disease or injury (primary prevention) or to detect and treat risk factors for disease or injury (secondary prevention).

PREVENTIVE HEALTH CARE: CLINICAL AND COST EFFECTIVENESS

Establishing the impact of prevention on health has preceded establishing its impact on economics. The clinical effectiveness of prevention was identified in the U.S. Preventive Services Task Force (1989) report *Guide to Clinical Preventive Services*. This report provided age-, gender-, and risk factor–specific recommendations for the prevention of more than 60 major causes of morbidity and mortality. The methodology of the report involved a thorough examination of the quality of scientific evidence for the effectiveness of screening tests, immunizations, and counseling interventions. A principal finding relevant for nursing was that counseling to change personal health behaviors long before the onset of clinical disease is the most promising role for prevention in current health care practice. The task force report indicated that both practitioners and clients must assume responsibility for health promotion, with the client being empowered for behavioral change.

The belief that prevention should be judged on the criterion of whether the gains in health are a reasonable return for the costs occurs at a time when the nation continues to endure the economic burden of preventable illness, injury, and disability. The portion of the gross national product (GNP) spent on health care rose from 5.3% in 1960 to 12.2% ($666 billion) in 1990 (National Center for Health Statistics, 1992). The cost for diagnosis and treatment of such conditions as heart disease, cancer, injuries, and low birth weight, have exceeded society's ability to pay for what are essentially preventable conditions.

The reality of skyrocketing health care expenditures has ushered in cost-effectiveness analysis as an approach for determining how financial resources are—and should be—used in health care. The specific purpose of cost-effectiveness analysis is to help clinicians and policymakers focus on investments that bring the most health for the required expenditure, with outcomes reported either as a single measure (e.g., years of life saved) or as several measures combined on a single scale (e.g., quality-adjusted life years) (Eisenberg, 1988). Thus far, cost-effectiveness analyses of preventive services have included lead screening, cholesterol screening, cervical cancer screening for older, low-income women, and mammography screening for women 65 years and older. The fact that most counseling interventions have not yet undergone cost-effectiveness analysis may explain why the 1989 National Ambulatory Medical Care Survey (Woodwell, 1992) showed that primary care physicians spent less than 15% of their time counseling clients on weight reduction, cholesterol reduction, smoking cessation, and breast self-examination.

A number of fundamental questions remain concerning the cost-effectiveness of preventive health care. It has been estimated that providing coverage for preventive services is likely to increase costs in the short term (Russell, 1986), which is problematic given the current era of unrestrained health care costs. Furthermore, preventive services may vary in clinical effectiveness and cost effectiveness when performed by health care providers using different techniques. Another consideration involves the differential costs per year for services that have undergone cost-effectiveness analysis, suggesting that personal and social values may influence whether a preventive intervention is judged to be cost effective.

Because the U.S. health care financing system has evolved historically with a bias toward coverage for acute illnesses, it has been difficult to include coverage for preventive services in most public and private insurance plans. Among public plans, which are relevant to underserved populations, Medicare provides coverage for only a limited number of preventive services: pneumococcal and hepatitis B vaccines, cervical cancer screening, and mammography. Medicaid mandates two major types of preventive services be available for individuals under 21 years of age: family planning services; and early/periodic screening, diagnosis, and treatment (EPSDT). Other services, such as wellness checkups, immunizations, and dental care, are offered only as optional services in some states.

A core package of preventive services for Medicare- and Medicaid-eligible adults is undergoing internal review within the U.S. Department of Health and Human Services (1991). This package, which is based on the recommendations of the U.S. Preventive Services Task Force (1989), provides a minimum set of age- and gender-specific services (risk assessment, immunizations, physical examinations, and risk-specific counseling) for inclusion in periodic health visits. How such recommendations will yield lower incidences of infant mortality and chronic morbidity for underserved groups is yet to be determined.

HEALTH AND PREVENTIVE CARE PROFILES OF UNDERSERVED GROUPS

The accurate assessment of health status and preventive care patterns of the underserved has been hindered by the heterogeneity of these groups, as well as by the limited data systems for tracking preventive care access. Two national reports, *Health United States 1991* (National Center for Health Statistics, 1992) and *Health Status of the Disadvantaged: Chartbook 1990* (Health Resources and Services Administration, 1990), illustrate some of the disparities in health status and overall health care utilization rates among various populations. For example, between 1980 and 1989 the age-adjusted percentage of individuals under age 65 without any health insurance increased from 13% to 16%. Among those persons most likely to be uninsured were blacks (22%), individuals with incomes below the poverty threshold (36%), the unemployed (39%), and persons with less than 12 years of education (30%). The health status–adjusted physician utilization rates of ethnic minority groups were lower than the rate for whites. Between 1984 and 1989, persons with higher incomes were more likely to receive their care through ambulatory visits, whereas persons with lower incomes were more likely to use hospital outpatient services for their primary source of care. In 1990 less than 1% of Medicaid funds was directed to early and periodic screening, rural health clinics, and family planning services.

According to a report on the 1987 National Medical Expenditure Survey (NMES) (Agency for Health Care Policy and Research, 1991), individuals who are uninsured or who have inadequate coverage may well forego primary and preventive health care. Additional evidence of this primary care underservice is found in The Robert Wood Johnson Foundation's (1978; 1983; 1987) National Access to Care Surveys, which identify factors associated with utilization of health care services. The most recent survey indicated that 43 million Americans (18% of the population) did not have a health care provider, clinic, or hospital as a regular source of health care, representing a 7% increase over an earlier survey. At the same time, the percentage of individuals who reported having no ambulatory visit in the prior 12 months rose significantly—from 19% to 33%. Underserved populations were affected disproportionately, with a significantly higher percentage of poor, uninsured, and ethnic minority individuals reporting no regular source of care, no ambulatory visits within the preceding 12 months, and fair or poor health status.

The health and preventive care profiles of the following underserved groups provide a context within which to review policies and programs for promoting health through preventive health care. Statistics are provided to the extent that they illuminate the issues, identify more clearly the areas that need attention, and help direct efforts and resources.

Infants

Perhaps no other indicator of health is as dramatic for underserved populations as the infant mortality rate. Although the mortality rate for American infants dropped from 29.2 per 1000 live births in 1950 to 9.1 per 1000 live births in 1990, the U.S. infant mortality rate continues to rank among the highest of industrialized nations. Despite an overall downward trend, the infant mortality rates for several ethnic minority groups have remained consistently higher than the national average. For example, black infants are twice as likely as white infants to die before their first birthday and twice as likely to be born weighing less than 2500 grams (National Center for Health Statistics, 1992).

Poor pregnancy outcomes are influenced by late or no prenatal care, ethnicity, low income, low educational level, unemployment or low occupational status, being unmarried, and teen pregnancy (Institute of Medicine, 1985). Women living in poverty are 3 times more likely than nonpoor women to obtain late prenatal care or none at all. In 1989 early prenatal care was used by only 57% of Mexican American and Native American women and 62% of black, Central and South American, and Puerto Rican women compared with 79% of white women (National Center for Health Statistics, 1992).

Children and Adolescents

As in the case of underserved mothers and infants, the adverse health status of disadvantaged children is associated with an array of social circumstances, including poverty, limited parental education, extramarital births, single and/or adolescent parents, nonwhite ethnicity, and limited access to primary and preventive care. Underserved children are more likely to die during early childhood; more likely to experience acute illnesses, injuries, lead poisoning, or child abuse; and more likely to suffer from nutrition-related problems, chronic illnesses, and developmental disabilities (Klerman, 1991a).

The 1986 National Access to Care Survey (The Robert Wood Johnson Foundation, 1987) revealed that 15% of all poor children under age 17 lacked a regular source of health care—twice the percentage as among nonpoor children. An analysis of preventive care use by school-age children demonstrated that those in families with incomes below the poverty level were 52% less likely to receive routine medical and dental examinations; only 22% of all Medicaid-eligible children made frequent use of preventive care (Newacheck & Halfon, 1988). In 1985, whereas more than 60% of white children were reported to have been immunized against communicable diseases, less than half of all other children received any immunizations (Health Resources and Services Administration, 1990).

Poor families are more likely to seek their care in settings that are not designed to provide primary or preventive services (e.g., hospital emergency rooms). Yet, because they engage in fewer health-promoting behaviors than the nonpoor, families living in poverty are in greater need of preventive health care. Inadequate knowledge of the importance of preventive behaviors and services, insufficient funds, preoccupation with immediate survival issues, and feelings of powerlessness are all cited as reasons these families do not have life-styles and preventive care patterns that are favorable to the health of infants and children (Klerman, 1991b).

For the leading causes of death among adolescents—unintentional injuries, homicide, and suicide—ethnic minority groups experience disproportionately higher rates. Between 1985 and 1989 the homicide rate for black males ages 15 to 24 years increased by 74% to 114.8 deaths per 100,000—almost 9 times the homicide rate for white males in this age group. Since the mid-1980s the suicide rate among adolescent black males has been increasing faster than the rate among adolescent white males. The suicide rate for Native American youth is nearly twice the rate as for white youth (National Center for Health Statistics, 1992).

The role of economics in adolescent health care is demonstrated by low-income adolescents being more prone to adverse health outcomes than are nonpoor adolescents. Low-income adolescents have significantly higher rates of sexually transmitted diseases, unintended pregnancy, depression, and substance abuse (U.S. Public Health Service, 1990). Adolescents without health insurance, often from poor working families, are more likely to delay seeking health care. Adolescent access issues include specific concerns about location of health care facilities and their hours of operation, as well as the ability of minors to consent to their own health care (Jenkins, 1991).

Adults

The health and preventive care patterns of adults, like those of infants and children, are shaped by a mosaic of economic, ethnic, and other social characteristics. For example, health disparities between black and white adults are demonstrated by a shorter life expectancy for blacks, as well as a higher incidence of preventable conditions, such as cardiovascular disease, certain cancers, diabetes, and homicide. Obesity and cigarette smoking are among the health risks seen more frequently in ethnic minority and low socioeconomic groups. For example, black women have a higher prevalence of being overweight and a reduced likelihood of weight loss than white women (Kahn, Williamson, & Stevens, 1991). In 1987 the smoking rates of black men (39%), Native American men (37%), and Puerto Rican men (37%) were higher than the rate for white men (29%) (National Center for Health Statistics, 1992).

Although ethnic minority groups are more likely to require health care, they are less likely to receive it. Between 1985 and 1986 the number of ambulatory visits decreased for blacks (6.8) and Hispanics (8.6) in fair or poor health, whereas the average number of visits for whites (10.1) increased. For the adult poor, the number of ambulatory visits declined 30% between 1982 and 1986 (The Robert Wood Johnson Foundation, 1987). As in the case of other underserved groups, low-income adults and those with public aid/self-pay status are more likely to use hospital emergency rooms as their routine source of health care and more likely to delay seeking needed care than higher-income and fully insured adults (Pane, 1991). The Hispanic Health and Nutrition Examination Survey, sponsored by the National Center for Health Statistics from 1982 through 1984, showed that the use of preventive health services (physical, dental, and eye examinations, Papanicolaou test, and clinical breast examination) among Mexican American, Cuban American, and Puerto Rican adults was less for those without a routine place for health care, no health insurance coverage, and no regular primary care provider than for those who did not experience these access barriers (Solis, Marks, Garcia, & Shelton, 1990). The tendency for adult populations at greater risk for disease to be less likely to receive preventive services has been observed for specific screening procedures.

This "reverse targeting" tendency was predicted primarily by inadequate insurance coverage in a sample of middle-aged women who received four screening tests: blood pressure check, clinical breast examination, Papanicolaou test, and examination for glaucoma. Lack of insurance was more prevalent among blacks (20%), the poor (35%), those without a high school education (19%), and those in fair or poor health (18%)

(Woolhandler & Himmelstein, 1988). The impact of insurance status and other socioeconomic factors has also been demonstrated in studies of screening mammography, which showed that having no insurance and being non-white, poor, and older were all associated with less likelihood of receiving a screening mammogram in the past year (Anda, Sienko, Remington, Gentry, & Marks, 1987; Zapka, Stoddard, Costanza, & Greene, 1989).

Among all age-groups, older adults represent those who are most in need of clinical preventive services to offset disabling and life-threatening conditions. Especially important for this age-group are screening tests for cardiovascular disease and breast, cervical, and colorectal cancers, as well as immunizations against pneumococcal disease and influenza (U.S. Public Health Service, 1990). Yet public and private insurers traditionally have not covered the costs of primary and secondary preventive services. As a result, the delivery of health care to older adults often is fragmented, with individuals having no primary care provider as case manager. For example, Medicare is currently prohibited by law from offering coverage for preventive services, except for vaccines for pneumococcal pneumonia and hepatitis B and screening for breast and cervical cancers (Office of Technology Assessment, 1990).

Approximately one third of black and Hispanic older adults have private insurance in addition to Medicare, compared with three fourths of white adults (National Center for Health Statistics, 1992). Between 1982 and 1986 ambulatory health care visits for poor older adults declined 20% (The Robert Wood Johnson Foundation, 1987). Self-reported utilization rates for selected screening tests indicated that increasing age was associated with a decline in the number of women who had practiced breast self-examination or who had received a screening mammogram or Papanicolaou test in the previous year. Having a regular physician was highly correlated with receipt of screening services (Chao, Paganini-Hill, Ross, & Henderson, 1987). These findings suggest that the opportunity for older Americans to access preventive care is not universal.

The Medicare structure leaves older women especially vulnerable because of the inadequate coverage of chronic conditions typically experienced by more women than men. Older women who have only Medicare coverage are more likely than men to have illnesses with moderate to high out-of-pocket expenses (Horton, 1992). Given the predominance of poverty among older women, out-of-pocket expenses become more of a hardship in this population, with limited or no coverage for primary and secondary preventive services.

For some underserved populations, unstable or dangerous physical environments, isolation, and the lack of adequate and available health services exacerbate the already high rates of preventable illness and death. For example, data obtained over the past decade show that women in rural areas are less likely to receive early prenatal care than are women in urban areas. The race-specific infant mortality rates are slightly higher and physician visits for children and adolescents somewhat lower in rural areas than in other areas (Klerman, 1991c). Access barriers faced by rural families, especially those who are poor, include declining numbers of primary care physicians, reductions in the National Health Service Corps, inadequate state-supported maternal and child health services, and insufficient funding of community and migrant health centers (Hughes & Rosenbaum, 1989). Yet a study of a rural clinic population in the Midwest demonstrated that despite physicians' underestimation, clients are interested in a broad range of preventive services, including periodic health examinations and life-style counseling interventions (Stanford & Solberg, 1991).

Numerous reports illustrate the health and social problems of ethnic minority populations living in urban areas of concentrated poverty. Crime, unemployment, dropping out of school, and teenage pregnancy all are higher in urban areas than elsewhere (Klerman, 1991c), as are the adverse health conditions noted earlier, such as infant mortality, injuries, and life-style–related diseases. Many health care practitioners have moved away from inner-city areas, which have high concentrations of poor families, to the suburbs. For those practitioners who have stayed in the inner city, the Medicaid reimbursement level often deters them from providing primary health care to these families (Klerman, 1991b). For example, data from a survey of primary care physicians in New York City showed that those with predominantly black and Hispanic patient populations who were 65 years of age or older were less likely to recommend screening mammography (7% versus 23%) or influenza vaccination (48% versus 74%) than those with predominantly white patient populations of the same age group (Gemson, Elinson, & Messeri, 1988).

Perhaps for no other group is the convergence of economic hardship, social isolation, and physical and mental disability more apparent than for homeless individuals and families. The Institute of Medicine's (1988a) report *Homelessness, Health, and Human Needs* states that families with children are the fastest-growing subgroup among the homeless. Data indicate that homeless children have a higher incidence of upper respiratory infections, malnutrition, skin diseases, and traumas. In addition, these children have immunization delays, elevated blood lead levels, and increased rates of child abuse and hospital admissions (Klerman, 1991c). A study of homeless adults in Charleston, South Carolina found that the majority of respondents had no insurance coverage, knew little about availability of health services, and had no regular source of primary health care (Malloy, Christ, & Hohloch, 1990). A survey of shelters serving women in Chicago revealed that most of the women did not view prenatal care as a high priority—in large part because they were fearful of losing their infants if they listed the shelter as their place of residence (Barge & Norr, 1991).

IMPROVING PREVENTIVE CARE ACCESS: POLICY AND PROGRAM DEVELOPMENT

Disparities in health and preventive care access between majority and underserved populations highlight the need for a multifaceted approach to promote access to preventive health services. In recent years numerous public and private strategies have been designed to correct inequities in health care access. Some policies have focused on improving the environment of care, whereas others have promoted adoption of preventive health behaviors and services. Most programs for the underserved have addressed either specific services for general groups (e.g., cancer prevention for low-income adults) or comprehensive services for specific populations (e.g., mothers and infants).

The year 2000 national health objectives provide a comprehensive framework for narrowing the gaps in health status, risk factors, and preventive services delivery between the total population and those who experience excessive rates of premature morbidity and mortality (U.S. Public Health Service, 1990). The *Public Health Service Action Plan for Women's Health* (U.S. Public Health Service, 1991a) is another goal-driven blueprint for addressing a variety of women's health issues in the areas of prevention, research, education, and service delivery. Additional policy trends in recent years include the access-to-care legislation and position statements developed by professional health organizations, the health insurance industry, and academic health settings. For example, the American Medical Association (1990) has called for greater access to care for the uninsured, greater awareness of and responsiveness to racial disparities in health care access, and development of practice parameters that will prevent racial disparities. The American Nurses Association's (1991) report *Nursing's Agenda for Health Care Reform* endorses the integration of public and private strategies in providing health care packages that emphasize primary and preventive services. The Health Insurance Association of America's proposal advocates worksite health reforms, as well as government responsibility for the primary health care of the poor and near-poor (Schramm, 1991).

The idea that large-scale financing reforms will automatically yield broadened access to primary and preventive health care has recently been challenged (Ginzberg & Ostow, 1991; Menken, 1991). The health and preventive care profiles described earlier suggest that barriers related to cost, sociocultural context, and provider availability have each contributed to the imbalances in health care access. The following examples illustrate policy and programmatic initiatives that consider a range of barriers in an effort to narrow the health and preventive care gaps between majority and underserved populations.

Public Initiatives

The Institute of Medicine's (1988b) landmark report *The Future of Public Health* maintained that the Federal government has ultimate responsibility for assuring equitable access to health care for all citizens. The Health Resources and Services Administration (HRSA) is the U.S. Public Health Service agency responsible for assuring the availability of preventive and primary care services, especially to the underserved. Underserved populations are the targets of numerous HRSA programs, including the Community and Migrant Health Centers, Rural Health, Maternal and Child Health block grants, and Health Care for the Homeless (Harmon & Carlson, 1991; Sundwall & Tavani, 1991).

In addition to the responsibility for a broad range of primary and preventive care programs, HRSA sponsors initiatives for training health professionals, including the Health Professions Training Program and the National Health Service Corps (Politzer, Harris, Gaston, & Mullan, 1991). Mechanisms for improving preventive care access also have included grants to primary care associations and cooperative agreements between community and migrant health centers and state and local health departments. The purpose of these agreements is to support state leadership in providing comprehensive primary care services to underserved populations. HRSA also has collaborated with The Robert Wood Johnson Foundation on a number of projects, including the *Healthy Generations* initiative. This initiative is designed to improve access and quality of preventive services for pregnant women and infants through outreach and coordinated systems of care (Crane, 1991).

Maternal-Infant Health

Reducing infant mortality remains one of the nation's highest priorities. In addition to the HRSA programs just described, a number of public health programs have focused on underserved mothers and infants in the areas of injury prevention, lead poisoning prevention, nutrition supplementation and counseling, immunizations, and newborn screening (Klerman, 1991d). The report of the U.S. Public Health Service Expert Panel on the Content of Prenatal Care (1989), as well as a report prepared for the Interagency Committee on Infant Mortality (Culpepper, 1991), highlight the need for health and psychosocial interventions and health services research in the prevention of infant mortality.

The National Commission to Prevent Infant Mortality was established by Congress in 1987 to develop and implement a national strategic plan for reducing infant mortality and morbidity. The Commission's (1991) report *One-Stop Shopping: The Road to Healthy Mothers and Children* outlines a national strategy for coordinating the health and social services for pregnant women and their families. Emphasis is placed on a public-private sharing of accountability in the ongoing assessment of local needs and the delivery of client-centered care. The strategy is designed to help locate, enroll, support, educate, and provide preventive, primary, and referral services to underserved mothers and children.

Cancer Prevention Programs

The *National Strategic Plan for the Early Detection and Control of Breast and Cervical Cancer* (U.S. Public Health Service, 1991b) provides a comprehensive approach for assuring that all women receive regular screening for breast and cervical cancer as needed and that tests are performed in accordance with quality assurance guidelines. The plan outlines mechanisms by which the early detection and control of breast and cervical cancer can best be achieved through integration of services, public and professional education, and quality assurance and evaluation of programmatic efforts. Target populations for this plan include older, poor, less-educated, and ethnic minority women.

The National Cancer Institute (NCI) (1991) has established the multi-year *Prescribe for Health Program*, a large-scale initiative to evaluate methods for implementing NCI's working guidelines on early cancer detection. The focus of the program is on improving physicians' skills in early detection of the major types of cancer: breast, skin, colorectal, testicular, oral cavity, and uterine cervix. A total of 348 medical practices—approximately 1000 physicians and 60,000 patients—will be studied in four geographical areas of the country. A principal hypothesis is that the program will have a significant impact on those populations most in need of early cancer detection services, including low-income, older, and ethnic minority individuals.

Older Adult Health

The Health Care Financing Administration is supporting six demonstration projects that offer clinical preventive services to Medicare beneficiaries (Office of Technology Assessment, 1990). The purpose of these projects is to evaluate the health and cost effects of offering packages of preventive services to older Americans. These projects provide a mix of physical examinations, immunizations, screening tests, and counseling. The primary goal of all six projects is to demonstrate both clinical and cost effectiveness of preventive services for the targeted population. Thus far, one of the six projects is yielding significant data on effectiveness, and the other five projects are providing information on the feasibility of access to and utilization of these services by older adults.

State Examples

The Institute on Health Care for the Poor and Underserved was established in 1988 to focus attention on the health status and health care needs of the poor and underserved (Meharry Medical College, 1990). Supported in part by the Tennessee Department of Health and Environment, the Institute seeks solutions to the health problems of underserved populations through research and evaluation and provides information and learning experiences to those involved in solving these problems.

The *Texas Primary Health Care Services Program* involves a partnership between public and private providers to deliver primary and preventive health care to underserved communities (Begley, Aday, & McCandless, 1989). Since its inception in 1985, the Texas Department of Health has contracted with community health centers, local health departments, and private clinics to provide a broad range of primary care services. Preventive services—screening, immunizations, family planning, and health education—represent approximately 56% of all services delivered.

A Private Effort—The Robert Wood Johnson Foundation (1991)

Improving the health and the delivery of health care to the nation has been the mission of The Robert Wood Johnson (RWJ) Foundation since its inception in 1972. In its nearly two decades as a national philanthropy, the Foundation has invested more than $1 billion in three categorical areas: service demonstration programs, research, and training. Among the three primary objectives currently pursued by RWJ is assuring access to basic health care for all Americans. Recognizing the multifaceted nature of health care access, RWJ has implemented a three-pronged grantmaking strategy: (1) reducing financial barriers by exploring options for expanded coverage for uninsured and underinsured persons; (2) reducing distributional barriers by strengthening the location and supply of primary care; and (3) reducing sociocultural and organizational barriers by fostering the capacity of communities to address their health concerns.

Following are examples of prevention-oriented programs targeted to achieving the goal of assured health care access:

1. *Community Care Funding Partners*—primary and preventive care projects for underserved groups in Kansas City, Dallas, Chicago, and rural Georgia.
2. *Healthy Futures*—a multiyear initiative to support new efforts in southern states to coordinate and improve maternal, perinatal, and infant care services.
3. *Homeless Families Program*—initiative to help homeless families in eight cities obtain needed health and social services. Grantees are located in Baltimore, San Francisco, Denver, Nashville, Houston, Atlanta, Portland, and Seattle.
4. *Program to Strengthen Primary Care Health Centers*—initiative to improve the capacity for self-sufficiency of not-for-profit primary health care centers in Oakland, Honolulu, Santa Fe, Arizona, and Colorado.
5. *Health Care for the Uninsured Program*—a 5-year effort to provide support to state and local entities for the implementation of innovative public/private financing and service delivery arrangements designed to improve access to care for uninsured populations. Most of the projects have involved development of health insurance mechanisms for small businesses and include some preventive services in their benefits packages: well baby care, routine physicals, immunizations, and hearing and eye examinations.

STRATEGIES FOR CHANGE

The health concerns and preventive care barriers experienced by underserved groups pose a dramatic challenge for clinicians, scientists, and policymakers alike. As this report indicates, health problems of the underserved range from infant mortality to excessive rates of preventable illness and death. Access limitations—cost, distribution of services and providers, and diverse patient demographics—underscore the need for a comprehensive approach to correcting the disparities in health status and preventive care delivery for currently underserved populations.

Given the importance of preventive care in promoting the health of the public, it is critical for nursing to articulate an agenda that will ensure equitable delivery of preventive health care for all Americans. The beginning of such an agenda is evident in the report *Nursing's Agenda for Health Care Reform* (American Nurses Association, 1991), a broad-based strategy that calls for a nationally defined standard package of primary and preventive health services. A central theme in this report is the development of provider/client relationships targeted to activities that will improve health outcomes in a cost-effective manner. By acting on this agenda in a timely and constructive manner, nursing can assume a position of leadership in promoting the health of underserved Americans. The policy guidelines and programmatic approaches cited in this report suggest three principal goals for nursing to consider in correcting preventive care access inequities.

Participate in Health-Promotion Policy Development

Cultivating nursing leadership in health policy development involves time, funds, expertise, authority, and education (Milio, 1989). While nurses continue to focus on the care of individuals in acute settings, there should be equal support for altering the contexts that result in preventable illness and disability. Professional attention to health-promoting environments and behaviors provides an entry point to the development of community-based models of primary care that emphasize health promotion and disease prevention.

Manuscripts, monographs, and other formal viewpoints should be developed by nursing groups concerned with economic, practice, education, or research issues in prevention. In an effort to build strong collaborative linkages with others, clear and realistic position papers should be presented before a variety of professional and governmental groups. One approach is to evaluate the *Healthy People 2000* report (U.S. Public Health Service, 1990) and identify how nursing initiatives support achievement of the national health-promotion and disease-prevention objectives. By directly linking disciplinary policies and programs with the broader prevention agenda, nursing is enabled to more fully participate in policy decision making and implementation.

Influence Consumer Expectations About Health Promotion

Presentations and other forms of public dialogue and education will help to raise public awareness of the value of prevention in promoting individual and community health. Nursing has the collective capacity to change the basic philosophy of the system from selling health care in the marketplace to creating a milieu for health behavior change. Encouraging meaningful community participation in addressing health issues provides a significant opportunity to narrow the gap between what is possible in terms of health promotion in this country and what is the reality.

Increasing consumer demand for preventive care and provider willingness to offer such care is influenced largely by covering preventive services in health insurance plans. Nursing should participate in a broad range of activities that evaluate options for expanding coverage of preventive health care. As long as fee-for-service remains the dominant method of payment for health care services, nursing should continue to lobby for equitable reimbursement. A preferable approach might be to establish a periodic preventive health visit fee that would specify an effectiveness-based package of preventive services for different population groups.

Increase the Availability of Preventive Health Care

Given the higher rates of preventable conditions among underserved populations, there is a justified need to promote the distribution and utilization of clinical preventive services. Community-based endeavors that combine public and private resources should be targeted to those most in need of preventive care. Delivery models that focus on the integration of preventive and primary care should be expanded into more areas. The current examination of relationships between community and migrant health centers and local health agencies should help direct future distribution, functioning, and financing of government-funded primary health care facilities.

Preventive health care delivery should be based on a broad research agenda that encompasses multiple health and social science perspectives. Nursing should participate in areas of research that will influence both personal and community health in a cost-effective manner. Service delivery also can benefit from an expanded health services research agenda that fosters collaboration with other disciplines, such as nutrition and education. Most important, preventive care should be adapted to the health and social problems of specific groups and supplemented as needed by the services of social workers, nutritionists, translators, and outreach workers. Alternative forms of preventive service delivery should be examined likewise, including mobile vans, school and worksite clinics, and other community-based sites.

In summary, improvements in the nation's health depend on reducing the health problems and preventive care barriers experienced by underserved populations. Evidence in this chapter demonstrates that several constituencies are already committed to realizing an equal opportunity for improved health for all through preventive care. The time is now for nursing to respond—through a combination of leadership, creativity, and determination—to establish a healthier future for all Americans.

REFERENCES

Agency for Health Care Policy and Research. (1991). *National Medical Expenditure Survey: Health insurance, use of health services, and health care expenditures*. Rockville, MD: U.S. Public Health Service.

American Medical Association. Council on Ethical and Judicial Affairs. (1990). Black-white disparities in health care. *Journal of the American Medical Association, 263*(17), 2344-2346.

American Nurses Association. (1991). *Nursing's agenda for health care reform*. Kansas City: Author.

Anda, R.F., Sienko, D.G., Remington, P.L., Gentry, E.M., & Marks, J.S. (1987). Screening mammography for women 50 years of age and older: Practices and trends. *American Journal of Preventive Medicine, 6*(3), 123-129.

Barge, F.C., & Norr, K.F. (1991). Homeless shelter policies for women in an urban environment. *IMAGE: Journal of Nursing Scholarship, 23*(3), 145-149.

Begley, C.E., Aday, L.A., & McCandless, R. (1989). Evaluation of a primary health care program for the poor. *Journal of Community Health, 14*(2), 107-120.

Chao, A., Paganini-Hill, A., Ross, R.K., & Henderson, B.E. (1987). Use of preventive care by the elderly. *Preventive Medicine, 16*, 710-722.

Crane, A.B. (1991). HRSA's collaborative efforts with national organizations to expand primary care for the medically underserved. *Public Health Reports, 106*(1), 10-14.

Culpepper, L. (Unpublished, 1991). *Reducing infant mortality: The research gaps*. A background paper for the Interagency Committee on Infant Mortality.

Eisenberg, J.M. (1988). Discussion of economic barriers to preventive services: Clinical obstacle or fiscal defense? In R.N. Battista & R.S. Lawrence (Eds.). *Implementing preventive services* (pp. 121-126). New York: Oxford University.

Friedman, E. (1991). The uninsured: From dilemma to crisis. *Journal of the American Medical Association, 265*, 2491-2495.

Gemson, D.H., Elinson, J., & Messeri, P. (1988). Differences in physician prevention practice patterns for white and minority populations. *Journal of Community Health, 13*(1), 53-64.

Ginzberg, E., & Ostow, M. (1991). Beyond universal health insurance to effective health care. *Journal of the American Medical Association, 265*(19), 2559-2562.

Harmon, R.G., & Carlson, R.H. (1991). HRSA's role in primary care and public health in the 1990s. *Public Health Reports, 106*(1), 6-10.

Hawkins, D.R., & Rosenbaum, S. (1992). *Lives in the balance: A national, state and county profile of America's medically underserved*. Washington, DC: National Association of Community Health Centers.

Health Resources and Services Administration. (1990). *Health status of the disadvantaged: Chartbook 1990*. Washington, DC: U.S. Public Health Service.

Horton, J.A. (Ed.). (1992). *The women's health data book: A profile of women's health in the United States*. Washington, DC: The Jacobs Institute of Women's Health.

Hughes, D., & Rosenbaum, S. (1989). An overview of maternal and infant health services in rural America. *Journal of Rural Health, 5*, 299-319.

Institute of Medicine. (1985). *Preventing low birth weight*. Washington, DC: National Academy Press.

Institute of Medicine. (1988a). *Homelessness, health, and human needs*. Washington, DC: National Academy Press.

Institute of Medicine. (1988b). *The future of public health*. Washington, DC: National Academy Press.

Jenkins, R.R. (1991). Social dynamics and health care in adolescence. *Journal of Health Care for the Poor and Underserved, 2*(1), 106-112.

Kahn, H.S., Williamson, D.F., & Stevens, J.A. (1991). Race and weight change in U.S. women: The roles of socioeconomic and marital status. *American Journal of Public Health, 81*(3), 319-323.

Klerman, L.V. (1991a). The health problems of children in poverty. In *Alive and well? A research and policy review of health programs for poor young children* (pp.19-40). New York: National Center for Children in Poverty, Columbia University School of Public Health.

Klerman, L.V. (1991b). The impact of poverty on health. In *Alive and well? A research and policy review of health programs for poor young children* (pp.51-59). New York: National Center for Children in Poverty, Columbia University School of Public Health.

Klerman, L.V. (1991c). Children with special problems that affect their health. In *Alive and well? A research and policy review of health programs for poor young children* (pp.41-50). New York: National Center for Children in Poverty, Columbia University School of Public Health.

Klerman, L.V. (1991d). Programs that have improved the health of children in poverty. In *Alive and well? A research and policy review of health programs for poor young children* (pp.73-92). New York: National Center for Children in Poverty, Columbia University School of Public Health.

Malloy, C., Christ, M.A., & Hohlock, F.J. (1990). The homeless: Social isolates. *Journal of Community Health Nursing, 7*(1), 25-36.

Meharry Medical College. (Unpublished, 1990). *Institute on health care for the poor and underserved*. (Fact sheet).

Menken, M. (1991). Caring for the underserved: Health insurance coverage is not enough. *Archives of Neurology, 48*, 472-475.

Milio, N. (1989). Developing nursing leadership in health policy. *Journal of Professional Nursing, 5*(6), 315-321.

National Cancer Institute. (Unpublished, 1991). *NCI launches Prescribe for Health program*. (Fact sheet).

National Center for Health Statistics, Centers for Disease Control. (1992). *Health United States 1991*. Hyattsville, MD: U.S. Public Health Service.

Newacheck, P.W., & Halfon, N. (1988). Preventive care use by school-aged children: Differences by socioeconomic status. *Pediatrics, 82*(3), 462-468.

Office of Technology Assessment. (1990). *Preventive health services for Medicare beneficiaries: Policies and research issues*. OTA-H-416. Washington, DC: U.S. Government Printing Office.

Pane, G.A. (1991). Health care access problems of medically indigent emergency walk-in patients. *Annals of Emergency Medicine, 20*(7), 730-733.

Pepper Commission. Bipartisan Commission on Comprehensive Health Care. (1990). *A call for action*. Washington, DC: U.S. Government Printing Office.

Politzer, R.M., Harris, D.L., Gaston, M.H., & Mullan, F. (1991). Primary care physician supply and the medically underserved: A status report and recommendations. *Journal of the American Medical Association, 266*(1), 104-109.

Russell, L. (1986). *Is prevention better than cure?* Washington, DC: Brookings Institution.

Schramm, C.J. (1991). Health care financing for all Americans. *Journal of the American Medical Association, 265*(24), 3296-3299.

Solis, J.M., Marks, G., Garcia, M., & Shelton, D. (1990). Acculturation, access to care, and use of preventive services by Hispanics: Findings from HHANES. *American Journal of Public Health, 80*(suppl), 11-19.

Stanford, J.B., & Solberg, L.I. (1991). Rural patients' interests in preventive medical care. *Journal of the American Board of Family Practice, 4*(1), 11-18.

Sundwall, D.N., & Tavani, C. (1991). The role of public health in providing primary care for the medically underserved. *Public Health Reports, 106*(1), 2-5.

The National Commission to Prevent Infant Mortality. (1991). *One-stop shopping: The road to healthy mothers and children.* Washington, DC: The National Commission to Prevent Infant Mortality.

The Robert Wood Johnson Foundation. (1978). *A new survey on access to medical care. Special report.* Princeton, NJ: Author.

The Robert Wood Johnson Foundation. (1983). *Updated report on access to health care for the American people. Special report.* Princeton, NJ: Author.

The Robert Wood Johnson Foundation. (1987). *Access to health care in the United States: Results of a 1986 survey. Special report.* Princeton, NJ: Author.

The Robert Wood Johnson Foundation. (1991). *Annual report 1990: Change amid change.* Princeton, NJ: Author.

U.S. Department of Health and Human Services. (Unpublished, 1991). *Financing clinical preventive services for adults.* (Draft).

U.S. Preventive Services Task Force. (1989). *Guide to clinical preventive services: An assessment of the effectiveness of 169 interventions.* Baltimore: Williams & Wilkins.

U.S. Public Health Service. (1990). *Healthy people 2000: National health promotion and disease prevention objectives.* Washington, DC: Author.

U.S. Public Health Service. (1991a). *PHS action plan for women's health.* Washington, DC: Author.

U.S. Public Health Service. (Unpublished, 1991b). *National strategic plan for the early detection and control of breast and cervical cancer* (Draft).

U.S. Public Health Service Expert Panel on the Content of Prenatal Care. (1989). *Caring for our future: The content of prenatal care.* Washington, DC: U.S. Public Health Service.

Woodwell, D.A. (1992). Office visits to internists, 1989. *Advance Data, Vital and Health Statistics, 209,* (National Center for Health Statistics Pub. No. 216).

Woolhandler, S., & Himmelstein, D.U. (1988). Reverse targeting of preventive care due to lack of health insurance. *Journal of the American Medical Association, 259*(19), 2872-2874.

Zapka, J.G., Stoddard, A.M., Costanza, M.E., & Greene, H.L. (1989). Breast cancer screening by mammography: Utilization and associated factors. *American Journal of Public Health, 79*(11), 1499-1502.

CHAPTER 8

The Continuity Versus Episodic Care Battle Continues

John Feather

Most health care professionals agree that continuity of care (i.e., providing and coordinating the care that is the most appropriate to the patient's changing health care and social needs over a long period) is preferable to "episodic care" that concentrates on solving problems, usually those most pressing or acute, as discrete episodes. Reasons for lack of continuity include the fragmented health care financing system, vested interests, conflict between disciplines, and the regulatory environment. However, providing continuity of care requires an honest appraisal of fundamental questions about health care today. The complex reality of the issues involved in continuity of care belies the simple rhetoric of "good" continuity versus "bad" episodic care. Fragmented health care reimbursement is usually blamed for this "bad care," but the current pattern of care is both deeply rooted and effective in its own way. A "reform" of health care that gives incentives for organizations to ensure continuity would inevitably cause changes that would have unintended consequences. Control over resources involved in continuity of care is also a central question; professionals often object to fragmentation but would be dissatisfied with a system in which an all-powerful gatekeeper would decide reimbursement levels for any services needed. In addition, it is not clear that the patient would gain in power over health care decisions in a system that provided complete continuity of care. Continuity of care will always be difficult to achieve, because, by definition, it links together disparate and sometimes conflicting organizations and services. Providing greater incentives in the context of a reformed health care system will help to integrate care, but the main goal must be to balance the need for continuity with the legitimate need to provide excellence in care in each phase or episode of care.

Director, Western New York Geriatric Education Center; Co-Director, Primary Care Resource Center, State University of New York, Buffalo, NY 14214

Series on Nursing Administration—Volume 6, 1994

In a course on health care organization for first-year medical students, the following example is used:

Mrs. Smith is an 80-year-old white female patient who has a history of osteoporosis and rheumatoid arthritis. She lives alone in her own home and has no family or close friends who live nearby, although neighbors check on her occasionally. As she came down the front porch stairs, Mrs. S. slipped and fell, fracturing her hip and right wrist. After careful assessment and consultation with the patient care team (nursing, social work, physical and occupational therapy), you (the physician) recommend that Mrs. Smith have the following continuous pattern of care:

- Hip replacement surgery followed by an acute care stay of approximately 2 weeks
- Intensive hip and wrist rehabilitation for 3 weeks on the skilled care unit of a nursing home specializing in rehabilitation
- Less intensive rehabilitation and recuperation for approximately another month on the intermediate care unit of the nursing home
- Transfer to patient's home with skilled nursing visits three times per week and a home health aide 12 hours per day for a month
- Continuing home health care aide 8 hours per day indefinitely, with Meals-on-Wheels and other auxiliary services provided

The medical students are asked "What are the factors that might impede this reasonable and continuous pattern of care for Mrs. Smith?" and "How likely is it that she will receive the services in an integrated and smooth pattern of services?" As most health care professionals will recognize, unless Mrs. Smith has substantial private resources, the answer to the latter question is "not very likely." Some of the medical students are shocked that the pattern of care that best suits the needs of the patient is in reality impossible to provide, even if the physician orders it. More important, they begin to understand that providing excellent separate services (such as intensive wrist rehabilitation) during specific episodes of need will not provide the complex and interconnected pattern of care most beneficial to this patient.

Everyone agrees that continuity of care (i.e., providing and coordinating the care that is the most appropriate to the patient's changing health care and social needs over a long period) is preferable to "episodic care" that concentrates on solving problems, usually those most pressing or acute, as discrete and relatively unconnected units. Why, then, is most care still episodic? Once the usual scapegoat (the fragmented health care financing system) is blamed, an honest appraisal raises fundamental questions about health care today, including the following:

- What are the impediments to providing continuity of care?
- Who controls resources and makes decisions about continuity of care?
- What are the political realities and proposals affecting continuity of care?
- What is the role of nursing in fostering effective continuity of care?

Each of these questions is addressed in turn.

IMPEDIMENTS TO CONTINUITY OF CARE

Since continuity of care has become the functional equivalent of "a chicken in every pot" for the 90s, it is hard to examine the issue critically. The growth of hospital discharge planning, case management, and integrated health care systems is an important positive step that has improved the provision of coordinated care to patients, and yet the system as a whole remains focused primarily on episodic and loosely integrated care. What are the impediments to providing continuity of care?

Financing

Although the nation's fragmented health care financing system does not deserve all the blame for the current problems, it is certainly the most important single factor. The best example is that the federal government, the largest single payor of health care services, spends most it its health care money on two institutional health care programs—acute care hospitalization under Medicare and nursing home care under Medicaid—with only a tiny percentage funding home health care or other services. Private insurers typically have followed the government's lead and have been as slow (and sometimes slower) in providing the financing for all levels of care that would allow the smooth transition between needed services.

More important, the funding is provided for the specific service rather than following the patient's changing needs. That is, rather than money being available for the patient's needs (whatever they may be), the money is used if, and only if, the patient qualifies for the particular service, such as acute care hospitalization under Medicare. In a system of patient-driven funding, a "gatekeeper" decides what services the patient needs and buys them from providers. This provides a financial incentive to look at the patient's long-term needs and plan for continuity of services rather than trying to put the patient in a setting where services will be paid for.

Given the gaps in the financing system, especially for home care and non-medical programs such as social day care, patients, family members, and professionals have an enormous incentive to find a way to place patients in the high-level institutional care that is funded by the system, since the only alternative often is no service or service paid for out-of-pocket. Because "prevention," in both the limited sense of disease prevention and the broader sense of preventing a breakdown of either the physical or social support system that allows the patient to function independently, is almost never funded, it is not surprising that the system encounters patients only when immediate attention is needed, in which a comprehensive pattern of care is not the goal.

Payment for care one episode at a time is the tradition in the United States and is the basis of the fee-for-service structure. The major reimbursement reform of the past decade—prospective payment using diagnosis-related groups (DRGs) for Medicare acute care hospitalization—strongly reinforced this pattern of episodic care both by basing payment on each hospital admission and by rigorously enforcing the acute care standard, causing patients to leave the hospital as soon as these services were no longer appropriate. Ironically, prospective payment also indirectly improved discharge planning and case management for continuity of care, as hospitals and other health care organizations scrambled to finds ways of addressing the needs of patients who were being discharged "quicker and sicker." The new system provided few incentives for coordination of care; however, it did provide penalties for patients readmitted because of premature discharge. Because the stick can be as effective as the carrot in changing behavior, many hospitals have invested in continuity of care programs to avoid patients "backing up" in the hospital. Without either strong incentives or penalties specifically focused on continuity of care, the natural tendency of the fragmented payment system has been to improve episodic care and provide continuity of care as an occasional by-product.

Even if financing for all levels of care is provided through insurance or private funds, the coordination of care is difficult to achieve. Indeed, the entire industry of case management has developed in response to the lack of coordination in the system. Once again, the fragmented financing system, in which patients must qualify for each program and its particular set of services separately, is in large part responsible. However, full funding of all programs would not guarantee coordination, as is sometimes implied. As long as separate and competing institutions provide care, the difficulty of coordination will remain.

Vested Interests

Americans spent more than $600 billion on health care in 1991, or more than the assets of the 15 largest U.S. corporations combined. Health care is big business, and many people, including most of those reading this book, make their living from it either directly or indirectly. Although we usually think of "vested interests" as heartless corporate plutocrats squandering millions of desperately needed dollars, most of us feel that our segment of the health care industry is filled with dedicated professionals providing quality care for too little money. The truth, of course, is that we all have vested interests in the current health care system and are reluctant to change a system that, for all its faults, does in fact provide high quality care to millions of people.

Many of the factors that would lead to better continuity of care would require major changes in health care organizations. For example, a "capitated" payment system (similar to the one in use by health maintenance organizations) in which a single organization would be responsible for all health care and social needs of a patient in return for a single flat fee per year, would provide an incentive to the organization to provide continuity of care so that the patient could remain out of expensive institutional care as long as possible. However, such a system would force many single-purpose organizations out of business or at least give outside case managers or "gatekeepers" much more power over what services would be provided—a result they are not likely to let develop without opposition.

Organizational resistance to change is to be expected bureaucratically, but also can always be partly justified by the successful care already provided to patients. Why change a system that (to some extent) "works" for one that is untried? Would a greater emphasis on coordination of services lead to a weakening of the individual services themselves? The word "gridlock" often is used to describe our government, but the same can be said of the health care system. Someone will lose in any major health care reform, and, given the huge sums of money involved, those groups will fight the change. Without a clear mandate and incentive to provide coordination, organizations will continue to provide care in the patterns they have developed—primarily in providing episodic care.

Discipline Divisions

Similarly, each of the professional disciplines has a vested interest in maintaining its own profession's particular niche in the health care system. Although interdisciplinary teamwork has become an accepted concept, it often is more honored in theory than in practice. As organizations try to institutionalize interdisciplinary practice patterns, they often meet resistance and hostility for the discipline-specific departments into which medical institutions have traditionally been divided. Hospital discharge planning and community case management have been and continue to be dominated by the disciplines of nursing and social work. Although very few professionals would argue publicly against interdisciplinary cooperation, a hospital attempting to merge the social work department under the nursing service (or vice versa) to achieve organizational interdisciplinary collaboration might meet resistance. As continuity of care becomes more visible and important, some professions are reasserting their profession's rights and historic claim on the field as a way of defending territory that it perceives to be under attack. If the assertion of rights leads to organizational roadblocks to integrating the transition between levels of care, continuity of care will suffer.

Regulatory Environment

Health care is perhaps the most highly regulated segment of the U.S. economy, and rightly so, since it impacts literally on life-and-death issues. Although regulation is essential, it also plays a major role in fragmenting the system and thereby making continuity of care more difficult to achieve. Every health care professional has his or her personal favorite horror story of regulations in the hospital that contradict those in the nursing home or home care setting, making a smooth transfer between levels of care impossible. Health care organizations are regulated by local, state, and federal agencies, with as many as 40 regulatory agencies impinging on the average hospital. The different regulatory bodies have not only different legislative mandates, but often different philosophies about the role of health care institutions and the role of government in managing them. Most important, many of the regulatory bodies are organized as separate entities for each level of care—with one agency regulating hospitals, another regulating nursing homes, and yet another regulating home care. Being part of the same state government does not guarantee a unity of approach to regulation.

As in the reimbursement system, the fragmentation of regulation is not the full cause of the difficulty in providing continuity of care; rather, the fragmentation is part of a system of care that has both positive and negative aspects. For many patients the fragmented system provides what they need; the question then becomes, Who really benefits from continuity of care?

RESOURCE CONTROLS AND DECISION MAKING

I recently went along on a home visit to "Mrs. Jones," an elderly woman who had a number of chronic conditions but who was managing well in her home with the assistance of her sister, her main caregiver. As we sat in the kitchen, I noticed a chart on the refrigerator and asked them about it. They replied that it was the schedule of all the services Mrs. Jones was receiving, along with the names of the staff members from each agency, because, without the chart, the two elderly women found it hard to remember who was supposed to be in the house at any time. Small wonder—Mrs. Jones received services from ten agencies and had four case managers! Although it is wonderful that she can receive the services she needs, her case illustrates the complex reality behind the rhetoric of "continuity of care." Continuity of care is a widely accepted goal, but the delivery of continuing care implies control over resources and control over choices. Who makes those decisions, and who do those decisions serve?

Organizations are more powerful than individuals in any setting, but health care is in some ways unique. On the one hand, patients traditionally have looked to health care professionals to tell them what they should do; on the other hand, no decisions are more personal and individual than health care decisions. Finding the balance between these two conflicting forces rarely has been achieved, but clearly, within the past few years, patients have been effective enough in expressing their frustration with their lack of input to be given substantial new authority over decision making. Health care proxies, do-not-resuscitate orders, and patient bills of rights have been mandated in most health care settings.

The growth and controversy over the role of case management highlights many of the conflicts. Case management has been so loosely defined that it can be applied to almost any activity that tries to match patient needs with available services. However, for the purpose of this analysis, it is important to distinguish three types of case managers:

- Case managers who are paid by and work directly for the patient
- Case managers who work for health care providers
- Case managers who work for payors (e.g., insurance companies)

All of these are "gatekeepers" between the patient and the services, but they clearly have different pressures and motivations. Case management is an attempt to remedy the fragmented system that matches patients with services one at a time, as if the need for hospitalization and the need for home care were not connected; that is, case management tries to be longitudinal rather than episodic. However, Mrs. Jones had four case managers, each of whom worked for an agency providing service. Their main focus was not to provide an integrated overall plan of care, but to ensure that the services provided by the agency were appropriate and reimbursable. Does Mrs. Jones benefit from this pattern, and is this really any different from the traditional episodic pattern that case management is supposed to avoid? Mrs. Jones happens to be one of those "perfect" clients—just poor enough and just sick enough to fit into every funding program, and with a cheerful personality and a loving caregiver as added bonuses. No one will "let go" of her. Although she certainly benefits from the services and the case management, her case is an illustration of how complex the issues behind continuity of care can be.

Many critics have said that a universal health care system in which a case manager finds and buys the services needed for the patient would solve this problem, but that system also has its price—the specter of the omnipotent gatekeeper who has ultimate authority over every decision to provide services. If Mrs. Jones hires her own case manager, she essentially is buying an advocate who will be more knowledgeable and forceful than she can be, but it will not ensure that the power to decide will remain with her. The purpose of this discussion is not to disparage case managers, who are dedicated professionals trying hard to make a dysfunctional, fragmented health care system work, but to remind us of the complexity of the economic, professional, and personal pressures under which we all work, which makes easy distinctions between "bad" episodic care and "good" continuity of care hard to come by.

POLITICAL REALITIES OF CONTINUITY OF CARE

As a new administration begins, health care remains one of the most pressure-filled issues on the political agenda. Will we finally see continuity of care addressed as an explicit goal of health care policy? That is unlikely, but many of the proposed reforms would have a major impact on the incentives and disincentives to providing continuity of care. Although the specific program that will finally be adopted is impossible to foresee at the moment, the broad issues have been clearly delineated in proposals already introduced into Congress. The dozens of different bills in Congress can be distinguished primarily by their response to the issues addressed in the following discussion.

Access to Care

Approximately 35 million Americans have no health insurance, and another 30 million have only minimal insurance (e.g., major hospitalization coverage only). Most of these individuals are working full time and traditionally have received health care coverage through their employer. The breakdown of the traditional employer mechanism has put tremendous political pressure on health care reform, because most of these people vote and they are frightened by the prospect of having no protection. Most bills, therefore, address the issue of how to best provide universal access to care for all individuals, either through a uniform health care system or provisions to provide a true "safety net" for those without other types of insurance coverage.

Payor of Service

Central to any health care reform is the issue of the fragmented reimbursement system. Each program provides a mechanism to pay for health care services, which ranges from the federal government being the only source of payment to reform of the private insurance industry to provide the bulk of the payment. An auxiliary question is whether the payment will be capitated (i.e., a single payment per client, such as the payment to HMOs or in the prospective payment system using DRGs) or a fee-for-service system, in which each service is paid for separately.

Provider of Service

Health care services are provided by a variety of types of institutions with different types of ownership structures. For example, some bills propose a system in which the government would have a more active role in actually providing care, as well as paying for it. Some bills discuss the organizational structure of health care and how it might be reformed to better provide continuity of care.

From the dozens of bills before Congress and the dozens more likely to be introduced in the next session, it is possible to distill three main groups of proposals for health care reform, each of which would have a major effect on the ability to provide continuity of care. The proposals are as follows:

- Reform of the Current System. The major reform element on these proposals would be a reform of the private insurance industry to encourage or force insurance companies to provide coverage for a larger percentage of Americans, especially those now working, thereby providing greater access to care. Some proposals also call for tax incentives or subsidies to poorer persons who fall above the Medicaid level—to allow them to purchase private insurance. The current payment system, with the mix of government and private payment sources, would remain substantially the same, as would the service provider system.

- "Play or Pay" System. The second set of proposals, which seems to be receiving attention as the most "politically feasible," would require employers to provide insurance of at least a minimum standard to all of their employees ("play") or put an equal amount of money into a new federally administered health care insurance fund ("pay"). Most employers would continue to buy from the private insurance companies but would have the option of buying coverage from the federal programs, as would self-employed persons. A variety of tax incentives and/or subsidies would be provided to small companies, who have been hit hardest by rapidly rising health insurance premiums. The unemployed and those covered by Medicaid would have their premiums to the federal program paid directly by the federal government. The federal government would therefore become an even more dominant payor of services, in effect becoming the largest insurer in the country. The provision of health care, however, would remain essentially the same. The central reform in this plan is to ensure that everyone is covered by some health care insurance, either federally or privately provided, that meets uniform minimum standards, thereby ensuring universal access to care. Most of the provisions of these proposals were developed by the U.S. Bipartisan Commission on Health Care (the Pepper Commission).
- Universal Health Care. For want of a more precise term, the last group of proposals is often labeled "universal" care and is the most radical in its approach to reform. The basic proposition is that a fragmented reimbursement system always will result in a fragmented health care delivery system. Therefore a single federal payment system, into which employers, individuals, or the government itself would pay, is proposed. Universal access to care would be ensured because payment for all individuals would be paid from the same source, which would establish uniform rules for all. Services would continue to be provided by the wide range of organizations now in existence. This is similar to the "Canadian system," in which the government is the sole payor for services but not the provider of service, but distinct from the "British system," in which the government is both the sole payor for services and *also* the primary provider of services. The service providers are severely constrained by this system, since they do not have an alternative purchaser of their services, but the system eliminates discrimination against types of clients based on their payment source (such as Medicaid), since everyone has exactly the same payment source operating under the same regulations. It also cuts down on costly reimbursement administrative costs (shown to be a major difference in the cost of U.S. health care as opposed to that of other developed nations) because of the uniformity of payment.

Each of these groups of proposals would have a different impact on continuity of care, although the exact implications will not be clear until a specific bill is signed into law. Reform of the current system would have the least impact, because it leaves the fragmented reimbursement system and service provision system in place. No specific incentives for continuity of care are envisioned in most of the proposals being offered, although improving the access to private health care insurance would alleviate the critical problem of the growing population that "falls through the cracks" of the current system. "Play or pay" is more unpredictable in its effect on continuity of care. Providing universal access to care through a federally sponsored insurance program would aid continuity by ensuring that every client would have access to the services provided under the program. Because those services have not been spelled out, it is impossible to know whether they will be comprehensive enough to provide the range of reasonably funded services for clients with complex continuing care needs; however, it is encouraging that the second major part of the Pepper Commission report dealt with providing comprehensive long-term care. It is possible (even likely) that private insurers will follow the federal insurance program's regulations and funding levels, thereby providing some standardization of the system, but, once again, it is impossible to determine without a specific proposal.

Universal health care would clearly be the most likely to promote continuity of care, since all clients would be under the same payment system with the same regulations. The federal government, as the sole payor of services, would have a financial incentive to find ways to effectively link parts of the system to avoid use of the most expensive parts of the system—institutional care in hospitals and nursing homes. However, with the incentive comes the necessity for control, since the government cannot allow universal access and payment to lead to unrestrained use of services. The gatekeeping function of the government case manager becomes an all-powerful tool, because the client has no alternative if the case manager decides that certain services are not needed. This, of course, is the greatest criticism of this system, since the government can use its tremendous power as the sole purchaser of services to control utilization and distribution. For example, the government can dictate how many CT scanners are available and where they are located, as the Canadian government currently does. Advocates for the patient will find it more difficult to "work the system" if only one system is available.

THE ROLE OF NURSING

Nurses have an important part to play in the debate over and the implementation of the health care reform that will certainly follow in some form in the next 4 years. First, nurses need to be involved in the political process of the legislation itself, because, both individually and collectively, they have a credibility perhaps unmatched by any other professional group. Physicians, unfortunately, have too often advocated for positions that seem to serve mainly their power position or income (e.g., the American Medical Association's recent opposition to a grossly distorted version of the

Canadian system). Nurses are perceived as being patient advocates and the group most closely associated with the hands-on care of patients in the widest variety of settings. It is essential that the organized professional groups in nursing be actively involved in developing a unified position and an effective lobbying strategy on proposed legislation. However, individual nurses also have an important role with their own legislators. Providing timely and specific individual input to legislators can be much more successful than most people think. Legislators are elected by their constituents, and they are more interested in what their constituents think than the constant barrage of mail they receive from organized lobbyists. A well-told story of a patient who received poor service because of the fragmented health care system can be effective because it is different and because legislators are people oriented—they will remember the story about their 80-year-old constituent Mrs. Jones far longer than the mounds of statistics they see each day. If that story can then be linked to a current legislative proposal, individual advocacy becomes a powerful tool for change. It requires that each individual stay abreast of current proposals, usually through professional newsletters (see Periodicals list at the end of this chapter) and that each individual take the initiative to write. Nursing groups must also continue to be involved in collaborative arrangements with other health care organizations. Service providers see the advantage of allying themselves with nursing in developing coalitions because of the added credibility that the association gives them.

Legislation is the key to all health care reform, but regulation is perhaps more important and more likely to have a direct impact on continuity of care. Legislation passed by Congress and signed by the President generally provides only broad guidelines; the specific program is defined through regulations developed by the Department of Health and Human Services in its Health Care Financing Administration. These are the specific rules that health care professionals must follow. Every proposed regulation must be published in preliminary form for public comment, and, perhaps surprisingly, these public comments are taken seriously. Often the comments alert the regulators to potential pitfalls they simply did not think about or to rules that would be politically difficult to implement, and the regulations are changed accordingly. It is critical that nursing organizations and individual nurses continue to be actively involved in the development of regulation, because it is often inconsistencies in regulations that make continuity of care difficult to achieve. Only in these ways will a balance between excellence in episodes of care and continuity of care be achieved.

READING LIST

American Nurses Association. (1973). *Standards of nursing practice.* Kansas City, MO: Author.

Berger, C.S. (1990). Enhancing social work influence in the hospital: Identifying sources of power. *Social Work in Health Care, 15,* 77-93.

Brown, D.G., & Groves, A. (1988). A tale of two states: Chronology of legislation. *Discharge Planning Update, 8,* 10-13.

Evanshwick, C.J., & Weiss L.J. (Eds.). (1987). *Managing the continuity of care.* Rockville, MD: Aspen.

Feather, J., & Nichols, L. (1984). Hospital discharge planning for continuity of care: The national perspective. In E. Hartigan & D.J. Brown (Eds.), *Discharge planning for continuity of care.* New York: National League for Nursing, publication no. 20-1977:71-77.

Fethke, C.C., Smith, I.M., & Johnson, N. (1986). "Risk" factors affecting readmission of elderly into the health care system. *Medical Care, 24,* 429-437.

McClelland, E., Kelly, K., & Buckwalter, K.C. (Eds.). (1985). *Continuity of care: Advancing the concept of discharge planning.* Orlando, FL: Grune & Stratton.

Hanson, P.C. (1988). *Quality assurance: A strategic guide for discharge planning professionals.* Buffalo, NY: Western NY Geriatric Education Center.

Joint Commission on the Accreditation of Health Care Organizations. (1987). Discharge planning AMH standards revised. *Joint Commission Perspectives, 7,* 9-10.

K.M. McKeehan (Ed.). (1981). *Continuing care: A multidisciplinary approach to discharge planning.* St. Louis: Mosby Year–Book.

Reichelt, P.A., & Newcomb, J. (1980). Organizational factors in discharge planning. *Journal of Nursing Administration, 10,* 36-42.

Rossen, S., & Coulton, C. (1985). Research agenda for discharge planning. *Social Work in Health Care, 10*(4), 55-61.

PERIODICALS

Newsletters of the professional nursing organizations.

AACCESS. Published as the journal of the American Association for Continuity of Care. IMPAACCT, also published by the Association, concerns recent legislative and regulatory issues. Write: AACC, 1730 N. Lynn Street, Suite 502, Arlington, VA 22209.

The Case Manager. Published quarterly. Focuses on case management. Write: Individual Case Managers Association, 10809 Executive Center Drive, Suite 105, Little Rock, AR 72211.

Contemporary Long Term Care. Published monthly. Focuses on clinical and business issues. Write: Bill Communications, Inc., 341 White Pond Dr., Akron, OH 44320.

Continuing Care. Published monthly. Covers discharge planning and case management. Write: Stevens Publishing Corp., 225 N. New Road, Waco, TX 76710.

Discharge Planning Update. Published six times per year. Focuses on a wide range of discharge planning issues. Write: American Hospital Publishing, Inc., Circulation Dept., P.O. Box 92567, Chicago, IL 60675.

Health Care Financing Administration. Published quarterly. The official research and policy journal of the Health Care Financing Administration. Write: Superintendent of Documents, P.O. Box 371954, Pittsburgh, PA 15250-7954.

Hospitals: The Magazine for Health Care Executives. Published twice monthly by the American Hospital Association. Excellent coverage of general health care policy issues. Write: AHA, 737 N. Michigan Avenue, Chicago, IL 60611.

Journal of Case Management. Published quarterly. Focuses on case management research and policy. Write: Springer Publishing Company, 536 Broadway, New York, NY 10012-3955.

Long-Term Care News. Published monthly. Focusesing on long-term care management and business issues. Write: McKnight Medical Communications, 1419 Lake Cook Rd., Deerfield, IL 66015.

SECTION THREE

Proactive Management Innovations and Strategies

The final section of this volume offers proactive approaches for nurse administrators to use in facing the paradox and dilemmas inherent in rationing efforts. In Chapter 9 Jones challenges nursing to develop innovative work redesign strategies and to consider the implications of restructured health care delivery for our approach to health care education. The chapter offers examples of work redesign and the nurse manager implications associated with each. (Note that Volume 7 of *SONA* will focus on Health Care Work Redesign).

In Chapter 10 Maguire and McFadden discuss the inherent ethical problems in health care rationing and the problems associated with short-sighted solutions. Four categories of effective resolution to ethical problems are discussed.

An important aspect of any consideration of health care reform and rationing is managing care across delivery boundaries. In Chapter 11 Falk and Bower use their extensive knowledge and experience in managing care to develop a transitional approach to a continuum of care. They propose that the end result of such an effort would be a system of care rather than a series of isolated events that now make up individual health care.

In Chapter 12 McKenzie and Ray identify research as a critical response to any health care reform effort. In keeping with the section's purpose to offer proactive strategies for addressing rationing, the authors propose a model for the study of rationing. The model incorporates public values and preferences, clinical effectiveness, and cost efficiency.

The capstone for this section is Chapter 13—a stimulating "revisit" by Crossley to each chapter. In this process he highlights the value of each author's contribution to nursing administration as each deals with health care reform. The reader is reminded that as this volume is being written, many decisions are not yet made that are likely to be a reality when the volume is published. He predicts that the information in this volume has a long "half-life" and therefore is useful in future strategizing to influence and respond to health care policy reform.

CHAPTER 9

Restructuring Health Care Services

Katherine R. Jones

Structural responses by the health care system to increased competition and constrained revenue have included diversification, merger, vertical integration, work and role redesign, automation of information systems, and decentralization. Much restructuring activity has involved redesign of nursing care delivery systems, with the goal of creating environments that facilitate professional nursing practice.

Restructuring of health care delivery systems occurs on many levels. This chapter discusses organizational restructuring and work redesign at the individual role level, the unit delivery system level, and the health care organization and system level. Specific examples of several innovative strategies are provided, and where possible, implementation issues and problems are identified. Implications for nurse managers and executives are discussed, as well as recommendations for nursing and nursing management education in the future.

Band-Aid solutions to U.S. health care system needs are not working. The system is therefore setting its sights on longer-term restructuring and rethinking of the processes of care delivery. Systems, structures, tools, and roles are being redesigned to better fit the demands of today's environment (Zander, 1988). Structural responses by the health care system to increased competition and constrained revenue have included diversification, merger, horizontal and vertical integration, downsizing and rightsiz-

Associate Professor, The University of Michigan School of Nursing, Ann Arbor, MI 48109

Series on Nursing Administration—Volume 6, 1994

ing, work redesign, automation of information systems, and decentralization. The direction of planned changes is being determined by top leadership, while implemention and coordination are being achieved through shared goals and values (Dienemann & Shaffer, 1992).

A U.S. Department of Health and Human Services research report indicated that major restructuring of health care settings and organizations, including redesigning of nursing care delivery systems, was needed to create environments that would facilitate professional nursing practice (DHHS, 1988). In 1989 The Robert Wood Johnson (RWJ) Foundation and Pew Foundation challenged hospitals to strengthen the practice of nursing. The goal of this major funding program was to change the structures and processes associated with the delivery of nursing care in a way that would improve patient and family outcomes. This program enabled hospitals to engage in interdisciplinary planning, development, and implementation of innovative models of practice.

Fralic (1992) identified the increasingly high cost per nurse as the major driving force behind hospital restructuring and work redesign. This high cost presents an availability/affordability dilemma to hospital and nursing executives. The institution simply cannot afford to have the same number of nurses on the payroll as in the past. The solution, according to Fralic (1992), is to use the scarce, finite, and expensive professional nurse in only the most appropriate ways, in a work setting that has well-designed clinical and nonclinical support services.

In designing and implementing new structures, nurse executives must make sure they are creating institutional models, not nursing models (Fralic, 1992). The institution as a whole, not just the nursing department, is providing patient care. This is an important strategy for gaining institutional support and commitment. Everyone must feel ownership of his or her part of the restructuring and redesign effort (Fralic, 1992). Multidisciplinary caregiver teams are increasingly an important facet of hospital restructuring. This approach to care delivery requires increased communication and coordination among physicians, nurses, and ancillary staff, as well as increased patient participation in care. It is hoped that the multidisciplinary team strategy fosters mutual respect and appreciation for all team members and their contributions to care (Donaho & Kohles, 1992).

Restructuring of health care services can occur on many levels. This chapter discusses organizational restructuring and work redesign at the individual role level, the unit delivery system level, and the health care organization level.

RESTRUCTURING OF CAREGIVER ROLES

McClure (1991) wrote that nurses have a twofold role: that of caregiver and that of integrator. The caregiver function ranges from basic patient dependency needs to sophisticated patient monitoring and evaluation; that is, the function is hierarchical in terms of knowledge and skill required. The integrator function allows the work of different departments and services to come together and create a specific product. Nursing has long undervalued the integrator responsibility, but it is central to the care of patients (McClure, 1991). The economic constraints in the health care system along with the shortage of professional nurses have combined to generate new caregiver roles that either contain a balance of caregiver and integrator functions or are differentiated by the extent of integrator versus caregiver functions embodied in the role.

Aiken (1990) has called for the development of additional career tracks in hospital nursing that create new roles for the professional nurse. She proposes organizing nursing similar to the organization of medical care, with an attending nurse comparable to the attending physician. These attending nurses, drawn from the ranks of the senior nurse clinicians, would be organized by clinical service, with group practices consisting of nurse/physician teams. The attending nurse would have 24-hour responsibility for patients on the service and would have on-call responsibility. Staff nurses would continue to cover each hospital shift, providing basic nursing care and carrying out the plan of care developed by the medical and nursing attendings.

A different category of nurses would be called *intensivists*. These nurses would provide acute, high-technology care in the critical care units and would assume responsibility for the patient during this period, rather than the attending nurse assuming the responsibility. The intensivists also would work in partnership with the attending physician. Another nursing role in Aiken's model is the subspecialist consulting nurse, who would cut across clinical specialty areas. For example, there might be a subspecialist for patients experiencing psychologic manifestations of illness. These nurses would hold appointments on a clinical service and would have on-call responsibilities. Nurse managers in Aiken's system would provide for staff coverage, communicate the needs of clinicians to hospital management, and help the clinicians adapt to institutional priorities.

This model has yet to be implemented in a clinical setting. One might question the cost of such a system, given the seemingly large number of advanced practitioners. But these costs might be offset by savings generated from better-managed care processes. There are also political issues involved with this model, including overlapping areas of responsibility between the attending nurse and attending physician, as well as between the attending nurse and the staff nurse. The attractiveness of the attending nurse role to nurses is another important issue. It might not work well with part-time nurses or with 12-hour shifts. On the other hand, it might draw nurses back into the profession or into full-time practice because of its higher level of practice and collaboration.

The Clinical Nurse Specialist

The clinical nurse specialist (CNS) role increasingly is being expanded from the individual patient and nurse level to the unit and system level. More and more frequently CNSs are called on to identify and correct systemwide factors that contribute to problemmatic patient care outcomes, such as extended length of stay (LOS) or hospital-acquired complications (Wolf, 1990). In addition, CNSs are asked to identify and correct systemwide factors that contribute to inefficient and ineffective nursing practice (Wolf, 1990). In many settings CNSs are given the responsibility to lead the development of coordinated care and critical pathways for selected patient populations. In other settings they are asked to develop, implement, and evaluate the training programs for cross-trained, multiskilled employees. Wolf (1990) describes responsibilities of this second generation CNS as including development of innovative approaches to care delivery systems, evaluation of new technologies and equipment, and development of new programs and strategies that support a resource-driven model of care. It is probable that schools of nursing are not preparing their CNS graduates for these new roles. Most graduate programs have an extensive focus on the clinical aspects of care, with little or no content on delivery systems, health and patient care costs and financing, and management. In addition, many CNSs would not welcome these nonclinical activities into their sphere of practice.

Head Nurse/Unit Manager

The traditional head nurse role in most settings has been or is being converted into an expanded unit nurse manager role, which carries greater authority and responsibility. The new role must deal with the dual challenges of managing the restructuring of care delivery systems, as well as managing a new breed of nurse (Adams & Rentfro, 1991).

Newly defined managerial positions have been extended to include responsibility and accountability for financial planning and control, capital equipment expenses, employee evaluations, quality of staff work life, quality assurance and patient care outcomes, medical staff relations, professional development, and clinical practice decisions. Unit-level nurse managers now have critical responsibility for improving patient care processes and outcomes while also controlling costs. The unit manager, in effect, translates the hospital's strategic goals into direct care delivered to patients on the nursing units (Eubanks, 1992).

The new role has been compared with that of a chief operating officer (COO) of a department. The manager carefully controls unit finances, develops liaisons with other department heads, and coordinates institutional resources around patient needs (Eubanks, 1992). With downsizing and decentralization, it is not unusual for the nurse manager to have responsibility for more than one unit and to have 24-hour accountability.

Decentralization also has led to unit-based staffing, scheduling, and staff replacement. The average span of control for a unit manager has increased from 25 to 75 employees. In addition, nurse manager positions are being converted to salaried rather than hourly positions (Kramer, 1990).

Flattened structures and participative management approaches empower managers by increasing their discretion and authority (Dienemann & Shaffer, 1992). All grantees under the RWJ Strengthening Hospital Performance program are pushing decision making and authority down to unit level—where care is rendered and therapeutic judgments are made (Donaho & Kohles, 1992). These decentralized systems demand expert interpersonal skills for managers so they can provide leadership through coaching, facilitating, educating, and providing appropriate resources. The middle manager role also facilitates others in the organization by managing interactions and functions across departments (Donaho & Kohles, 1992). This liaison function involves helping other departments become effective partners with nursing (Eubanks, 1992). Because the nurse manager will be leading the change process in his or her area of responsibility, the ability to manage change will be an especially valuable skill.

Nurse managers will need preparation at the master's level, preferably in a nursing systems or nursing administration program. Special emphasis needs to be placed on team building, conflict resolution, negotiation, budgeting, and managing change. The chief nurse executive must interpret this new nurse manager role to physicians, the chief executive officer, and others (Eubanks, 1992) to reduce resistance, clarify expectations, and enhance the chances of success.

The newly defined responsibilities of the nurse manager also require assurances that direct caregivers are "empowered" by top administration to perform such activities as self-scheduling and peer review (Eubanks, 1992). This requires a change from the traditional hierarchical method of organizing to a matrix and team approach. Hospital governance, as reflected in the institutional authority and control structures, must shift from centralized, bureaucratic structures to increased committee participation, formal shared governance, or self-managed units (Eubanks, 1992). Kramer (1990) reported that most magnet hospitals have adopted a self-governance/shared-governance system of autonomous, self-managed, self-governed operations at the unit level. There is systematic, participative, representative involvement by unit nurses in nursing department-wide governance issues.

Staff nurses will therefore need increasing competence in both clinical decision making and organizational decision making. Undergraduate curricula must go beyond the typical "leadership course" and offer meaningful clinical management experiences to the students before they graduate. Working in teams and the art of delegation must be emphasized, with at least observational experience in these areas.

RESTRUCTURING OF CARE DELIVERY SYSTEMS

There are six organizational approaches to cutting cost: across-the-board percentage cuts; cutting out fat in specific services; reducing services; reducing quality; increasing volume; and changing production processes (Zander, 1985). The last strategy, changing production processes, is the most meaningful approach but is also the most complex (Zander, 1988). It is the strategy behind the many attempts to restructure and redesign patient care delivery systems. Changing production processes also means eliminating some of the traditional boundaries between specialized departments, with a goal of satisfying patient care needs rather than department needs (DiMola & Burns, 1991).

Restructuring of care delivery systems begins with a systematic analysis of the work of patient care delivery on each unit (Fralic, 1992a,b). New patterns of staffing and task assignment should emerge from this analysis (DiMola & Burns, 1991). Jobs that contain meaningful and satisfying work and a manageable workload must be designed. Each job needs to be assigned an appropriate level of authority and responsibility. Moreover, there must be clear accountability for patient and organizational outcomes. Even though most new delivery systems use fewer registered nurses per unit, the essence of nursing practice can be preserved through delegation of carefully selected clinical tasks and nonclinical activities (Fralic, 1992a,b). The final step in the restructuring process is reintegration of the new roles into one high-performance team (Fralic, 1992a,b).

The Secretary's Commission on Nursing (1988) recommended preserving nurses' time for patient care by (1) providing adequate support services, (2) implementing new staffing patterns that use differences among RNs and between RNs and other nursing personnel, and (3) recognizing appropriate clinical decision-making authority of RNs. Curtain (1990) identified three "arenas of practice" that demonstrate the differentiation of RN roles:

1. *Clinical Nurses*—design and deliver direct patient care and collaborate with the case manager.
2. *Case Managers*—coordinate the design, delivery, and evaluation of care for a specific caseload of patients in collaboration with other health professionals.
3. *Nurse Specialists*—midwives, nurse anesthetists, and nurse practitioners.

Much differentiation in nursing roles has taken place in the magnet hospitals since the first study (Kramer, 1990). Some of the magnet hospitals have all RN staffs, with nursing assistants assigned to the RN for non-nursing/environmental tasks. Others have differentiated RN roles. The most effective and prevalent differentiation of the RN role, according to Kramer (1990), is into a professional case manager role, with a unit staff nurse or case-care associate having shift responsibility for care.

Case Management

Case management is a delivery system in which a nurse is responsible for a patient's care across an episode of illness. The case manager emphasizes assessment and prescription, delegation to co-workers, and collaboration with physician and other relevant health care professionals (Kruger, 1989). Some common characteristics of case management are the following (Kruger, 1989):

- Preadmission or admission assignment of a clinical case manager
- Assignments made based on subspecialty medical practices
- Cases managed for an episode of illness over time, including inpatient and outpatient management
- Case managers working with specific physicians to share the same patients
- Critical pathways, care maps, or protocols established as guidelines for the anticipated plan of care

McClosky (1991) identified four key concepts that are common to all models of case management: standardization, efficiency, continuity of care, and interdisciplinary collaboration. Usually, more highly educated and experienced staff members are better able to assume this role because of its high-level clinical management decision making (Kruger, 1989).

The New England Medical Center defined case management as a restructuring of the clinical and production processes of care delivery in a way that facilitates achievement of cost and quality outcomes (Zander, 1988). This assumes that length of stay (LOS) and resource allocation represent costs that clinicians can control through timing, sequencing, and better coordination of their practice patterns (Zander, 1988). At the New England Medical Center, case managers are responsible for achievement of both clinical and financial outcomes within the DRG-allotted time frame and are held responsible for the continuity of nursing care (Adams & Rentfro, 1991). Case management plans (comprehensive protocols) and shorter versions of the case management plan, called *critical paths*, are employed as tools to define standards and identify variations from these standards (Zander, 1988). Critical paths highlight key events and time intervals and allow visualization of highly technical and interpersonal interactions during an entire episode of care. Zander (1988) believes that critical paths give the clinician, patient, and administration a new sense of positive control. They assist in the concurrent management of care, facilitate revision of patterns of care, and increase the quality of care through allowing fewer problems in the production process (Zander, 1988).

Both the Primm/Differentiated Case Management Model and the Robert Wood Johnson Hospital/Professionally Advanced Care Team (ProAct) Model maximize the use of ancillary staff roles (Adams & Rentfro, 1991). Features of the ProAct model include two distinct professional nurse roles: primary nurse and clinical care manager (CCM) (Ritter & Tonges, 1991).

The CCM is an RN who manages the entire hospital stay of a caseload of patients (Adams & Rentfro, 1991). Other aspects of the system are supervised utilization of assistive personnel in the delivery of direct patient care and expansion of clinical and nonclinical support services at the unit level to relieve nursing staff of inappropriate tasks (Ritter & Tonges, 1991).

Additional models are appearing in the literature. One is called *Multidisciplinary Collaborative Case Management*, implemented at the Tuscon Medical Center (Adams & Rentfro, 1991). In this model the clinical manager manages cases plus functions as a staff or charge nurse. The management action plan (MAP) delineates the essential, patient-specific care activities that are to take place within specific time frames (Gwozdz & Togno-Armanasco, 1992). The model functions independently of established delivery systems and varies according to the unit and physician practice patterns within a unit (Adams & Rentfro, 1991).

Case management differs from primary nursing by being more deliberative in planning for resource use and by involving interdisciplinary collaboration. It differs from primary nursing also in that it emphasizes care management for a sizable group of patients, encourages several layers of direct care providers, and is not expected of all registered nurses on the staff (Kruger, 1989).

There are several potential barriers to successful implementation of case management. Physician collaboration is necessary, since physicians are key stakeholders in care delivery. In many settings the clinical care protocols or critical pathways used for case management are developed by physicians, nurses, and other health care providers as a joint project (Ritter & Tonges, 1991). Discussion of critical path variances then occurs at interdisciplinary meetings. The result is integrated care made possible by the cooperation of medicine, nursing, pharmacy, physical therapy, support services, and other relevant departments (Donaho & Kohles, 1992). Case management may fail also if physicians and nurses lack knowledge of the disease process, goals of therapy, or patient response to therapy (Kruger, 1989). Case management has been found to help decrease length of stay and to increase nurse autonomy (Ethridge & Rusch, 1989), but it is also expensive to implement and is probably not justified for all patients (ANA, 1988; Morlock, 1990). The implementation of this new delivery system requires staff nurses to have additional skills in interdisciplinary collaboration and negotiation, as well as better knowledge of the financial aspects of care and organization and community resources.

The models that rely heavily on nurse extenders (ProAct) enable the nurse to provide a larger volume of services (McCloskey, 1991). However, nurse delegation of tasks to various extender groups is causing concern among nursing groups. These models demand a clear definition of nursing—and determination of what nursing tasks, treatments, and decisions can be performed by nonlicensed personnel with limited education (McCloskey, 1991).

Examples of case management model implementation. The Dartmouth-Hitchcock Medical Center designed and implemented a case management nursing care delivery model called the *Patient Care Management Model* (Cronenwett, Clark, Reeves, & Easton, 1991). Nurse case managers are salaried, have varied hours, work full-time, cover weekends, and have 24-hour and LOS accountability for nursing care of patients in their caseload. Each case manager caseload matches that of one or more attending physicians to facilitate physician-nurse collaboration. Role responsibilities include assessment and care planning, teaching, evaluation and revision of the care plan, preparation for discharge, timely coordination of services, and documentation. In this model, RN patient care coordinators have shift patient care responsibilities with a geographic-based caseload.

In evaluating their new structure, the authors believed it to be successful because of the strength and vision of the nursing managers. The managers made a commitment to involve staff in all decisions at all stages of the transition. There were multiple retreats for values clarification and communication and for development of conflict resolution skills.

Several implementation issues arose including concern about the relative value placed on each role, concern about how nurses would be chosen for the patient care management positions, and some resentment over splitting responsibility for patient care (the previous commitment was to total patient care) (Cronenwett et al., 1991). There were also physician adjustment problems—attending physicians, house staff, and other nurses in the hospital were not positive about the new care delivery model (Cronenwett et al., 1991). However, per diem and float nurses expressed greater satisfaction working in the new environment, recruitment of BSN nurses improved, quality of care improvements were noted, and average length of stay was down (Cronenwett et al., 1991).

Evaluation also revealed that further management development is needed. The change process slowed down when managers were not able to follow through (Cronenwett et al., 1991). According to these authors, managers need to be able to develop concrete budget proposals for the desired models, deal with the stresses of role transitions on the part of nursing and the medical staff, and make the transition to letting go of the clinical management aspects of the managerial role. They recommend that education of nurse managers include content on interactive planning processes, managing role change transitions, and differentiated practice goals and models.

At Sioux Valley Hospital the role of nursing was expanded to that of professional business partner, based on the belief that balancing clinical and business competencies is necessary to help integrate nursing units into the decision-making arena of the health care industry (Koerner, 1991). The Sioux Valley model consists of four components identified as essential to professional practice: a participative management structure, a comprehensive care delivery system, collaborative professional relationships, and opportunities and rewards for professional growth.

Additional features of the Sioux Valley Hospital system have been described by Koerner (1991). It has two distinct roles for nurses: case manager and care associate, building on the Primm model. The revised care delivery system is called *integrated care*. The primary nurse is the integrative force, and the registered nurse is the care deliverer. Integrative pathways are the primary work tool used to facilitate client movement through the acute episode. Primary nurses are the critical force in providing managed care within the hospital setting. A critical skill for the case manager is longitudinal thinking: the ability to plan discharges and consider care needs that extend beyond the hospital walls. In addition to the primary nurse/case manager, the clinical nurse specialist in this system designs a unique pathway for each patient needing specialized services—such as those with a chronic illness or those who have a significant financial or knowledge deficit.

Hartford Hospital developed a collaborative practice model that integrates the functions of nurses, physicians, and others (Cohen, Armstrong, Koerner, & Soukup, 1991). This model includes concurrent and retrospective multiprofessional patient record reviews, implementation of a patient care team coordinator role, advances in automated information systems, and interactive collaborative practice and management (Cohen et al., 1991). Standardized protocols have been developed for predictable patient patterns. Unique to this model is its redefinition of career ladders: selected personnel categories have been combined and cross-training carried out. Multiskilled, nonprofessional workers are prepared for a broadened scope of work responsibilities and assignments. Direct patient care tasks are delegated through cross-training methods. Job enrichment has been provided for a wider variety of technical personnel.

The Community Setting

Case management can be community based, as well as institutional. It often is employed when patients require substantial medical and social intervention over a long period, such as with AIDS or severe mental illness. These patients have wide-ranging health care, psychologic, and social service needs. Typical case management functions include client intake and assessment; service planning, referral, and system linkages; service receipt and client status monitoring; and advocating on behalf of clients (Mor, Piette, & Fleishman, 1989). The two primary goals of case managed systems of care in the community setting are to link clients with the appropriate community-based services and to rationalize the provision of services by reducing the inappropriate use of expensive inpatient care and the total cost of care (Mor et al., 1989). It remains unresolved whether these goals are being achieved. In one randomized clinical trial with the severely mentally ill, the treatment group did not improve significantly in terms of psychosocial adjustment and reported satisfaction with their lives (Jerrell & Hu, 1989). There was a desirable reallocation of costs among types of services, with a shift away from expensive 24-hour and ER care and an increase in outpatient services and case management. However, the new treatment program was more costly in total than traditional care.

Case management has been applied also to posthospital, community-based care of frail, elderly patients (MacAdam, Capitman, Yee, Prottas, Leutz, & Westwater, 1989). The five basic steps of case management under the RWJ Program for Hospital Initiatives in Long-term Care were comprehensive functional assessment; care planning; service arrangement; monitoring; and periodic reassessment. The evaluators of this program found two views of the role of case management: it was seen as an adjunct to the adequate provision of medical care; and alternatively, it was seen as a combination of an extension of the hospital's mission of community service provision and also as a tool to meet an organizational imperative to attract new users.

The success of case management in this study depended on several factors (Mor et al., 1989). It was important to create a role and presence of the case manager within the existing, complex service network, and goals, scope of services, and criteria for participant admission to the service had to be decided before implementation of the program. Difficulties arose when the case management role and functions were poorly linked to medical care delivery. Most of the experimental programs also could not document changes in outcomes as a result of the provision of case management (MacAdam et al., 1989).

Creating New Care Environments

Approaches to reducing costs while maintaining quality of care include creating new care environments, as well as designing new care delivery systems (such as those just described). Changes in health insurance and escalating financial pressures on hospitals to be less costly and more efficient have led to closer examination of high-cost patients, such as those who are ventilator-dependent. These patients have extended hospital stays with total costs usually exceeding total revenues to a substantial degree. One response has been the initiation of a special care unit for chronically, critically ill patients who are ventilator-dependent (Daly, Phelps, & Rudy, 1991). This nurse-directed unit established a new system of care consisting of case management along critical paths because of the high need to plan and coordinate the care of these patients with consultants and primary care providers. The unit omitted many standing orders and care protocols and used no interns or residents. Costs were lower and patient and family satisfaction higher than in the traditional intensive care environment (Daly et al., 1991).

WORK REDESIGN

Other hospitals have focused on streamlining the operating systems that extend across traditional departmental boundaries. Some have restructured departments into a single patient care organization that manages all nursing and support staff on each floor. In one hospital this was called an *integrated patient care system* (Didier & Jennings, 1990). All support services—couriers, escorts, housekeeping, discharge cleaning—were placed under the direction of frontline nursing staff. Two new management positions were created on each floor: a director of patient care services and a director of support services. The director of patient care services had total operating authority for the floor, including budgeting and financial performance, personnel management, and quality assurance. These positions were filled by former associate directors of nursing service. The director of support services coordinated housekeeping, patient escort, and logistical activities. Staff was cross-trained, scheduling was made flexible to meet varying workload demands, and shifts were staggered for better coverage. A rapid courier system for each floor provided continuous pickup and deliveries every 20 minutes, and phlebotomists were unit-based for the peak day and evening hours. The benefits of the redesigned hospital include simpler and better understood communications among departments and better operational effectiveness (Didier & Jennings, 1990).

Strasen (1991) developed an innovative strategy for restructuring how work is organized within hospitals. She proposed four major initiatives to redesign the traditional hospital: downsizing management, decentralizing ancillary and support services, centralizing the distribution of supplies, and organizing specific ancillary labor around expensive technology.

Many hospitals have pursued a decentralizing and flattening strategy. Kanter (1989) advocates reducing managerial levels so that there are only four or fewer levels. Under this strategy, firstline managers would have a span of control from 50 to 75 employees, whereas senior managers would have a span of control from 15 to 20 direct reports (Strasen, 1991). More decentralization of ancillary and support services would reduce the approximate 40% "down time" associated with transportation of patients and equipment, telephone coordination, and so on (Strasen, 1991). Services would be organized around the patient, instituting a true customer focus consistent with total quality initiatives. Cross-training of personnel would be used to maximize the presence of more ancillary staff on the nursing unit. The third strategy would centralize supplies so that one department would stock, deliver, and charge for all supplies used.

The final strategy recommended by Strasen would establish specific high-technology areas with appropriate ancillary services assigned to each area. For example, ancillary/diagnostic services would have personnel categories such as physical therapists and respiratory therapists; the imaging services area would have radiology technicians and nuclear medicine technologists.

Evaluation Component

The initiation of these many innovative care delivery systems and structures requires careful, thorough evaluation efforts. Aspects to be assessed include the care delivered, continuity, cost, quality, and communication. One approach is to track cohorts of patients. Patient experiences are profiled both before and after the organizational restructuring. Data are collected to determine differences in quality, communication, efficiency, coordination, and continuity of care. Quality may be measured by analyzing clinical expertise, accountability, professional attitudes, interdependency, group decision making, negotiation, and conflict resolution. Costs associated with deviations from established critical paths or protocols can be analyzed using analysis of variance. Patient outcomes may include incidences or measures of medication errors, fall rates, skin breakdown, wound or respiratory infections, readmissions, depression, pain management, and length of stay. Staff outcomes may include job and work satisfaction, retention, vacancies, and nursing documentation. Financial outcomes may include hours per patient day, overtime, supplemental agency use, and salary costs per patient day. The multiple dimensions to be measured support the need for multidisciplinary studies of patient outcomes.

Integrated computer systems that link financial, personnel, and patient information are a vital resource for organizational improvement initiatives (Dienemann & Shaffer, 1992). Data must be linked in a meaningful and timely way to the needs of clinicians and managers. Managerial decisions must be based on and monitored through relevant, timely information. Nursing unit managers and clinical nurse specialists need to get involved in helping create these data bases (Dienemann & Shaffer, 1992). In addition, hospital administration needs to implement some method of regular data collection on selected variables—organizational demographics, staff satisfaction, commitment, professionalism—to facilitate continuous monitoring of the responses to organizational innovations (McCloskey, 1991).

Although many organizations succeed in changing their shapes, few achieve the equally important goal of altering employees' behavior (Bice, 1990). Why does restructuring fail to bring about the anticipated changes? According to Bice, it arises from management's not putting enough time and effort into aligning the organization's culture with the new structure. Management culture is one of the most powerful's tools to promote organizational integration (Williams, 1992). Changing culture is time consuming and hard—but it must be done (Williams, 1992).

Most attempts at organizational redesign have at least one thing in common: synergy—getting more for less by more efficiently structuring the workforce and work production support systems (Bice, 1990). Bice (1990) calls for development of horizontal cultures that can better meet customer needs and improve organizational synergy. This means removing layers of management, which reduces the opportunity for system blockage, distortion, and filtering of information and empowers employees to give better service.

Williams (1992) suggests the following steps for managing the organizational culture:

1. Assess and monitor the culture on a regular basis—it sends the message that you care.
2. Focus culture changes on areas that will truly further integration—decision making, organizational integration, management style, management compensation, management development.
3. Implement a human resource planning process that is linked to the overall strategic plan.
4. Invest wisely in training and development processes—these should be ongoing and consistent with the values of a learning organization and the principles of continuous quality improvement.
5. Change the criteria for performance planning and appraisal; it should be an ongoing process rather than episodic and should include effectiveness in team participation as one criterion.
6. Build strong teams—clarify roles, responsibilities, and job interrelationships and build camaraderie and cohesion.

RESTRUCTURING THE HEALTH CARE DELIVERY SYSTEM

The revolution in health care organization and financing catapulted hospitals into a highly regulated, intensely competitive marketplace (Horwitz, 1988). Health care experienced fundamental changes marked by prospective payment for services based on fixed rates, increased competition, new technologic developments emphasizing outpatient care, and growing employer and consumer demands for more cost-effective care. Existing organizational structures were ill-suited for this new environment. The net result was profound changes in the strategies, structures, and underlying power relationships of the industry (Shortell, Morrison, & Hughes, 1989). Strategies have changed from an internal operations focus to an external, market-driven focus. Structures have changed from functionally oriented service lines to services organized along divisional or product lines. Power has shifted from providers of care to purchasers and consumers. Hospitals have responded by diversifying into new services and markets. The objectives were to add additional revenue streams, gain operational flexibility, attract physicians and patients, preempt the competition, feed the core business through referrals, facilitate earlier discharge, and develop integrated packages of services that could help contain cost, promote continuity, and be marketable to local employers (Horwitz, 1988; Shortell et al., 1989).

Diversification and Corporate Restructuring

Diversification is the process of developing a new product or service line or breaking into a new market; it is a strategic decision that can spread an organization's risk or improve its market position (Liszewski, 1988). Corporate restructuring, on the other hand, is a change in the structure or organization of a corporation. It typically involves moving away from a single organizational entity toward creation of additional corporations. The parent holding company model seems to offer the best structure in terms of regulatory, reimbursement, tax, and management advantages (Horwitz, 1988). The reorganized hospital becomes a nonprofit subdivision of the parent company. The parent may have several nonprofit and for-profit subsidiary supporting organizations (Horwitz, 1988), which may be health-related or non-health-related.

Restructuring should be considered only as a component of the health care organization's strategic plan. The institution must ask itself: Does a corporate reorganization better position the organization to accomplish its goals and objectives and to fulfull its mission; and Is a different structure needed for the new activities under consideration? (Liszewski, 1988). Feasibility studies should be done and corresponding business plans developed for each proposed corporate entity. Outside expertise should be sought to address the legal, tax, and reimbursement issues.

Diversification became common in the early 1980s as the health care industry responded to major regulatory and competitive challenges. Many of these diversification activities failed because hospitals got into businesses they did not understand (Johnsson, 1992). Hospitals now see diversification as one means to manage patient care over the continuum of required services (Johnsson, 1992). A recent survey shows that hospitals more frequently are diversifying into health-related businesses (Sabatino, 1990). In terms of financial success, the most advantageous new lines of business are outpatient surgery, inpatient physical rehabilitation, cardiac rehabilitation, industrial medicine, home health care, women's health, preferred provider organizations, psychiatric services, substance abuse treatment, and outpatient diagnostic centers. However, some of these lines of business are becoming less profitable over time (substance abuse treatment, psychiatric services, and outpatient diagnostic centers), and some are more successful in certain settings (cardiac rehabilitation programs are more profitable in hospitals with more than 500 beds (Sabatino, 1990).

As members of the executive decision-making team, nurse executives must be informed of the financial responsibilities and opportunities associated with joint venture and diversification activities, as well as their impact on the day-to-day operations of the hospital (Pelfry & Theisen, 1989). New activities should be compatible with the long-range plans of the hospital and should not drain human, physical, or financial resources (Horwitz, 1988).

Ives and Kerfoot (1989) believ that hospitals have to develop entrepreneurial cultures. They recommend diversification activities that could be undertaken within nursing services departments. For example, hospitals could market their cardiac rehabilitation and home health services to outside groups. They could market consultation services by using the expertise of their clinical nurse specialists. They also could market their managerial expertise and specific educational programs. Several hospitals have been packaging and selling their case management and shared governance programs. For example, Carondelet St. Mary's Hospital and Medical Center in Tucson has established a professional nursing network with nurse case managers at the hub. In 1990 this network won a contract for managing the care of 10,000 elderly patients in the "senior plan" of an HMO (Schorr, 1990). In addition, nursing personnel could be doing their own product testing and development. Many innovations are simply given away to drug companies and hospital supply companies—innovations that, instead, could have generated substantial revenue for individuals and their institutions (Ives & Kerfoot, 1989).

Vertical Integration

The recent strategic thrust in health care organizations is to strengthen the traditional business—a back-to-basics approach (Fox, 1989). Vertical integration is used to secure and retain customers for the traditional business, either by upstream integration (securing control over raw materials or supplies that differentiate the core business product) or by downstream integration (securing control over distribution channels that provide advantageous access to customers) (Fox, 1989). There are two critical differences between vertical integration and the diversification strategy of the 1980s (Fox, 1989):

1. Diversification implies moving away from a declining core business; vertical integration implies support of the core business.
2. Diversification requires complete ownership of the new business; vertical integration allows limited ownership through partnerships and contractual arrangements.

A vertically integrated health care system is an arrangement whereby a health care organization offers a broad range of patient care and support services operated in a functionally unified manner (Conrad & Dowling, 1990). The range of services may be preacute, acute, or postacute organized around an acute care hospital, or the delivery system may specialize in offering a range of services related to a particular area, such as long-term care or mental health.

A vertically integrated system requires both administrative and clinical integration. Managing integration is necessary for the success of health care organizations that are linking multiple service lines and several delivery points in pursuit of a continuum of care strategy (Williams, 1992). The system must be managed in such a way that permits each service line to realize its potential contribution. The operating cultures and types of talent required are different from those of the hospital setting, yet it is also important not to isolate the new businesses from the core business (Fox, 1989).

Williams (1992) identified several strategies for managing a complex, vertically integrated system. Structural considerations include the following:

1. *Streamlining*—the organization needs to eliminate management positions, reduce layers of management, and increase spans of control. This reduces the number of links in the chain of decision making, leading to quicker decisions and empowered managers.
2. *Decentralization*—there should be fewer people providing a broader array of clinical services at the unit level.
3. *Developing the Key "Make or Break" Jobs*—in a vertically integrated system, vital managerial positions are the top geographic executive (who will direct the integration of various business units), the head of physician networking, and the head of medical affairs. Vital staff roles are the chief financial officer, the director of management information systems, and the director of human resources.

Management systems and processes include the following:

1. Linking TQM/CQI with other management and human resource processes.
2. Developing meaningful business plans, both annual and long-term, that are linked to the budget and long-term financial forecasts.
3. Developing effective information systems that are well linked and user friendly.
4. Using communications to reinforce a sense of integration and systemness: memos, newsletters.
5. Budgeting for integration by breaking traditional processes and incorporating nonfinancial measures into the budget process (quality of care, customer satisfaction, market share).

CONCLUSION

Aydelotte (1991) identified four classes of nursing roles that will be needed in the future: the provider of direct services to clients; the researcher and developer of new knowledge and techniques; the case or panel manager; and the executive. Case managers and direct caregivers will be scholarly clinical practitioners and scientists who use highly sophisticated information systems in their practice. Nurse executives will be concerned with securing and allocating resources, policy development, evaluation, and revision, as well as the distribution of services.

Nurse managers of the future will be accountable for facilitating cooperative and collaborative relationships among departments and disciplines (AONE, 1992). The management of clinical nursing practice and patient care will be coordinated within a framework of all disciplines participating in patient care activities. The nurse manager will also play a pivotal role in promoting collegial relationships based on mutual respect and trust (AONE, 1992).

Three areas of decision making are critical for nurse executives in the future: the interface of the organization with the environment, organizational design, and managerial strategy (Fralic, 1992b). Managerial decisions that concern the interface with the external environment include the development, implementation, and evaluation of the institution's mission, goals, and objectives (Fralic, 1992b; AONE, 1990). In designing organizational structures, nurse executives will develop compatible policies and programs that reflect utilization of available personnel and a responsiveness to the personal and professional development of the nursing staff (AONE, 1990). Managerial strategies will be either formal technologies (budget systems) or informal management processes (leadership) (Fralic, 1992b). The nurse executive will participate in the institution's strategic planning activities and interpret the role of nursing in the organization's strategic plan. Such planning will reflect the economic environment and include resource allocation, selection of planning alternatives, and trends forecasting (AONE, 1990). The nurse executive of the future will be more accountable, more influential, more corporate in mindset, and more competitive in acquiring resources for patient care (Fralic, 1992b).

REFERENCES

Adams, R.A., & Rentfro, A.R. (1991). Strengthening hospital nursing: An approach to restructuring care delivery. *Journal of Nursing Administration, 21*(6), 12-19.

Aiken, L.H. (1990). Charting the future of hospital nursing. *Image: Journal of Nursing Scholarship, 22*(2), 72-78.

American Nurses Association (ANA). (1988). *Nursing case management.* Kansas City, MO: Author.

American Organization of Nurse Executives (AONE). (1990). *Role and functions of the hospital nurse executive.* Chicago: Author.

American Organization of Nurse Executives (AONE). (1992). *Role and functions of the hospital nurse manager.* Chicago: Author.

Aydelotte, M.K. (1991). Nursing's preferred future. In M.J. Ward & S.A. Price (Eds.), *Issues in nursing administration: Selected readings.* St. Louis: Mosby–Year Book.

Bice, M. (1990). Culture can make or break a restructuring. *Hospitals, 64*(18), 60.

Cohen, J.R., Armstrong, D.M., Koerner, B., & Soukup, M. (1991). Hartford Hospital's patient care delivery programs. In I.E. Goertzen (Ed.), *Differentiating nursing practice into the twenty-first century.* Kansas City, MO: American Academy of Nursing.

Conrad, D.A., & Dowling, W.A. (1990). Vertical integration in health services: Theory and managerial implications. *Health Care Management Review, 15*(4), 9-22.

Cronenwett, L., Clark, K., Reeves, S., & Easton, L. (1991). Building on shared values: The Dartmouth-Hitchcock Medical Center approach. In I.E. Goertzen (Ed.), *Differentiating nursing practice into the twenty-first century.* Kansas City, MO: American Academy of Nursing.

Curtain, L.L. (1990). Designing new roles: Nursing in the 90's and beyond. *Nursing Management, 21*(2), 7-9.

Daly, B.J., Phelps, C., & Rudy, E.B. (1991). A nurse-managed special care unit. *Journal of Nursing Administration, 21*(7/8), 31-38.

Department of Health and Human Services (DHHS). (1988). *State of the Science Invitational Conference: Nursing resources and the delivery of patient care.* Bethesda, MD: National Institutes of Health.

Didier, G.B., & Jennings, W.R. (1990). Floorwide organization at South Hills Health System. *Healthcare Productivity Report.* Ann Arbor, MI: Chi Systems, Inc.

Dienemann, J., & Shaffer, C. (1992). Manager responsibilities in community agencies and hospitals. *Journal of Nursing Administration, 22*(5), 40-45.

DiMola, M.A., & Burns, S. (1991). Development of a differentiated practice model. In I.E. Goertzen (Ed.), *Differentiating nursing practice into the twenty-first century.* Kansas City, MO: American Academy of Nursing.

Donaho, B.A., & Kohles, M.K. (Eds.). (1992). Multi-disciplinary caregiver teams: A key to patient-centered care. *Strengthening, 1*(1), 1-8.

Ethridge, P., & Rusch, S.C. (1989). The professional nurse/case manager in changing organizational structures. In M. Johnson (Ed.), *Series on Nursing Administration*, Vol. 2. Redwood City, CA: Addison-Wesley.

Eubanks, P. (1992). The new nurse manager: A linchpin in quality care and cost control. *Hospitals, 66*(8), 22-29.

Fox, W.L. (1989). Integration strategies: More promising than diversification. *Health Care Management Review, 14*(3), 49-56.

Fralic, M.F. (1992). Creating new practice models and designing new roles: Reflections and recommendations. *Journal of Nursing Administration, 22*(6), 7-8.

Gwozdz, D.T., & Togno-Armanasco, V.D. (1992). Streamlining patient care documentation. *Journal of Nursing Administration, 22*(5), 35-39.

Horwitz, M. (1988). Corporate reorganization: The last gasp or last clear chance for the tax-exempt, nonprofit hospital? *American Journal of Law and Medicine, 13*(4), 527-559.

Ives, J.E., & Kerfoot, K. (1989). Pitfalls and promises of diversification. *Nursing Economic$, 7*(4), 200-203.

Jerrell, J.M., & Hu, T. (1989). Cost-effectiveness of intensive clinical and case management compared with an existing system of care. *Inquiry, 26*(3), 224-234.

Johnsson, J. (1992). Dynamic diversification: Hospitals pursue physician alliances, seamless care. *Hospitals, 66*(3), 20-26.

Kanter, R. (1989). *When giants learn to dance.* New York: Simon & Schuster.

Koerner, J. (1991). Building on shared governance: The Sioux Valley Hospital experience. In I. Goertzen (Ed.), *Differentiating nursing practice into the twenty-first century.* Kansas City, MO: American Academy of Nursing.

Kramer, M. (1990). The magnet hospitals: Excellence revisited. *Journal of Nursing Administration, 20*(4), 35-44.

Kruger, N.R. (1989). Case management: Is it a delivery system for my organization? *Aspen Advisor for Nurse Executives, 4*(10), 4,5,8.

Liszewski, D.M. (1988). Diversification and corporate restructuring revisited: Back to square one? *Nursing Clinics of North America, 23*(2), 399-413.

MacAdam, M., Capitman, J., Yee, D., Prottas, J., Leutz, W., & Westwater, D. (1989). Case management for frail elderlies: The Robert Wood Johnson Foundation's program for hospital initiatives in long-term care. *Gerontologist, 29*(6), 737-744.

McCloskey, J.M. (1991). Differentiated practice: Response from a researcher. In I.E. Goertzen (Ed.), *Differentiating nursing practice into the twenty-first century.* Kansas City, MO: American Academy of Nursing.

McClure, M.L. (1991). Introduction. In I.E. Goertzen (Ed.), *Differentiating nursing practice into the twenty-first century*, Kansas City, MO: American Academy of Nursing.

Mor, V., Piette, J., & Fleishman, J. (1989). Community-based case management for persons with AIDS. *Health Affairs, 8*(4), 139-153.

Morlock, L. (1990). Dialogue: A case for case management. *Focus on Mental Health Services Research, 3*(1), 1-2.

Pelfrey, S., & Theisen, B.A. (1989). Joint ventures in health care. *Journal of Nursing Administration, 19*(4), 39-42.

Ritter, J., & Tonges, M.C. (1991). Work redesign in high intensity environments: ProAct for critical care. *Journal of Nursing Administration, 21*(12), 26-35.

Sabatino, F. (1990). Survey: Managed care led '89, diversification improvements. *Hospitals, 64*(1), 56-59.

Schorr, T.M. (1990). Nurse-run managed care. *American Journal of Nursing, 91*(10), 25.

Secretary's Commission on Nursing. Final Report. Vol. 1. (1988). Washington, D.C.: U.S. Department of Health and Human Services.

Shortell, S.M., Morrison, E., & Hughes, S. (1989). The keys to successful diversification: Lessons from leading hospital systems. *Hospital & Health Services Administration, 34*(4), 471-492.

Strason, L. (1991). Redesigning hospitals around patients and technology. *Nursing Economic$, 9*(4), 233-238.

Williams, J.B. (1992). Guidelines for managing integration. *Healthcare Forum Journal, 35*(2), 39-49.

Wolf, G.A. (1990). Clinical nurse specialists: The second generation. *Journal of Nursing Administration, 20*(5), 7-8.

Zander, K. (1985). Revising the production process ... when more is not the solution. *Health Care Supervisor, 47*, 1-4.

Zander, K. (1988). Nursing case management: Resolving the DRG paradox. *Nursing Clinics of North America, 23*(3), 503-520.

CHAPTER 10

The Ethics of Health Care Rationing: The Missing Voice

Daniel C. Maguire
Edith A. McFadden

A massive change in the philosophy of health care is under way in the United States. Shortsighted rationing solutions based on categories such as age have appeared. These solutions are constricted by zero sum thinking, a lack of alternative-consciousness, and an implicit bias against the elderly. The opinion of nurses is rarely sought in this debate even though nurses' role as participants in health care and as health care educators is crucial to the solution to the current health care crisis. The solution to the crisis lies in new attention to (1) education and communication in the health care setting, (2) a renewed commitment to professionalism, (3) the restriction of useless procedures, and (4) a healthier and new public-private partnership.

There currently is much discussion of health care rationing and cutbacks in the United States. The allegedly richest nation in the world is concluding that it cannot afford the care of its sick. Health care costs are escalating at a reckless rate that cannot be sustained. In 1960 health care costs in the United States were 5.2% of the gross national product (GNP). By 1985 this had more than doubled, reaching 10.5%, and some projected the figure for 1992 at 13% (Callahan, 1990). One economist estimates that if

DCM: Professor of Ethics, Marquette University, Milwaukee, WI 53226
EAM: Assistant Professor of Otolaryngology, Medical College of Wisconsin, Milwaukee, WI 53226

Series on Nursing Administration—Volume 6, 1994

the accelerating medical portion of the GNP continues unabated, by the year 2057 health care costs will consume 100% of our GNP, leaving nothing for housing, food, and other necessities (Kissick, 1988).

From 1973 to 1986 the percentage of the GNP devoted to education actually dropped—from 6.4% to 6.2%. The number of children in poverty rose in the 1980s from 13% to 20% (Callahan, 1990). Thus health care is not seizing a bigger piece of an expanding pie; it is gobbling up more and more of a stable or shrinking pie.

In much analysis of health care rationing, the competitive, simplistic spirit of "zero sum" thinking—*if you win, I lose*—is active. Aside from being economically and sociologically short-sighted, such a spirit always spawns incriminatory comparisons. Hostile, pointing fingers are appearing around the table. Many of them are pointing to the elderly, and the term "greedy geezers" began to appear in this context in 1988. The facts that children have no lobby comparable to that of retired people and that they cannot vote have been noted. There are 30 million people over 65 years of age today, and the number is expected to double in the next 25 years. In a "zero sum" spirit, Menzel (1990) asks: "Do we really care enough about open-heart surgery for ourselves at age 75 to continue paying for it but refuse funding for better prenatal care?" Former governor of Colorado, Richard Lamm, is quoted as saying that the terminally ill have a "duty to die" and get "out of the way." There is some tendency for recommended solutions to be extreme, and creative alternatives are often lacking.

Public attention has been focusing on the fact that a few people are eating most of the health care pie. Ten percent of patients are responsible for as much as 75% of the health care costs (Garfinkel, Riley, & Iannocchione, 1988). And, again, the elderly loom ominously in this statistical assessment. Ten percent of our health care dollars and more than 1% of our GNP is consumed by elderly people in their last year of life. Other statistics emphasize the imbalance. Eighteen percent of medical expenses occur in the last year of life and 12% of that in the last month (Menzel, 1990). Clearly, this outpouring of money has minimal success, since death is then the sequel to these expenditures.

Selfish motives are sometimes attributed to those who consume resources in the final weeks of life. Barrington's (1980) speculative, futuristic question actually contains a present tense indictment: "What if a time came when...the decision to live on for the maximum number of years were considered a mark of heedless egoism?" Is it "heedless egoism" that brings the old to health care? Are the elderly using too many health care resources at the expense of educating children, relieving the poverty of all age-groups, and meeting other social needs? We are told that 30% of European dialysis centers exclude patients who are older than 65 (Menzel, 1990). Whether we should do likewise is a question that more and more persons are considering.

THE SILENT PARTNERS

The voices of nurses tend to be muted in debates about health care. This is true not only in the critical issue of rationing, but also in most of today's contested issues of health care. Health care is being completely rethought (Maguire, 1986). And in all of these debates nurses are *talked to* much more than they are *heard from*. Many of the volumes on the rethinking of health care do not even allude to nurses. The role of sexism in the omission of nurses from the health care dialogue and from acknowledgment of their contributions to health care must be noted and corrected.

Nurses are not distant adjuncts to the medical scene. The word *medicine* comes from the Latin *mederi*, meaning *to heal*. Healing is complex, involving many aspects—from technical procedures to hands-on care. Henderson's (1966) well-received definition of nurses is that they are those persons who provide "that service to the individual that helps him/her to attain or maintain a healthy state of mind or body; or, where a return to health is not possible, the relief of pain and discomfort." To fulfill that broad and noble function is not to stand at the periphery looking at the real medical action through binoculars. To be a nurse in Henderson's definition is to be involved in the entire enterprise of curing and caring. The definition puts the nurse in a key place in primary, secondary, or tertiary care, in prevention or in long-term care. Nursing in its various specializations is intrinsic to health care at every juncture.*

The various nursing roles, which have become increasingly complex and responsible, are relevant in all phases of the healing process. If the theoreticians and health care experts from various disciplines who are pontificating on the need to *do this* or *ration that* are not clued into the important contributions of nurses, their decisions will not be sound.

Some of the problem here lies with nurses. Nurses have accepted the silent role too passively. Volumes like this one seek to fill this void, but more active participation in the debates and more well-organized lobbying are needed if the voice of nurses is to help direct the future of health care. After all, it is nurses who usually will explain the decisions about rationing and other health care policies to the public and to patients.

ECONOMIC RATIONING

No discussion of health care rationing is accurate if it does not acknowledge that *de facto* rationing is a current feature of modern life. Egalitarian

---

*The Washington State Board of Nursing says that "the practice of nursing means the performance of acts requiring substantial specialized knowledge, judgment and skill based upon the principles of the biological, physiological and social sciences." They take the position, for example, that nurses can inject epidural narcotics. See L. Brian Ready et al. (1988). Development of an anesthesiology-based postoperative pain management service. *Anesthesiology, 68,* 104.

health care delivery may have existed in simple times, but it has never been a feature of industrialized societies. Some dimensions of health care have long been beyond the grasp of the poor and the underinsured. Thus the current discussion inappropriately views rationing as a novelty rather than as a redefinition of who will be the objects of rationing.

The claim that this country has "the best health care system in the world" is specious. We have at least four types of hospital health care systems, and current rationing methods affect them all.

The Boutique Hospital

The first health care system involves what health care economist Uwe Reinhardt refers to as "boutique" hospitals. These hospitals, probably the best in the world, are found in various places in the United States, and from their physical appearance to their technical equipment—and even to their food—are outstanding. These beautifully appointed, affluently ensconced institutions enjoy a certain geographical immunity to indigency and the problems thereof. They are not centers of reflection on the ethics of rationing.

The Private Community Hospital

This is the kind of hospital that the adequately insured and well located among us enjoy. It tends to be far enough removed from large numbers of the uninsured to enjoy adequate prosperity, and the care is first class. It approximates in many aspects the "boutique," even though it does not enjoy as much immunity to the demands of the uninsured and underinsured. It is precariously well off.

The Large Urban Hospital

A number of hospitals in large urban areas could be used to illustrate this type. These are the crowded city hospitals with overworked and often heroic staffs who bear undue burdens of care for AIDS victims and for uninsured patients suffering from illnesses often related to the pathology of our neglected cities. These hospitals are strained by persons who have no personal physician and who therefore come to emergency rooms for simple primary care problems. One New York City physician described his summer venue there as "a madhouse." A nurse in Philadelphia described her overworked city hospital as "a zoo," but even zoos are better financed and pleasant.

The Socialist Hospital

Most of these hospitals are not involved in rationing health care or in haggles over insurance and cost. They operate out of public funds on an entirely different financial base. The largest hospital system in the United States, the Veterans Administration Hospitals, is based on socialist theory.

The anomaly of a huge socialist hospital system in the midst of our capitalistic world goes almost unnoticed. Not all of these socialist hospitals are good or in a category with the first two systems just listed in terms of the quality of care or attractiveness of their environments. Some pick up the uninsured, veteran or not, simply because there is no other place for them to go and so, in various ways, are involved in forced rationing. However, our finest socialist hospital is certainly Walter Reed. At that hospital many physicians pour over the President's latest illness, there is no concern for DRGs or insurance, and there is certainly no rationing. The moral theory that operates there is that politicians and former soldiers should receive unrationed care at public expense. At that level, rationing is excluded on principle. Our society does not apply that principle elsewhere to persons who might be at least as deserving as politicians and soldiers, such as elementary school teachers, nurses, or all American children. This well-established system of military and political socialism can be viewed as a sign of moral disarray and national dishonesty, a point that is worth pondering without implying that the veterans' health care system is a paragon.

Thus our health care system is more an aristocracy than a democracy. Rich people and highly placed politicians have access to almost unlimited care. Many others scramble to get what care heroic professionals can give them in less-than-ideal circumstances. Economic and class rationing are as American as apple pie. Our leaders feast on it and seem to assume it is an inevitable fact of life.

This oligarchic health care system affects nurses and should be addressed by their spokespersons and lobbies. Class rationing leads to unfair forms of hidden taxation. Physicians must do much work *gratis*, and hospitals are forced to contribute space or service, often in an atmosphere of stress, because many persons are uninsured. The insured are overcharged. There is no justice or moral intelligence in this arrangement of indirect and scattered taxation.

The first author's son Tom went to a hospital recently with meningitis. On the chance that the meningitis was bacterial, he was given penicillin for a short time as a precaution. The cost for a few doses of penicillin, one of the least expensive antibiotics, was $2000. At issue here is not penicillin but taxation—indirect taxation. Tom had good health insurance coverage, whereas some patients down the hall were uninsured and penniless. The costs of the uninsured were transferred to Tom by a hospital trying to stay in business while also giving essential care to indigent persons, many of them children. In place of a national health care plan, in which the government would act as the insurer of last resort, hospitals must play these games.

RATIONAL RATIONING?

Rationing certain kinds of health care is as immoral as rationing literacy, the right to police protection, or the right to vote. Because health care should be a basic human right, it should not be rationed.

Ethics is the art and science that seeks to discover what persons deserve (Maguire & Fargnoli, 1991). Persons are precious, and deciding what befits them is the work of ethics. The two indispensable human needs are *respect* and *hope* (Maguire, 1981). The opposite of respect is insult, and the opposite of hope is desperation. If our essential needs are not met, our humanity is insulted and our hope is squelched. We are violated as persons. The work of ethics is to discern what needs are frivolous and what needs are essential, that is, needs without which hope and respect are denied.

Human beings often are slow to admit the essential needs of others. For a long time literacy, the right to vote, the right not to be bought and sold as property, the right of handicapped to enter buildings, and the right to legal representation at trial were not considered essential basic needs or rights. Gradually these rights became viewed as basic, not optional. Denial of these rights to anyone insults personhood at its core.

Most civilized nations have decided that basic health care is one of these basic rights. In the United States, we have not so decided. To some degree health care is treated as a commodity or consumer item, to be purchased if one can afford it. Nurses, physicians, and others try, often heroically, to meet the essential health needs of the poor, but they cannot do it in the absence of a rational system of distribution. They can no more do this than teachers could provide literacy for all or lawyers could provide representation for all without some societal commitment. *Again, there is no moral way to deny or ration basic rights*, and economics based on such a denial cannot long endure.

Basic health care is a basic human right. It is not a basic human right to receive everything modern health care can provide. "There are worse things than dying" an old Irish saying has it. And too much health care can give us those "worse things" when we would be better off dead. There is "a time for dying." But while we live and have prospects for great joy, we should have the staples of sound health care. That is a basic human right without which the human essentials, respect and hope, are not possible.

How can the basic human right to reasonable health care be realized in our society? We can start with common sense. Private enterprise is geared to profit and growth, and therefore it is not naturally drawn to the poor. Government, however, is the prime agent of the common good, and its primary purpose is the creation of peace through the elimination of poverty (Maguire, 1993). The poor are government's natural business, and if it does not attend to them, the results are noxious for the poor and for the common good. Thus the government's role is the elimination of the "uninsured patient."

The healers in our society should never face an uninsured patient when they are called on for the "ordinary means" of health care (Maguire, 1984). Only the government, as the insurer of last resort just as it is the pensioner of last resort in Social Security, can make this happen. The "ordinary means" of health care are those that impose no unreasonable burden on persons or society. Deciding the reasonable and essential kinds of health care that are the basic human rights is a challenge to our ethics, but nonetheless necessary.

Callahan (1990) distinguishes six levels of care—ranging from such things as relief of pain and hospice care, through nutrition, sanitation, immunization, and emergency medicine—to advanced forms of medical cure or restoration. He emphasizes the first four levels and concedes that government must play a major role in health care. "Both the complexity and the expense of modern healthcare require a central government role even if considerable room can be made for the private sector." Callahan's is a good effort, but there is nothing tidy about it. Disputes can range over all six levels. Still, we have no choice but to struggle with the fact that although some people will always be able to afford all the health care they desire, we must seek to define and provide *basic* health care for all citizens, regardless of their ability to pay.

States such as Oregon are making a noble effort to discern priorities. Pure success will not be achieved, what will be covered and considered "basic" will be contested, and line-drawing will be complicated by the fact that treatments once considered extraordinary become ordinary. For example, blood transfusion, once considered risky, became a simple office procedure but is again shifting away from simplicity because of the AIDS threat. So even when we draw the lines, the lines shift. Still, drawing lines is what ethics (like art) is all about. While the process of discerning what is basic and not to be denied to anyone is difficult and complicated, we must confront the issue to have a civilized and moral health care system.

Thurow (1985) predicts that if we do nothing, we will drift into three tiers of very different kinds of health care. The first tier will be one in which the government is the payor, and it will cover care for the poor in some minimal fashion. The second tier will be the coverage offered workers by business. This probably will be more generous but still in the DRG spirit of the first tier. The third tier will be the free market system where "Cadillac" health care can be found. Thurow says that in the current system, where costs are spread over a number of payors after the treatment has been delivered, there is no motive to set realistic limits on costs. In this atmosphere the experimental may be used with little concern for good effect and soon become "normal care."

ZERO SUM MYOPIA

There is danger that rationing-talk will distract us from stopping the financial hemorrhages that are built into the current health and social systems. Those hemorrhages are not just matters of inefficiency. They are caused by attitudes and myths, unchecked greed, and long-term irrationality. If we can attend to these with any success—and it will not be easy—we will discover that we can care for our sick of any age and do so generously.

Talk of rationing health care, if it is to occur, should come after we have tackled the irrationalities of our current health care systems. We are not in a situation of irremediable triage. We have not even caught up with the rest of the industrialized world in meeting basic health care needs. This is no time to pick out a whole category of people, for example, the elderly, and cut their medical rations *en bloc*. There are mean implications in this that suggest that limberness of limbs and efficiency of movement are the purpose of life. When Cicero wrote *De Senectute* (*On Old Age*), he lamented hyperbolically that his limbs were dead. Clearly his wit and wisdom and capacity for joy were alive. Wise cultures revere their aged and do not look on them as worn-out equipment.

SOLUTIONS

The four areas where the health care crisis can be eased if we have the imagination and moral will to address them are as follows:

- Education and communication in health care settings
- Professionalism
- Restricting useless procedures
- A healthy public-private partnership

Education and Communication in the Health Care Setting

Dentistry is a simpler terrain than most areas of health, but dentists have taught a grand lesson. People can learn preventive care. Through personal instruction and the use of film and written materials, dentists have taught and taught well. Some might feel they have taught too well, since dental schools are closing as fewer dentists are needed. What they have proved is that *people are educable*. Paternalistic medicine has not worked on that premise.

The ideal is for the physician and the nurse, in their distinct but complementary fashions, to be seen as trained experts and the patient to become an amateur expert with enough knowledge to make informed decisions. All health care personnel should see teaching as one of their prime tasks. Businesses that ask for discounts from a hospital—thus triggering an unprofessional and fatal price war—should instead be offered on-site education in health care, especially preventive care. This approach would save more money, discounting treatment that may not have been necessary if the illness was prevented.

To communicate with patients, doctors and nurses must learn to speak in understandable lay terms. When people speak English, it is wise to communicate with them in English. *Hepatosplenomegaly* can accurately be called *enlarged liver and spleen*. George Bernard Shaw said every profession is a conspiracy against the laity. Part of that conspiracy is befuddlement of the lay person by jargon. Medicine has indulged too often in this elitist behavior. People are interested in their health and can learn when the language is understandable. Communication in intelligible language gives people more responsibility for their health. It also may be part of the cure for malpractice fever: the propensity of persons to litigate when they are not satisfied with care.

One of the major educational tasks of medicine is to teach that enough is enough. This is not easily taught when the progress of medical technology seems to say that enough is never enough and *new and better* is the rule. Add to this the American bias for technical fixes and improvements, the American obsession with health (something noted by de Toqueville in the 1830s) (Starr, 1982), and our culturally phobic reaction to death.

When the first author's oldest son Danny was in the final years of a life shortened by Hunter's syndrome, his Irish grandmother would say when she heard he had been to the physician: "Don't take him to the doctor. Let the poor wee man go to God." She was satisfied on learning that the care was palliative, but her instincts were Irish, not American. She was culturally fitted to know when enough was enough; that is not true for U.S. culture. Medicine is not totally to blame for the proliferation of often fruitless treatments. Our culture drives them. Broad, sensitive education is the answer. There are hopeful signs that we can become sensitive and mature about life, death, and appropriate health care—with death, like birth, viewed as a natural part of life.

Professionalism

Health care is provided by professionals, and the values of the professions must supersede the values of business. Hospitals are not selling cars or tires. It is therefore anomalous at best to attend health care meetings and hear lectures by the same people who are advisors to car and tire sellers. Marketing experts tour the country telling health care professionals how to make their institutions meaner and leaner and thus beat out the competition. These models are wrong. The metaphors are wrong. Health care deals with patients, not customers.

If health care is just a business, competitors are enemies, customers must be charged "what the market will bear," and you have no real business dealing with consumers who have no money to pay for your product. Health care has a business dimension—supplies are to be purchased, bills are to be paid, people are to be hired—but health care is primarily the services of health care professions. The word *profession* comes from a Latin word meaning *to proclaim publicly*. Professionals profess two things: (1) they have finely honed skills in some specific area; and (2) they are committed to the highest moral ideals in the society. When we call someone "unprofessional," is it not true that most of the time we do so because of a moral failure? He or she has failed not in skills, but in commitment to persons, in respect for persons, in courage in the face of risk. We do not ask tire salespersons to take risks, but society expects it of professionals. Tire salespersons do not take oaths when they assume their posts, and we do not give them titles or trust them with our lives.

Competition in the health care system was proposed to reduce costs in accord with capitalistic values. Callahan (1990) said this was "a triumph of hope over logic." The result was to press one HMO to provide more and better than the other, and the race was on. Competition stifled cooperation, which is the undergirding of any health care cost containment.

Most seriously, the pure business paradigm reduces the patient to a customer, and that violates the patient in multiple ways. Increasing the number of customer visits makes money sense in business as does charging what the market will bear. However, it corrupts health care and introduces into the field fearsome expressions like "physician-induced demand" and is inflationary.

A recent issue of *Medical Economics For Surgeons* contains an article "Latest Fees for the Most Common Operations." The article asks no value question. It simply reports what people are charging for these operations. It does not interest itself in fair price but merely reports what people are managing to charge for operations that on a videotape would look the same. The range is enormous. Initial office visits cost from $30 to $180. Revisit charges range from $20 to $70. Cranioplasty ranges from less than $1500 to more than $5000; cervical dissectomy from less than $2000 to more than $5000; and coronary bypasses with three coronary grafts from less than $3000 to more than $7000 (Crane, 1990).

These prices signal a serious ethical problem. If the cost of the same operation from presumably competent doctors can vary 3, 4, or even 5 times, something is amiss. Business people would say *caveat emptor*—let the buyer beware. But the patient is not just a buyer and not just a customer. The patient is sick and often scared and does not have time to shop. If someone is shopping for an oriental rug, it is possible after many visits to various stores to become a minor expert and make an informed decision. This is in no way comparable to the patient arriving for an aortic valve replacement with cardiopulmonary bypass. There is no way the patient can put a price on this. Further, the patient *trusts* the hospital and the physician to charge reasonable fees. The patient *trusts* them to be professional.

The business paradigm does not work. Cooperation works. Education on prevention and treatment works. Avoidance of duplication of services in one geographic area works. Reasonable prices in a context where the patient has no choice works. Instruction on the naturalness of death and, in certain situations, on the lack of utility of "high-tech" medicine can work. Patients have a unique relationship with health care professionals, and much in current practice violates this relationship.

Restricting Useless Procedures

Why is it that health care costs in the United States are 3 times greater than those in Britain and more than 5 times greater than those in Japan and these nations are getting similar or better results (Menzel, 1983)? Rachel Lutner (Lutner, Roizen, Stocking, Thisted, Kim, Duke, Pompei, & Casel, 1991) in an article in *Anesthesiology*, a journal that represents a field that has led the way in reducing risks to patients (Pierce, 1991), says: "Approximately 50% to 70% of preoperative laboratory testing could be eliminated without adversely affecting patient care." Lutner also says that such testing might even be harmful to the patient because of false-positive results. She notes that Blue Cross/Blue Shield estimate that the cost of such testing in 1984 was $30 billion and that half of that could have been saved if only appropriate testing and evaluation were done.

The British use intensive care at less than one-fifth the frequency of Americans. Billions of dollars could be saved by even marginal changes here (Menzel, 1990). Menzel lists a number of "dubiously costworthy" procedures including some major surgery and argues that they accounted for 10% of the 1979 medical budget. Before we discuss rationing, this serious fiscal and medical problem must be addressed.

The incipient rediscovery of the body's healing powers also awaits attention. We are more expert in pathology than in health; more skilled in what can be done for the body than in what the body can do itself to limit disease. *The New York Times* (1991) reported on "a steady march of scientific findings demonstrating how heavily patients' emotional states can affect the course of their diseases." This insight, which can be greatly supplemented by nursing experience, can comfort patients and reduce costs. Emotionally supported patients also leave the hospital sooner.

A Healthy Public-Private Partnership

Government, as stated earlier, is the primary agency for the common good and the ultimate protector of the poor—especially children. A solid principle of ethics is that government should do nothing unless it is essential and will not otherwise be done (Maguire, 1993). Health care for the poor is beyond their means, even if it were attractive to health care professionals. A related principle of ethics is that what is good for children is good. More than 30% of the uninsured are children (Callahan, 1990). Clearly, that is not good for children, especially African American and Hispanic children who bear the greatest brunt of poverty. The government must be the bulwark preventing the medical abandonment and neglect of the poor, especially poor children. The U.S. government now pours $30 million an hour into military spending, even though the former archenemy, the Soviet Union, no longer exists. That same government finds huge amounts of money to pay for the savings-and-loan bailout. Government mismanagement resulting in a huge national debt and economic recession is not an acceptable excuse for ignoring the needs of the poor. It is the role of government to guarantee that all persons receive basic health care. It is the role of health care professionals to provide health care and to help define a system in which all persons have access to basic services.

However, professions have been negligent in assuming the social responsibility of developing a health care system that ensures basic health care for all persons, and nursing has tended to have little voice in these decisions.

THE MISSING VOICE

Nursing has been listed as one of "the ten worst careers for women" (McCandless, 1988). Enrollment in nursing schools declined by 50% between 1987 and 1989, while enrollment of women in schools of medicine, law, and engineering increased significantly (Kraegel & Kachoyeanos, 1989). A task force of nurses that convened in 1987 to study the drastic shortage of nurses reached some helpful conclusions. First, the task force noted that "perceived powerlessness is basic to much of the frustration in nursing" and that "shared governance, interdisciplinary collaboration, and open communication" are highly held values, mostly unrealized. Second, it insisted that "a baccalaureate degree should be the minimum education needed to practice as a professional nurse" (Donovan, 1990).

Both of those conclusions are important and connected. Nurses properly complain about "not being heard." Nursing suffers low prestige because its members are mostly women in a sexist society. But there is another reason. People cannot identify what a qualified nurse is because nursing lacks standards defining the profession. It is unfortunate that the 1990 task force of nurses should have to call for a "baccalaureate degree" as the "minimum education needed to practice as a professional nurse." Tradespersons are trained: professionals are educated. Experienced nurses may know more than anyone in certain clinical situations, but the insignia of knowledge is *a degree*, and degrees are respected as much as knowledge in professional settings. Add the fact that most nurses are women, and the need for advanced degrees becomes even keener.

Though progress is being made, the professional definition of a nurse is blurred. When one says "nurse," the reference may or may not be to a college graduate. The nurse might have a master's or doctoral degree. He or she may have advanced training in anesthesia or some other speciality. Nurses must demand full professional status in health care. The high level of education among many nurses is not widely known. The "Bedpan Sally" myth must still be assaulted. The myth that nurses are necessarily women and that these women enter their field only as a prelude to marriage must be corrected. Candidates will not be drawn to the field when nursing's professional status is misunderstood, nurses are not valued as committed professionals, and monetary rewards are disproportionately low compared with other health professionals.

The current crisis in health care, of which rationing is one symptom, would benefit from greater participation of nurses in developing solutions. One neurosurgeon, a reviewer for NIH grants, observes that "institutional support for nursing research is very low" (Kraegel & Kachoyeanos, 1989).

This is an example of the general low level of support for nursing development. Congressional appropriations for the Center for Nursing Research
(NCNR) increased the annual 1992 budget of $39,772,000 by only 1.4%
compared with the 1992 increase of 19.5% for the National Institute for
Aging (NIA) budget of $323,752,000. The NCNR budget appropriations
increase for 1992 was markedly lowest among 19 NIH agencies falling well
below the NIH average increase for all agencies of 8.86% (Center Report on
H.R. 2707, 1991).

Nursing is developing and diversifying. This is a secret that is too well
kept. For many patients, after surgery, it is nursing care that they rely on to
bring them back to health. These special caretakers must more precisely
define their public professional image if their voices are to be effective in
health care debates of today.

CONCLUSION

Areas of health care policy at local, state, and national levels await active
participation of nurses to identify problems and propose solutions. These
areas include the need to hold the patient's interests paramount as opposed
to financial gains, the need to constrain unlimited medical progress and
treatment, the need to address the health care needs of all persons with
insurance providers regardless of financial status, the need to be accountable professionals including holding peers and members of other professions accountable for their public trust, the need to advocate for cooperation among private and public approaches to the financing and delivery of
health care, and the need to educate and support all persons to develop
and maintain health, prevent illness, and encourage their participation in
the development of a more rational and egalitarian health care system.
Because nurse administrators are in positions of influence in their organizations and communities, they have the greatest responsibility to assume leadership in increasing nursing's voice and visibility and in facilitating its
involvement in changing the system and influencing health policy.

REFERENCES

Barrington, M. (1980). Apologia for suicide. In M.P. Battin & D.J. Mayo (Eds.), *Suicide: The
    philosophical issues*. New York: St. Martin's Press.

Callahan, D. (1990). *What kind of life: The limits of medical progress*. New York: Simon &
    Schuster.

Center Report on H.R. 2707, Health and Human Services, and Education Appropriations Bill
    (House Report 102-282); ADAMHA. NIH budget boost: Now you see it, now you don't. *The
    Journal of NIH Research*, December, 1991, Vol. 3.

Crane, M. (Sr. Ed.). (1990). Latest fees for the most common operations. *Medical Economics
    for Surgeons, 9*, 20-32.

Donovan, M. (1990). What we need to change about nursing: Staff nurses share their ideas.
    Journal of Nursing Administration, 20, 38.

Garfinkel, S., Riley, G., & Iannocchione, V. (1988). High-cost users of medical care. *Health Care Financing Review, 9*, 41-52.

Henderson, V. (1966). *The nature of nursing*. New York: MacMillan.

Kissick, W. (1988). Speech at a conference at The University of Iowa, Iowa City.

Kraegel, J., & Kachoyeanos, M. (1989). *Just a nurse*. New York: Dutton.

Lutner, R.E., Roizen, M.F., Stocking, C., Thisted, R.A., Kim, S., Duke, P.C., Pompei, P., & Casel, C.K. (1991). The automated interview versus the personal interview. *Anesthesiology, 75*, 394.

Maguire, D.C., & Fargnoli, A.N. (1991). *On moral grounds: The art/science of ethics*. New York: Crossroad.

Maguire, D.C. (1981). The nature of justice. In *A new American justice*. San Francisco: Harper & Row.

Maguire, D.C. (1984). *Death by choice* (Updated and Expanded Edition). Garden City, NY: Doubleday Image Book.

Maguire, D.C. (1986). The moral revolution in health care. In *The moral revolution*. San Francisco: Harper & Row.

Maguire, D.C. (1993). *The moral core of Judaism and Christianity*. Minneapolis: Fortress.

McCandless, H. (1988). The 10 worst careers for women. *Working Woman, 13*, 65-66.

Menzel, P.T. (1983). *Medical costs, moral choices: A philosophy of health care economics in America*. New Haven: Yale University Press.

Menzel, P.T. (1990). *Strong medicine: The ethical rationing of health care*. New York: Oxford University Press.

Pierce, E.C., Jr. (1991). Anesthesia patient safety movement—1991. *American Society of Anesthesiologists NEWSLETTER, 55*, 4-8.

Polister, S. (1992). Health care reform: The debate goes on. *Bulletin of the American College of Surgeons, 77*, 10-15.

Starr, P. (1982). *The social transformation of American medicine*. New York: Basic Books.

The New York Times. (1991, Nov. 26). *Doctors find comfort is a potent medicine*.

Thurow, L. (1985). Medicine versus economics. *New England Journal of Medicine, 313*, 611-614.

CHAPTER 11

Managing Care Across Department, Organization, and Setting Boundaries

Carol D. Falk
Kathleen A. Bower

An integral component of achieving the goals of quality and cost control in health care is managing care across provider boundaries. Contemporary health care delivery is a series of events—not a system. The need to reallocate health care resources is presented as an opportunity to move toward a true continuum of care, based on actual consumer needs. Care plans designed for each person within the parameters of care management will more accurately reflect the need and judicious application of resources rather than the priorities and resources of an individual, departmental, or organizational provider.

The management of patient care across boundaries such as departments, organizations, and settings is integral to the achievement of both quality and cost goals in health care today. When care is not managed effectively, it is likely to be fragmented and fraught with redundancy, omissions, and inconsistency. Patients struggle to negotiate a complex maze of providers, settings, and payors and often must overcome tremendous barriers to access needed care. As Berwick (1992) observes, what patients really need is a system; what they get is events.

CDF: President, Carondelet St. Mary's Nursing Enterprise, Tucson, AZ 85745
KAB: Principal, The Center for Case Management, Inc., South Natick, MA 01760

Series on Nursing Administration—Volume 6, 1994

Effective management of care across boundaries depends on the use of strategies to increase coordination and continuity. Coordination refers to synchronizing the care provided by multiple caregivers in multiple settings. Continuity shifts the focus from events to the continuum or the system; it creates an experience of seamlessness.

Creating new structures for coordination and continuity requires a change in vision for patient care. The resulting vision must then be translated into systems that restructure roles and processes to reflect coordination and continuity. This chapter discusses issues and concepts in managing care over the continuum. An approach to making a transition to continuum-focused care is presented. The approach includes changing the vision for care across the continuum, identifying the current organizational realities, and developing strategies for operationalizing continuous and coordinated care systems. Case management and critical path/CareMap™ systems are discussed as important methodologies for managing care across the continuum.

A NEW VISION

Managing care across the continuum demands expansion of the conventional concept of care to include a broader definition of health. In most environments the term *health care* is a misnomer in that the focus is not on health but rather on diagnosis and treatment of disease. Health care systems continue to evolve around acute illness with the major focus on curative medicine. According to Callahan (1991), curative medicine has been "designed to restore our body and its functioning to a state of normalcy in the face of illness, or to forestall a deterioration of capacity." Callahan proposes a shift in priorities from cure to care, observing that "what caring requires, for the most part, is concern and sympathy, time and personal attention." If health care is to achieve a blend of cure and care, the delivery of care will continue to take on new structures. These structures mandate a holistic model of care over the continuum, managed within and beyond traditional health care settings.

Essential approaches to *managing* care over the continuum are (1) strengthening the quality-cost link and (2) managing care and organizations as integrated, interdependent systems. One perspective of the quality-cost link is presented in Fig. 11-1. This perspective proposes that quality is a result of effective coordination and continuity of care. Quality enhancement in turn leads to better management of costs—suggesting that quality care is cost-effective care.

Continuity of care is based on adopting a systems perspective that includes all areas, settings, and departments where patients receive care. Experience continues to demonstrate that what happens in one area profoundly affects other areas—that care is a dynamic, interactive process. Most organizations currently are not structured as systems to ensure coordination and continuity of care across the continuum.

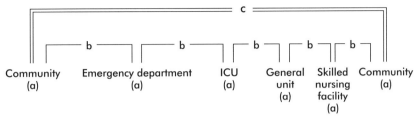

FIG. 11-1 Patient-focused care over the continuum. Care must be carefully managed within each area or segment (*a*), as well as between areas (*b*), with the ideal being continuum-focused care (*c*).

The goal of coordination and continuity of care over the continuum is realized by carefully redesigning structures, processes, and roles. In the redesign process three basic factors must be considered:

1. What are the needs and characteristics of the patient populations served by the organization?
2. What are the actual and potential resources within the organization?
3. What are the organization's goals for redesign?

Redesign at this nuclear level is a process that evolves over several years and, indeed, may never be completed. The process and its outcomes must be reexamined periodically to ensure that design continues to match need. Ideally, it involves becoming a "'learning organization'—an organization that is continually expanding its capacity to create its future" (Senge, 1990). The redesign process begins with an understanding of current reality as experienced by patients and the organization as discussed in the next section.

CURRENT REALITY: FOR PATIENTS AND ORGANIZATIONS

The Patient's Perspective

The current reality is a blend of how care is experienced by patients and the nature and characteristics of the patient populations served by the organization. Both of these perspectives are explored in this section.

What is the current reality for patients? Do they experience the organization as a seamless quilt or a fragmented maze? Current reality for many patients involves the following:

- Using the emergency department for primary or secondary care
- Having insufficient knowledge and/or resources to manage their care effectively
- Being the primary caregiver for another person yet needing time for their own convalescence
- Not qualifying for community services and yet temporarily needing support to recover from an acute illness episode

- Being delayed in discharge because tests and procedures are not obtained in a timely manner
- Being discharged on a last minute or "surprise" basis, creating confusion and crises
- Experiencing inadequate family support

In the case of the chronically ill these issues are exacerbated and include a high recidivism rate, necessitating critical care events and high resource utilization.

Most of these scenarios occur because health care systems continue to be built around acute illness services. Goldsmith (1992) points out that "as chronic illnesses . . . replaced the acute infection as our most significant health problem, the 'fit' between our healthcare needs and the health services framework worsened significantly." Failure to understand the current reality of patients and the organizations serving them merely creates patchwork solutions and will continue to promote event-driven, acute care structures.

An important step in understanding current reality is to identify the needs and characteristics of the patient population served by the organization. Essential questions for assessing the patient populations are outlined in the box on p. 165. The central issue is to thoroughly understand patient populations. This is the first step in creating a truly functional system in which services and resources are matched with patient needs.

The Organization's Perspective

As a profile of patients and their needs unfolds, the organization identifies current and potential resources for meeting those needs. Key issues for the organization include defining the following:

- What clinical and support services are required to meet identified patient needs?
- When in the trajectory are services most appropriately provided?
- How should the services be provided?
- Where are the services best delivered?
- Where are care and services best managed?
- Who are the most appropriate providers?

The evaluation also extends beyond the traditional walls of the organization and seeks information about what resources exist for care in the community, what resources are needed, what resources could be created, and how community resources will be linked to services within other settings. The information that emerges about the patient populations, the organization, and the community establishes a foundation for transforming the organization to provide care over the continuum.

Assessing Patient Populations: Focus Questions

1. What are the major patient populations/case types that receive care within the organization?

    a. By volume (e.g., diagnosis)

    b. By cost

    c. Payor mix

    d. High-intensity, high-resource users

2. What is the trajectory that the major patient populations follow?

    a. What is their entry point into the *health care system* and subsequently into the organization?

    b. Within the organization, what areas and departments provide service?

    c. Where do they go upon discharge from the organization?

    d. What is the recidivism rate?

3. How many and what groups of patients fall within high-risk categories?

    a. Chronic or terminal illness

    b. Lives alone or is caregiver for other family members

    c. Hospitalization within past 30 days

    d. Needs help with ADLs

    e. Needs help with meals, transportation, etc.

    f. Demonstrates knowledge deficit about disease process and related treatments and medications

    g. Cognitive impairment

    h. Emotionally challenged

    i. High probability for sudden physiologic imbalance requiring frequent emergency department and hospital use

    j. Inadequate family support

4. What patients are at risk for reaching less than desired outcomes including:

    a. Morbidity

    b. Mortality

    c. Infection rates

    d. Falls and other nosocomial traumas

    e. Clinical outcomes related to activity, health status, self-management ability, and prevention and management of complications

TRANSFORMING THE ORGANIZATION TO PROVIDE CARE OVER THE CONTINUUM

Changing the Organization's Vision

Central considerations in creating systems for care over the continuum are creating an organizational vision of patient care that incorporates continuity and coordination and reinventing the organization as a system. System thinking mandates that the interrelatedness of components (or segments) be acknowledged. An event in one area affects events in all other areas. As Senge (1990) observes:

> Business and other human endeavors are also systems. They, too, are bound by invisible fabrics of interrelated actions, which often take years to fully play out their effects on each other. Since we are part of that lacework ourselves, it's doubly hard to see the whole pattern of change. Instead, we tend to focus on snapshots of isolated parts of the system, and wonder why our deepest problems never seem to get solved.

This parallels the issues in managing care over the continuum. Many providers do not fully perceive the care that patients need throughout the continuum. As with other disciplines, nurses tend to specialize within segments of the trajectory (e.g., ICU, ED, ambulatory, home health) and their focus often is limited to that setting. Many nurses do not perceive how their work with patients within shifts or settings affects the whole. As a result, vision is fragmented and continuity and coordination are compromised.

To be transformed into a continuum-focused system the organizational vision must encompass the following:

- A holistic framework
- An outcomes focus
- Clearly defining and managing accountability
- Continuity of plan and provider
- Understanding and integrating patterns
- Creating partnerships

Integrating a Holistic Framework

A system of care over the continuum must be holistic in nature. A holistic approach integrates the psychosocial, emotional, and spiritual needs with physiologic and biologic needs and acknowledges the interrelationships between them. This integration is particularly important when addressing patient needs beyond those of the presenting illness and beyond the traditional walls of the organization.

Currently health care systems do not operate within a holistic framework. Rather, they address the presenting problem in isolation, diagnosing and treating illness as though the "problem" has a "fix." Although some patient problems are finite, increasing numbers of illnesses are chronic or recurring. These illnesses require continuity and coordination of care across settings and time, with special emphasis on patient responses and coping patterns. The continuum presents the need to promote and maximize health, as well as to respond to illness situations. As care moves across settings, patient needs change and thus the focus must be adjusted simultaneously.

Focus on Outcomes

In the future, successful clinicians and organizations will be defined by their ability to achieve effective long-term clinical and financial outcomes and not just to manage these factors in the acute care setting. When the concept of care is broadened to include management of the continuum, outcomes must be expanded as well. Within this context, outcomes are described as the realistic, desired, and measurable results of care stated in patient terms. At present, outcomes appear to be measured inconsistently at best. When they are measured, the timing and criteria are narrowly defined. For example, in the acute care setting, outcome criteria often are limited to factors such as morbidity, mortality, infection rates, and readmission rates and do not consider other essential criteria such as functionality and comfort. In addition, these criteria usually are applied during hospitalization or at discharge from the acute care setting without regard for longer-term measurement. In contrast, a continuum-based care system establishes measurement at various intervals before, during, and after the provision of care and in various settings. Measurement criteria are expanded to include functional status of the patient in terms of mobility, self-care ability, knowledge, and skill levels sufficient for self-management of an illness and its treatment, health status, comfort, and patient satisfaction. For example, the functional status, activity status, and comfort status of patients who have had total hip replacement are measured preoperatively, during hospitalization, at discharge, and at predetermined intervals postoperatively (such as at 3, 6, and 12 months).

Clearly Defining and Managing Accountability

The issue of accountability is fundamental to the process of managing care. In many organizations, staff responsibilities are clearly outlined and focus on the tasks within the various role descriptions. Most of these tasks are procedural. Essentially, assignments are allocated and accepted with the premise that everyone knows what is being done, when, and by whom. Accountability is missing in many organizations. As stated by Lewis and Batey (1982), "To be accountable is to be answerable for what one has done, to stand behind one's decisions and actions. It is a condition of being responsible for acts performed in a professional role, and it provides for a reckoning."

In the context of care over the continuum, accountability is for the *outcomes* of the care processes, which in turn implies that the system is designed to include strategies for measuring clinical outcomes. In addition, scope of authority needs to be clearly delineated because accountability without authority has a neutralizing effect. This type of accountability does not occur spontaneously; it must be designed, nurtured, and managed. The system for managing care over the continuum must clearly define the who, when, and what of accountability.

Continuity of Plan and Provider

A basic element in managing care across the continuum is continuity. Two aspects of continuity in this context are *continuity of plan* and *continuity of provider*. In systems for care over the continuum, continuity of plan synchronizes the contributions of the various disciplines within multiple settings. The plan in the acute setting, in addition to addressing current needs, considers at what point needed services can be safely provided in alternative settings or through community services. Alternatively, when patients are in the community setting, the plan of care reflects services needed to maintain and promote health outside the acute care setting.

Continuity of provider establishes a second thread through the care trajectory. There is a need for continuity of provider both at the unit or setting level, as well as at the continuum level. Within continuity of provider, an individual clinician or a small team of clinicians is identified to manage the care of a patient and perhaps to provide care across time and settings. It does not mean that this individual or team is the only clinician to interact with or care for the patient. It does mean that the clinician regularly interacts with the patient, providing a stable base for planning, evaluating, and modifying care. Continuity of provider is not restricted to nursing care although that is the focus here. For example, in many settings patients have a strong need for physician continuity. Likewise, progress of orthopedic patients may be enhanced by continuity of physical therapists.

Incorporating continuity of provider into system design has numerous benefits. The primary benefit revolves around the relationship that develops between the clinician and the patient. Trust, an essential component of a caring relationship, evolves over time and through continuing interactions or, as Callahan suggests, through "time and personal attention." This relationship greatly contributes to the management of care over the continuum in many direct and indirect ways. Clinicians who have a continuous relationship with patients are better positioned to observe changes in condition when they are most subtle. In addition, patients are more likely to provide information about their condition to a clinician they trust. Addressing subtle changes often will prevent crises. These clinicians also can identify patterns and trends in patient choices and responses to treatment and intervene with the patient or modify the plan. In all of these situations, patients and their support systems are involved in the care plan and process.

Understanding and Integrating Patterns

Identifying and analyzing patterns and trends are important steps toward acknowledging how they need to be changed. These patterns include the correlation between interventions and resulting outcomes, as well as variances from the usual and why they occur. Patterns are used in three contexts: individual patients, clinicians, and at the organizational level.

Patterning can be applied to individual patients as well as groups of patients. For individual patients, additional options become more apparent when patterns have been identified between decisions and related consequences. For clinicians, knowledge of the patterns of care and responses within a group of patients with a specific diagnosis leads to rapid identification of those patients who fall outside the usual response pattern. Changes can then be initiated promptly.

At the organizational level, patterns and trends of variances from the norm among groups of patients can be identified, analyzed, and addressed, becoming the basis for systemwide changes. For example, the trend of high recidivism among patients with chronic respiratory disorders may lead to identifying a need for enhanced support in the community to assist patients in managing their health concerns. Likewise, a hospital may observe that its patients with total hip replacement who have surgery on a Thursday or Friday typically have a longer length of stay because physical therapy is not available on weekends. Knowledge of this trend stimulates a discussion about the need to better match system resources to patient needs for quality, as well as cost. For the organization, early identification of issues related to patterns facilitates positioning resources where they are most needed and at the appropriate time. In managing care across the continuum, attention to discerning patterns and trends enables the organization to analyze and redesign itself continually.

Attention to patterns is accompanied by the need for information systems to manage the data. Unfortunately, information systems at this time tend to reflect data associated with the care segments rather than data related to the continuum.

Creating Partnerships Between Payors, Providers, and Patients

When addressing care across the continuum, the interdependent nature of the care system must be acknowledged. The current approach tends to envision episodes of illness necessitating episodes of care financed episodically. A key step to breaking through this traditional approach is to identify what formal partnerships are needed to provide continuum-based care. Partnerships are needed among patients, providers, and payors. This creates forums in which the vested parties negotiate and agree on the right care, at the right time, in the right place, by the right provider.

METHODOLOGIES FOR MANAGING CARE ACROSS THE CONTINUUM

The shift to managing care over the continuum and across boundaries means refocusing and in some cases creating new tools, systems, roles, and processes. This section presents specific tools and systems for continuum-focused care, including critical paths/CareMaps™, unit-based care coordination, and case management.

As discussed earlier, the central concepts in managing care over the continuum are coordination and continuity. A dynamic relationship exists between area-based or unit-based (e.g., telemetry unit or ambulatory clinic) coordination and continuity and between all the areas represented on the continuum. Care must be carefully managed within each area or segment and between areas, with the ideal being patient-focused care over the continuum (see Fig. 11-1). In addition, the aspects of continuity of both provider and plan must be addressed and integrated.

Unit-Based Management of Care

Fundamental coordination of care begins at the unit or area level. Coordination and continuity of care are elements that have been diluted in many nursing organizations. This dilution has at least three causes: marked reductions in length of stay among most patient groups; a shift toward part-time and alternative scheduling patterns that tend to fragment nurses' interactions with patients; and a shift toward increased administrative responsibilities among nurse managers who, in the past, often functioned as care coordinators.

In nursing, care coordination at the unit level is the function of the care delivery system. Although hybrids have been created, basically there are four nursing care delivery systems: functional, team, total patient care, and primary nursing. Case management, which will be addressed in the next discussion, is not a nursing care delivery system. Coordination and continuity have two facets: shift-based and unit-based. Functional, team, and total patient care are shift-oriented nursing systems with no *formal* or structured accountability for coordination and continuity from one day or time frame to the next within the length of stay. Primary nursing promotes formalized accountability of a specifically identified staff nurse for care outcomes of individual patients for the time that the patient is receiving care on the unit or area. As a plan evolves for managing care over the continuum, it is important for nursing organizations to identify the care delivery system in use and to assess the extent to which that system accomplishes the goals of coordinating care at the unit level. In situations where functional nursing, team nursing, or total patient care is the established delivery system, it will be necessary to develop a unit-based role with accountability for coordinating care across time. In organizations where primary nursing is the identified care delivery system, coordination of patient care is one of the role responsibilities of the primary nurse. Creating a tight system for unit-based care coordination is an important link in effectively managing care over the continuum.

Management of Care Over the Continuum

Case management is an effective strategy for managing care over the continuum. It can be defined as the following (The Center for Case Management, 1992):

> A clinical system that focuses on the accountability of an identified individual or group for coordinating a patient's care (or group of patients) across a continuum of care; facilitating the achievement of quality, clinical, and financial outcomes; negotiating, procuring, and coordinating services and resources needed by the patient/family; intervening at key points for individual patients; addressing and resolving consistent issues and problems identified in the care of case managed patients; and, creating opportunities and systems to enhance outcomes.

Case management is used for specific populations of patients and usually is not employed for all patients. Priority case types for case management include those who (1) experience frequent readmissions to the hospital or have numerous emergency department visits, (2) have unpredictable care needs, (3) experience significant variances in their usual care patterns or have significant complications or comorbidities, (4) fall within high-risk socioeconomic profiles, and (5) are high cost.

In case management, a process is established to identify patients who fall within the target populations as early in the trajectory as possible. Once patients are identified, a case manager is assigned and assesses patient needs, resources, and situations. The process continues by negotiating a plan of care with the patient, other clinicians, and, at times, the patient's payor. The negotiated plan includes anticipated goals, interventions, and time frames. In working with the patient over time and settings, the plan is implemented and evaluated on a consistent and timely basis, with revisions negotiated as needs and conditions change. Case managers may provide direct care to patients or negotiate and coordinate the care provided by others. In designing case management systems, the needs and characteristics of the patient populations to be case managed will suggest where case managers should be positioned along the care trajectory. For instance, chronically ill patients are most effectively managed through community-based case management, an example of which is presented in the next section.

Community-Based Nurse Case Management

The basic concept of community-based nurse case management at Carondelet St. Mary's Hospital, Tucson, was designed to enhance quality of care and to maximize accessibility to appropriate services—and to do so in a cost-effective manner. The process of working with patients is one of developing a collaborative relationship, understanding and honoring their choices about health care, and assisting them to recognize patterns in their choices and the relationship to resulting outcomes (Newman, Lamb, & Michaels, 1991). Overall, the community-based nurse case management model assists patients to develop greater self-care abilities and increased responsibility for their health care needs.

The creation of a nursing network allows patients to access services at several points along the health care delivery spectrum. The network comprises multiple nursing services, including acute care, home health, rehabilitation, long-term/skilled care, hospice, and community nursing care. The nurse case manager is at the hub of this network and moves across the continuum in partnership with patients, coordinating services for patient self-care and brokering support services when patients' self-care abilities are inadequate.

Most patients are referred to the nurse case management service during their inpatient admission. The referrals often come from acute care nursing staff, although they can originate from any part of the system, including physicians, social service, payors, or community organizations.

A nurse case manager screens the referred patient against high-risk profile criteria to determine that case management services are appropriate. Patients admitted into the case management service are generally (1) those at risk for managing health concerns related to chronic illness and (2) those temporarily needing community health services for recovery from an acute illness episode.

When the patient is admitted into the case management program, a nurse case manager is assigned. The nurse case manager meets with the patient to develop a relationship, to initiate a data base, and to develop an anticipated discharge plan in conjunction with the patient and other care providers. During the hospital stay the nurse case manager follows the patient on a daily basis and attends regularly scheduled, multidisciplinary discharge planning rounds. This concurrent interaction ensures that the discharge plan is current and that community support services are in place. When the patient returns to the community, the nurse case manager conducts home visits or telephones patients; negotiates, coordinates, evaluates, and modifies the effectiveness of provided care and services; and facilitates timely access to services through referrals to nursing centers, acute care services, or physicians. Intensity of services is directly related to assessed patient need and is modified to meet changing patient conditions. When case management services are no longer required, patients may be put on inactive status, discharged, or transferred to another provider. The nurse case manager updates information when case-managed patients are readmitted to the hospital and works with the inpatient staff to ensure continuity of care and to develop or confirm the plan of care for after discharge.

In providing services to patients and their families, nurse case managers may evaluate health status, screen for common health problems, teach self-reliance and monitoring, obtain community-based support, coordinate access to needed health services, facilitate short- and long-term planning for health management, make referrals to other health care providers, manage nursing care, coordinate other care, broker services, serve as a primary provider, and/or assist patients to negotiate the health care system. Nurse case managers do not duplicate services provided elsewhere in the system. For example, patients who meet Medicare criteria are referred to home health services.

Goals achieved through nurse case management include preventing admissions and interrupting a cycle of readmissions. When admission to acute care is necessary, nurse case management promotes a reduced length of stay through intervening at a lower point of patient acuity, which results in a decrease in critical care and emergency department use (Ethridge & Lamb, 1989). The effect is more appropriate utilization of resources, enhanced patient satisfaction, and improved health status.

Paying for Case Management Services

Developing reimbursement methodologies for case management services is an important consideration in system design. Reimbursement for case management is derived from two basic sources: internal and external. Internally, case management is financed through reduction in loses and/or enhanced volume. Enhanced volume may occur through supporting the organization's bid to be a preferred provider through an insurer or employer. Externally, funding may be realized through fee for case management services negotiated directly by the organization with payors (Michaels, 1992; Ethridge, 1991).

Tools and Systems for Managing Care Across the Continuum

Care over the continuum is facilitated by tools and systems that contribute to continuity of plan and to the coordination of care between disciplines and areas. The principal tool that has emerged is the critical path, especially the second-generation format called the CareMap™. Systems that support CareMaps™ include variance analysis and refocused communication and documentation structures.

As a tool, CareMaps™ organize and sequence care activities and the clinical outcomes associated with them. Focused on specific patient populations, CareMaps™ create a matrix on which interventions, intermediate goals, and outcomes are outlined. Although originally developed for the care of patients during hospital stays, CareMaps™ can be written to address care needs during each phase of the trajectory. In moving from one phase to another, the primary difference is in defining the time frame.

An example of an episode-based CareMap™ is one that was developed for pregnancy and childbirth, the framework for which is shown in Fig.

11-2. In this situation, the time frame moves between visits (or months and weeks) and blocks of hours. The problem statements remain the same throughout the trajectory. The outcomes for each phase become the intermediate goals for the continuum, and the discharge goals indicate the point at which the patient no longer requires care for this condition. Once the CareMap™ is developed for the continuum of care, CareMaps™ can be developed for each phase of the trajectory that outline the required care in more detail.

For CareMap™ development, patients are grouped by diagnosis (e.g., myocardial infarction), by procedure or surgery (e.g., total hip replacement), or by condition (e.g., failure to wean from ventilator or boarder baby). They are developed by the multidisciplinary team that usually provides care to the identified patient population. The CareMap™ establishes the usual patterns of care, reflecting the needs of most patients with the diagnosis.

Once developed, the CareMap™ becomes a template for the plan of care that is activated as patients are admitted into the system. It is then modified to reflect the needs of individual patients by adding, deleting, or changing components based on assessment data collected about the patient. The CareMap™ is discussed with patients and their families to ensure that their needs and concerns are being addressed and to provide

CARE TRAJECTORY

| Setting | OB clinic --> OB admitting --> Labor & Delivery --> Postpartum --> OB clinic |
| Time frame | Visits/ Months | Visits/ Months | Hours | Hours | Visits/ Months |

Intermediate goals   Intermediate goals   Intermediate goals   Intermediate goals   Discharge outcomes

Problem/Issue statements

• Actual and potential issues related to self-care

• Management of discomfort and pain

• Relationship issues: partner/ spouse, baby, family/friends

• Actual and potential problems related to pregnancy and childbirth

FIG. 11-2 CareMap™ components: perinatal patients. (Developed by Mae J. McCormick, RN, MS, and the Maternal and Child Health Nursing Department, District of Columbia General Hospital, Washington, DC.)

them with specific information about the course of care. This modified CareMap™ is then used as the multidisiciplinary plan of care, synchronizing the activities of all providers. It also serves as a baseline against which progress can be evaluated.

CareMaps™ cannot be used in a vacuum. Communication systems must be modified to reflect their use. The communication systems that need to be revised include intershift report in nursing, physician rounds, and interdisciplinary patient-focused meetings. In addition to communication systems, the system for documentation will ultimately need to incorporate the CareMap™.

CareMaps™ outline the care for most but not all patients within an identified group. Because of individual responses to illness and treatment, situations will occur in which the actual plan or course differs from the expected plan as described in the CareMap™. CareMaps™ are not formulas dictating the care of patients. They are treatment parameters that must be modified through clinician judgment based on the changing needs and condition of individual patients. The difference between the expected and actual trajectory is known as *variance*. The advantage of a CareMap™ is that variances can be identified and addressed promptly, minimizing unnecessary delays or interruptions.

As CareMaps™ are used over time, variance data from each case type are aggregated and then analyzed for trends and patterns. Experience with aggregate data suggests that the variance causes can be categorized into three major groups: patient, system, and clinician. As variance patterns build and are prioritized within the organization, quality improvement activities focus on issues that are known to affect patient care. Variance data can also be used to modify or revise the CareMap™ and to create high-risk profiles for screening specific populations of patients. This establishes a continuous feedback cycle regarding the care of patients, creating a clinical application of the continuous quality improvement process.

SUMMARY

The management of patient care over the continuum is essential for quality and cost issues. In far too many situations, patients must "connect the dots" or manage their care in near isolation. Although patient self-reliance is a desired goal, the health care system must provide a means for managing care in partnership with patients. Strategies that enhance coordination and continuity of care are fundamental to that process and create a seamless experience for patients. Currently most health care systems are focused inwardly and do not effectively manage care over the continuum. Increasingly, hospitals and other health care organizations are realizing that patient care and its management involve interventions beyond the traditional walls. Creating an organization that can accomplish that goal requires system redesign.

Unit-based or setting-based care coordination, case management, and CareMaps™ are approaches to providing coordination and continuity of care across the continuum. Each makes a different but related contribution to the process. System redesign must include a decision about which approaches will be used and their interrelationships.

Care over the continuum is a philosophy and vision, as well as a process. To transform the vision into a new reality, there must be commitment throughout the organization, especially at the administrative level. In addition to commitment, a plan for managing the transition is critical to ensuring that a common focus is maintained. This plan must include creating alliances among all constituencies. In the process, the organization assumes the characteristics of a learning system, ensuring its future.

REFERENCES

Berwick, D. (1992). Seeking systemness. *Healthcare Forum Journal*, March/April, 23-28.

Callahan, D. (1991). *What kind of life: The limits of medical progress*. New York: Simon & Schuster.

The Center for Case Management. (1992). *Case management definition*. South Natick, MA: Author.

Ethridge, P. (1991). A nursing HMO: Carondelet St. Mary's experience. *Nursing Management, 22* (7), 22-27.

Ethridge, P., & Lamb, G. (1989). Professional nursing case management improves quality, access and costs. *Nursing Management, 20*(3), 30-35.

Goldsmith, J. (1992). The reshaping of healthcare. *Healthcare Forum Journal, 35*(3), 19-27.

Lewis, F., & Batey, M. (1982). Clarifying autonomy and accountability in nursing service: Part 2. *Journal of Nursing Administration, 12* (5), 10-15.

Michaels, C. (1992). Carondelet St. Mary's nursing enterprise. *Nursing Clinics of North America, 27*(1), 77-85.

Newman, M., Lamb, G., & Michaels, C. (1991). Nurse case management: The coming together of theory and practice. *Nursing & Health Care, 12* (8), 404-408.

Senge, P. (1990). *The fifth discipline*. New York: Doubleday.

CHAPTER 12

Research: A Critical Element in Response to Health Care Rationing

Darlene A. McKenzie
Leslie N. Ray

Research efforts around health care rationing must address two important questions: (1) What health objectives should be met? and (2) What nursing interventions should be included in a rationing plan? The authors incorporate these questions into a model of rationing that considers three central factors: (1) public values and preferences around health care, (2) clinical effectiveness of interventions, and (3) cost efficiencies of the services. Nursing research that addresses each component of the model requires studies across disciplines and calls for collaboration between nurse researchers and nurse administrators for successful implementation.

In this chapter we present what we view as an emerging model for making health care rationing decisions within the public sector. We discuss the extent to which nursing research has addressed components of this emerging model and make recommendations for nursing research that will enhance nursing's ability to influence rationing decisions.

In the past, an informal rationing system based on ability to pay determined the allocation of health care resources. However, the number of

School of Nursing, Community Health Care Systems Department, Oregon Health Sciences University, Portland, OR 76201

Series on Nursing Administration—Volume 6, 1994

Americans who do not meet poverty criteria for government assistance, who do not receive health insurance as an employee benefit, and who cannot afford to purchase health insurance privately has swollen to 37 million. The exclusion of this number of Americans from access to fundamental health care has brought the system under heavy criticism (Rooks, 1990) and has stimulated a number of universal-access proposals at both the state and federal levels of government.

Although a variety of private-public payment formulas have been discussed, any plan that substantially increases the number of Americans covered will require limiting the number or type of services covered under that plan unless the available resources expand. Substantial expansion of resources is unlikely because although "health care for all" is a public concern, increasing the proportion of the gross national product (GNP) spent on health care beyond the current 13% (Grace, 1990) has little public support. Furthermore, savings generated through efficiencies are unlikely to be large enough to eliminate the need to limit or ration services. Aaron and Schwartz (1990) predicted that improved efficiencies in delivery systems will provide only a small and temporary reduction in the escalation of health care costs.

Therefore it appears that the nation is moving toward a change in public policy regarding the allocation of health resources. It seems likely that this change will be reflected in government-sponsored health plans such as the Oregon health plan (Garland, 1991) that proposes to increase the proportion of the public covered by the plan through decreasing the numbers or types of services provided. That is, the government resources allocated to health care would be distributed or rationed through a system that guaranteed a set of essential or minimum services to a larger proportion of the population. Within this set of services it also is likely that costly interventions will be rationed at the individual level through techniques such as case management.

This rationing at the governmental level would not preclude the purchase of basic or supplemental coverage outside the governmental plan. Thus the production of services not considered "essential" will undoubtedly continue through some form of privatization. However, private insurance companies may be influenced and thus model their basic health coverage on the government plan. Thus rationing within governmental plans will affect the type of care provided by nurses and other health care professionals by regulating what services are reimbursable for a large proportion of the population.

RATIONING MODEL

Rationing within governmental health plans requires making choices regarding the allocation of scarce or limited resources designated for health care, that is, choosing how these resources will be apportioned, or shared.

As illustrated in Fig. 12-1, rationing decisions within this context will require making choices at two levels. The first level requires choosing among alternative health care objectives, such as healthy babies or longer life for individuals with renal failure. This level also may be conceptualized in terms of programs or services generally associated with the objective, that is, prenatal and well-baby care for meeting the healthy baby objective. The second level requires choosing among alternative interventions necessary to attain a single objective, for example, ultrasound diagnostic testing versus nutritional counseling to promote healthy babies. Further, choices at both of these levels involve consideration of three major factors: (1) the values of the public, (2) clinical effectiveness of health care services and interventions, and (3) economic efficiencies.

Public values are emerging as important considerations in the development of a government-supported health plan. Policymakers are beginning to recognize that the public is unlikely to support a health care plan that does not include health care services, interventions, and procedures that are important to them. Public values were explicitly considered in decisions at the level of allocation of health care services within Oregon's proposed governmental plan (Capuzzi & Garland, 1990). Furthermore, the pro-

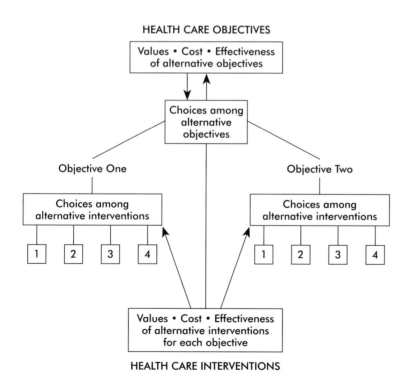

Fig. 12-1 Health care rationing decision model.

cess employed in the development of that plan recognized that the values of services need to be expressed relative to one another. It is interesting to note that the services valued by the public did not mirror the type of services generally funded. Palliative care and prevention programs, frequently underfunded in our current plans, ranked high.

At the level of choosing among alternative interventions, preferences or values usually are expressed individually. In the course of providing health care, providers elicit information from individuals regarding their treatment desires. However, with the implementation of a government-sponsored health plan, rationing decisions will need to be made for the aggregate about desired and thus potentially reimbursable interventions. Rationing decisions also may extend to establishing decision rules for determining who can receive a specific intervention. In either situation, we can expect the public to demand a say in those decisions.

Clinical outcomes or effectiveness is a second factor that influences rationing decisions. Everything else being equal, that is, values and cost, individuals generally choose the most effective intervention available to them, even if the effectiveness is low. Established clinical effectiveness of a health service or intervention is a strong argument for allocation of health care resources to one health objective over another objective or to one intervention over another under a government-sponsored health plan. We can expect that, as in Oregon (Capuzzi & Garland, 1990), relative clinical effectiveness will influence decisions about which health care objectives or services are funded. Insofar as a health plan specifies the types of covered interventions, we also can expect relative clinical effectiveness to influence decisions. Furthermore, using clinical effectiveness as a criterion for inclusion of services or interventions in a health care rationing plan may lead to the establishment of a minimum acceptable level of effectiveness. "Better than nothing" is not likely to suffice as a basis for funding a service or intervention.

Cost is a third factor that clearly influences rationing decisions. Within the resources allocated to health care, we want each health care service priced low enough so that we can afford to reimburse services across a range of health care objectives. Similarly, we want costs of alternative interventions to be such that they do not preclude consideration for use. Costs of alternative interventions are being examined increasingly (Drummond, 1980) and have been used to develop a government plan (Oregon Health Services Commission, 1991).

Although there seems to be general support for considering data on some combination of these three factors when making rationing decisions, the way data are linked to reach a decision varies. In Oregon (Oregon Health Services Commission, 1991), widely held health values and health care service priorities were incorporated with survey data on the clinical effectiveness of specific interventions to form a prioritized list of services. Actuarial and reimbursement data were used to estimate the cost of providing each of the services. Oregon proposed to pay for as many of the services as the budget or available resources allowed—beginning at the top of the list. Hadorn (1991) argued for use of "preference-weighted" outcomes to determine the relative priority of different health services. Preferences (value) for certain health outcomes across the population or identified sub-populations would be determined in relation to expected outcomes (effectiveness) for particular clinical conditions. Eddy (1991) proposed a similar process that would provide for patient input into rationing decisions and explicitly link value and cost at the level of individual interventions and patient conditions. A representative group of patients would be presented with data on the benefits, harm, and cost of alternative interventions and asked to make a choice. Linkage of these factors also is reflected in economic analyses that incorporate values and effectiveness, as well as costs (Drummond, 1980).

Just as cost or effectiveness data can be used to identify preferences, public values data can be used to influence which outcomes are studied. That is, public values identified through clinical practice can be incorporated into outcome studies. For example, it is generally accepted in practice that many patients with cancer in terminal stages of the disease accept chemotherapy with the goal of comfort or prolongation of life rather than recovery. This suggests that any evaluation of the effectiveness of chemotherapy under those circumstances would include comfort and longevity as clinical effectiveness outcome variables.

As illustrated in the model in Fig. 12-1, rationing decisions among alternative health care services and interventions are dynamic and iterative. Changes in values or costs or advances in practice may lead to reviewing decisions at either level. That is, changes in the values, effectiveness, or cost of alternative objectives may lead to changes in the objectives funded. The changes in these three factors also may lead to changes in the distribution of funds among the objectives. Similarly, changes in values, effectiveness, or cost of alternative interventions may lead to changes in the type of interventions funded or in the distribution of funds among the interventions. For example, technology will undoubtedly change the effectiveness and cost of some services, eliminate the need for others, and create the need for still others.

Furthermore, value, effectiveness, and cost data collected at the intervention level may influence subsequent decisions made at the objectives level. This can happen if data are aggregated across interventions and are thus available to provide an estimate of the value, cost, and effectiveness of meeting the associated objective. In response to these new data, the choice among alternative objectives may be revisited. For example, in the conduct of a study to evaluate alternative interventions for reducing child abuse, cost and/or effectiveness data for counseling as one of the interventions might lead to its inclusion as a reimbursable intervention under a currently funded service package, such as well-child care. It also might lead to prevention of child abuse being given a higher priority for funding relative to other objectives. Thus data gathered for the purposes of comparing alternative interventions may serve as an impetus for re-examining the funding priority of the associated health care objective.

As just discussed, when making rationing decisions about what services and interventions to include in a government-sponsored health plan, it is useful to recognize that decisions are made at two levels. Furthermore, within each level, data are needed regarding what is valued, what works, and what it costs. In other words, it is important to look at the effectiveness of services or interventions known to be of public value or to assign relative weights to services and interventions based on public values. In like manner, it is important to begin looking at the costs required to obtain the clinical effectiveness for valued services and interventions. It also is important to recognize that health care rationing decisions made within the emerging model are dynamic. Our health care priorities and the specific choices and decisions that follow are likely to change as our knowledge of values, effectiveness, and cost increases. It becomes imperative, then, that nurses consider the impact of research on not only individual care, but the health care of the nation as a whole.

NURSING RESEARCH AND ROLE IN RATIONING DECISIONS

Nurses have a key role in providing data for rationing policy decisions. To have an effective voice in influencing health care rationing policy, nurses need to conduct research that provides information useful in making decisions at both the first and second level. That is, nurses need to provide data that will help determine the priority of different health care objectives and thus the health care services included in a health care plan. This means nurses need to contribute to the data base concerning the value, effectiveness, and cost of the services required to meet alternative health care objectives. Similarly, nurses need to contribute to the data base concerning the value, effectiveness, and cost of interventions required to provide the services associated with each objective. Fortunately, because of the dynamic relationship between the decision levels, nurses can make a major contribution to decisions about alternative objectives by conducting research at the intervention level.

To what extent have nurses conducted research that will provide the type of data needed for rationing decisions? What can we do to enhance our ability to influence rationing decisions through continued research? In addressing these questions, we combine the two decision levels and present our recommendations in relation to each of the three factors influencing choice—values, effectiveness, and cost.

Determining Values

Determining what health care objectives and interventions are important to society as a whole is a formidable task in which nurses have not actively engaged. In attempting to determine what the public values in terms of health care, what gets asked and who gets asked are important issues and need to be considered in nursing research. Several scales are available to address what gets asked. They were developed and have been used to identify patient values regarding health outcomes (Hunt, McEwen, & McKenna, 1985; Kaplan & Bush, 1982; Stewart, Greenfield, Hays, Wells, Rogers, Berry, McGlynn, & Ware, 1989; Spitzer, Dobson, Hall, Chesterman, Levi, Shepherd, Battista, & Catchlove, 1981; Rosser & Kind, 1978). Unfortunately, these scales do not address value or preference for specific services or interventions and are, therefore, of limited value in helping us determine what the public wants. Furthermore, the scales do not present the values in such a way that we can measure how the public would like to make choices among alternative services and interventions.

With regard to who gets asked, nurses have provided policy makers with data on what the public values. However, like other health care professionals, nurses have collected most of the data on a patient-by-patient basis in the course of providing treatment. The data tend to focus on a particular incident, event, or decision point. Thus the data are primarily anecdotal. We do not know how complete the data are in terms of the type of the population, values, or alternatives represented.

What are the challenges to nurses arising from the need to understand public values, and how can nurses contribute to the collection of data on values? We recommend three considerations for nursing research:

- Develop scales that include nursing services and interventions in the choices the public is asked to value
- Sample patients and clients to obtain values information systematically
- Sample populations outside of the mainstream

In addressing the issue of what gets asked, nurses must open up rationing policy discussions to consider a broader range of health care objectives and interventions. There is a clear need to include nursing services and interventions beyond those delegated by physicians or related to care delegated by physicians. Independently managed nursing services and interventions such as continence care, restraint reduction, adjustment and coping with illness, and palliative care need to be considered explicitly as health care options by patients. Without such consideration, patients' options regarding valued care and services will be incomplete. If the services and interventions the public is asked to value are based on a medical model, many nursing interventions will be included or assumed by virtue of their association with an identified medical service or intervention. However, under a medical model, nursing services and interventions that are managed independently are less likely to be included. Nurses can address this concern in two ways. First, we can offer consultation to professionals and politicians generating the lists of options. Second, we can conduct additional studies of these independently managed services, which will serve to highlight their value and promote their being considered among the public choices.

Nurses also can take an active role in going directly to the public systematically to find out what is needed and wanted. Nurses can provide much of the data by including questions of choice in nursing research and by engaging in collaborative efforts in large population surveys mounted by other disciplines. Nursing intervention studies can incorporate questions on patient satisfaction and perceptions of the value of those interventions. Nursing administrators can gather similar data by asking about nursing interventions and outcomes explicitly in marketing and patient satisfaction surveys. Nurses also can encourage the use of secondary data currently not used as a data source for public values and priorities. For example, a readily available expression of the public's values regarding differing health care objectives is the check-off section of tax returns. Here taxpayers are allowed to indicate if they wish to allocate tax dollars to specific health care programs such as Alzheimer's disease. With appropriate analysis, these data could provide initial information regarding public priorities for health care.

In addressing the issue of who gets asked, nurses also have a responsibility for identifying the values and needs of the traditionally disenfranchised: the poor, elderly, and minority groups. The needs of some of these groups might be identified through oversampling in a large population survey. However, because of considerations such as education and language, methods other than surveys may need to be employed so that "outliers" and minority views are included in decision making. These methods might include interviews in the home, hospital, or workplace. Some of the questions and methods involved in these smaller, more closely focused efforts are appropriate to master's and doctoral level research. Student researchers under the direction of experienced faculty can make a valuable contribution to the data base regarding public values around health care.

In attempting to meet these research recommendations, nurses will be faced with methodologic challenges. Some of the more conspicuous include identifying appropriate population samples, determining which outcomes to include, describing outcomes, aggregating preferences, and developing tools for measurement (Hadorn, 1991). However, the payoff for meeting the challenges could be great. Data on differing preference patterns among sub-groups may lead to a rationing plan that offers a variety of packages, perhaps with different premiums.

Clinical Effectiveness

Although nurses historically have conducted clinical studies, our understanding of the effectiveness of nursing interventions has suffered from the unfocused approach to clinical research. In reviewing the publications of nursing research journals over 28 years, Brown, Tanner, and Patrick (1984) identified the noncumulative nature of the research as a major limitation. Haller, Reynolds, and Horsley (1979) identified only 10 clinical areas with a research base sufficient to develop practice protocols. A recent Medline search suggests that the volume of clinical research has increased in the past 5 years but stills remains relatively unfocused with regard to type of problems addressed. Such a shotgun approach to research has not facilitated choosing among alternative objectives or interventions based on effectiveness.

We can, however, expect our understanding of the effectiveness of nursing interventions to increase in the next decade. A more systematic evaluation of interventions within a specific problem area is being promoted at the national level. Setting priorities for outcomes research within both professional organizations and funding agencies has begun. The American Nurses Association (ANA), for example, is working with the National Center for Nursing Research (NCNR) to establish funding priorities in areas of practice that have a beginning but not definitive research base (K. O'Connor, personal communication, July 1992). To accomplish this goal, we may need to increase the overall funding base as well.

Our knowledge of effectiveness also will be increased by the promotion of interaction between practice and research by national organizations. For example, ANA has established a common language and framework to facilitate communication between practice and research and to provide a mechanism for collecting, analyzing, and retrieving data (McLoughlin, 1990). The Agency for Health Care Policy and Research (AHCPR) has established panels to develop guidelines for seven areas of clinical practice of great concern to nurses, e.g., pain, continence, and pressure sores (Koeppen, 1990). In addition to drawing on both practice and research, it is anticipated that the guidelines from ANA and AHCPR will generate feedback from the workplace, thus raising questions for additional outcome research and validation in practice.

What more can we do to increase our understanding of the effectiveness of nursing interventions and thus enhance our ability to make choices among alternatives? In addition to increasing our depth of knowledge within a problem area and strengthening the research/practice link, we recommend four considerations for nursing research:

- Create study designs that acknowledge interaction between intervention "packages" of multiple health care providers
- Ask "what works" in addition to asking "does X work"
- Frame studies in terms of course of illness or problem
- Increase the number of outcomes examined

Nurses have long recognized the contribution of other professional health care providers and the need to coordinate care to attain the desired outcomes. We also have recognized that the care provided by other disciplines can influence the care we provide. The care given in nursing is, to a large extent, context driven. That is, to achieve a specified outcome we provide nursing care not only in relation to what the patient wants or needs, but also within the context of what others are providing.

However, our research efforts often do not reflect this context or interaction. In our attempt to approximate an experimental design, we sometimes control through exclusion what we might more profitably be studying. That is, we often limit the intervention under study to a single intervention or variations of a single intervention. One approach to the seemingly competing demands of experimental control and clinical complexity is to build the complexity into the design. For example, by systematically creating different combinations of care, we can examine the relative effectiveness of varying combinations of multidisciplinary interventions.

The issues and implications for asking "what works" are similar to those for looking at interdisciplinary interaction effects. To achieve a better understanding of what might be effective in a practice setting we may need to expand our repertoire of research strategies. Although nursing is a practice discipline with a goal of conducting research that has implications for practice, we nurses tend to consider the experimental model used in basic science as the standard for our own research. In this model the intervention protocol is specified and procedures are established to ensure that the intervention does not alter during the course of the study. Specially trained research personnel frequently are used to implement the intervention. This model has two disadvantages. First, it does not allow the practitioner to improve on the intervention during the course of the study. Second, it is difficult to take implementation into consideration because the skills and motivation of the research personnel may differ substantially from those of a clinician. Similarly, the circumstances or protocol under which the intervention is conducted may be difficult to maintain in practice. Use of additional research strategies, such as action research (Peters & Robinson, 1984) and case studies (Yin, 1989), can expand our understanding of effectiveness in clinical practice.

One approach to improving interventions is to provide, as an ongoing part of practice, mechanisms for nurses to systematically document the nature and context of the intervention, as well as to evaluate the effectiveness of those interventions. These data, aggregated across nurses and institutions, could form the basis for an intervention that might be evaluated in a more traditional research design. This strategy currently is being used in a study on physical restraint reduction for nursing home residents (Rader, Semradek, McKenzie, & McMahon, in press). Along similar lines, Colling and her colleagues (Colling, Ouslander, Hadley, Eisch, & Campbell, 1992) gathered data on the extent to which staff followed an intervention protocol for urinary incontinence among nursing home residents. The investigators also gathered data on the reasons given for noncompliance. Those reasons or information on the barriers to implementation can be the basis for modifying the intervention or system context to support use of the intervention.

Evaluating the effectiveness of nursing interventions across the course of illness rather than the duration of stay is a critical dimension for nursing research. The effects of some interventions (either positive or negative) are not immediately apparent. Evaluations occurring too early may result in inaccurate assessments of effectiveness. This means that evaluations of interventions performed only during short hospital and specialty unit stays or single episodes of chronic illness may be insufficient. The impact of the care may manifest itself when the patient is in a different unit or after hospitalization. If we can presume that patients' outcomes at the time of discharge were acceptable, the negative posthospital outcomes attributed to early hospital discharge under diagnosis-related groups (DRGs) demonstrates the need for course-of-illness evaluation.

Looking at effectiveness of care across the course of the illness has implications for the way in which nurses conduct research. It also suggests the need for a common data base including the same patient identifier for use across settings and episodes. In addition, it suggests the need for common or compatible measures that can be used not only across care settings, but also across practice and research settings.

The last recommendation is to increase the range of service and intervention effects or outcomes nurses examine in relation to a given disease or condition. If we limit the measurement of effectiveness to a single outcome, we may miss other outcomes that may either be highly valued or influence our assessment of an intervention's effectiveness. For example, Jensen (1988), in a summary of medical studies on the treatment of peptic ulcers, reported that the effectiveness of the alternative intervention appeared inferior based on the single variable frequently employed (reoccurrence). However, with the inclusion of outcomes such as healing without complications, the alternative intervention appeared superior. Whether we employ a multivariate outcome approach within a single study or look at a range of outcomes across studies, this recommendation will be expensive to implement and suggests the need for increased research funding.

Cost Efficiencies

Much of the work that nurses have done in relation to establishing the cost of nursing services is of limited usefulness in comparing alternative nursing interventions. Methods such as process cost accounting recommended by Riccolo (1988) and others (Watson, Lower, Wells, Farrah, & Jarrell, 1991) for acute care settings were designed primarily for assuring unit or facility revenues sufficient to cover the costs of providing care in the aggregate. Under this method, unit level data are collected by cost categories such as staff and supplies and cannot be disaggregated by patient. Even when patient classification or acuity systems are used as the basis for process accounting, the data are unlikely to be sensitive to differences in resource use based on alternative interventions. Unless the activities or factors associated with the alternative interventions have widely varying points attached to them, patients are likely to be classified into the same care level and thus look the same with regard to resource use.

Nurses are only beginning to look at costs in relation to alternative interventions. A Medline search using nursing and clinical trials as key words identified 113 publications since 1987. Only five had MESH headings suggesting cost or resource consumption analysis. Only two addressed cost in relation to the intervention (Hu, Igfou, Kaltreider, Yu, Rohner, Dennis, Craighead, Hadley, & Ory, 1989; Hoepelman, Rozenberg-Arska, & Verhoef, 1988). A manual examination of the most recent 5 years of *Image, Western Journal of Nursing Research,* and *Nursing Research* failed to identify any studies that explored the relative costs of meeting differing objectives or providing different types of services.

What can we do to improve our understanding of the costs of nursing interventions and thus enhance our ability to make choices among alternatives? We recommend three considerations:

• Generate cost data related to service needs of patients rather than functional needs of the unit
• Develop a minimum data base for categories of costs
• Conduct studies within an economic analysis framework

The availability of service-based cost data could decrease the expense of conducting cost studies and could address design problems. In a service-based system, costs are documented in terms of what is required to provide a specific service to a specific patient or patient type. All occurrences of a task are counted separately and are charged for. For the purposes of budgeting, these data are likely to be aggregated across patients by type of treatment. However, in their original form, the data provide a rich source of secondary data for constructing individual patient cost profiles across alternative treatment modalities. In addition, access to a large, within-facility, secondary data set could resolve some methodologic problems associated with small sample sizes. The challenge to nurses in the use of a service-based or procedure-based model is to enumerate and develop standard definitions for the critical treatments and interventions. As noted by Hoffman (1988), nurses have yet to address the issue of professional services that are hard to measure.

The establishment and use of a minimum data set for the type of cost information that should be considered for inclusion in a study would also enhance our understanding of costs of alternative interventions. Drummond (1980) discussed relevant costs as changes in resource use in terms of both health services resources, other support services, and patient's (and family's) resources. Examples of health services resources include land, buildings, manpower, equipment, and consumable supplies. Support service resources could include volunteer and social services. Patient and family resources include, for example, personal time, transportation, and home adaptation. Use of such a data set would serve as a basis for critiquing the comparability of cost estimates across studies, facilitating metaanalysis. It also would serve as a guide to the type of data that might be relevant to the study. Jensen (1988), for example, reported that although indirect care costs are very relevant to the evaluation of interventions for peptic ulcer (78% of all costs), they were ignored in most studies.

Economic analysis is a useful tool for nurses to both identify the type of data needed and organize the data for analysis. For example, in an economic analysis the concept of benefit is expanded to include changes in productive output, as well as changes in health status. As noted by Schoenbaum (1980), attention to the cost-effectiveness implications of a study under design might result in an improved design.

Of the different methods available within the economic analysis framework, cost-effectiveness analysis and cost-benefit analysis provide the more balanced evaluations. Cost effectiveness is a method of comparing the costs of two ways of meeting the same objective when the value of the objective is assumed. If each intervention is equally effective in meeting the objective, the less costly intervention is chosen. Cost-benefit analysis is the method of choice when the value of societal goal, health objective, or treatment intervention is being questioned (Drummond 1980). Costs and benefits are converted into a common unit of analysis—usually dollars. A cost-benefit ratio is created for each alternative and compared across alternatives. By balancing the cost of the intervention with the perceived value of the outcomes, this method could produce a more positive score for the intervention that is more costly but also creates more highly valued outcomes.

IMPLEMENTATION OF RATIONING RESEARCH IN NURSING

Development of partnerships both within and outside of nursing is the key to providing the values, effectiveness, and cost data on which rationing decisions will be made. A partnership between nursing administration and academic nurse researchers to promote practice-based research is critical. The nurse administrator and nurse researcher bring different skills and perspectives that enable better information to be gathered.

Nurse administrators have the knowledge about which interventions might work in the practice setting and could, therefore, identify the most useful areas for study. They also have the authority to test alternative methods of providing service within their settings. Nurse administrators working collaboratively with researchers can assist in the development of practice-based data collection tools. These tools will aid both the nurse clinician in gathering information for delivering individual care and the nurse researcher in gathering data across groups of patients. Further, nurse administrators can provide essential support for nursing research in their facility and can argue for public access to institutional data for research purposes.

Nurse researchers have the knowledge and skills to evaluate different care methods and can assist nurses in the patient care setting to use this information to improve their practice. Nurse researchers also can use their voice in professional journals and presentations to articulate practice needs for improving patient care. Relying on advances in case study research (Yin, 1989), nurse researchers can use descriptions of what is being done currently to identify effective nursing care within the context of the practice setting.

In addition to forming a partnership with one another, nurse administrators and academic nurse researchers need to develop strong partnerships outside of nursing. Because of the complexity of a multivariate approach to health care rationing, our approach needs to be multidisciplinary. In developing institutional and research data sets to answer questions of values, effectiveness, and cost, we need to consult ethicists, sociologists, economists, and others. Similarly, in conducting nurse-initiated multivariate studies, we need to develop interdisciplinary research teams. This need is illustrated in a review of studies in which medical care was evaluated using economic analyses. Less than 25% identified appropriate costs and benefits, less than half allocated overhead costs appropriately, and most either did not perform sensitivity analyses or performed them incorrectly (Adams, McCall, Gray, Orza, & Chalmers, 1992).

The need for a multidisciplinary approach also suggests that nurses should be aggressively seeking participation in research studies initiated by other disciplines. As we know, much of the rationing-related research is conducted by health services researchers from economic and policy disciplines. And finally, the need for a multidisciplinary approach suggests that our efforts in developing minimum data sets and data-gathering tools should be directed toward maximizing their utility across disciplines, as well as across care delivery settings.

Nurse administrators and academic nurse researchers also may need to form political partnerships to emphasize and promote the value of rationing research and thus the need to increase rationing research funding. As noted, the type of research called for is expensive and may require the release of additional funding or the redistribution of existing funding. One approach that we might consider toward that end is increased communication with both funding bodies and the public regarding what is known about the values, effectiveness, and cost of alternative health care objectives and interventions. The development of a clearing house for study reports could serve both audiences.

SUMMARY

This chapter has presented a model for rationing policy decisions that can be used to guide nursing research. A multidimensional approach to research that considers the value, effectiveness, and cost of different health objectives, as well as different health care interventions, is necessary. There are serious consequences associated with not systematically gathering data within the rationing model as a whole. Without information on values and cost in addition to effectiveness, an optimal configuration for a health care plan will not be possible. This discussion is not meant to suggest that the value, effectiveness, and cost of nursing and medical interventions must be definitively established before their inclusion in a rationing plan. Rather, it suggests that providing even preliminary effectiveness and value data will enhance the probability of an intervention being considered for coverage in a rationing plan.

A partnership between nurse researchers and nurse administrators and between nurse researchers, ethicists, economists, and other professionals is essential to do the necessary research. The research recommendations in this chapter are consistent with nursing's agenda for health care (ANA, 1991) and a necessary step for making health care rationing. The next step is nurses' participation in the political arena to translate this agenda into an effective and efficient health care plan.

ACKNOWLEDGMENTS

We gratefully acknowledge John Collins, research assistant, for his assistance with reviewing the literature. In addition, we thank Julia Brown, Ph.D., for assistance in reviewing and refining this chapter.

REFERENCES

Aaron, H., & Schwartz, W. B. (1990). Rationing health care: The choice before us. *Science, 247*, 418-422.

Adams, M. E., McCall, N. T., Gray, D. T., Orza, M. J., & Chalmers, T. C. (1992). Economic analysis in randomized control trials. *Medical Care, 30*(3), 231-243.

American Nurses Association (ANA). (1991). *Nursing's agenda for health care.* Kansas City, MO: Author.

Brown, J., Tanner, C. A., & Patrick, K. P. (1984). Nursing search for scientific knowledge. *Nursing Research, 33*(1), 26-32.

Capuzzi, C., & Garland, M. (1990). The Oregon plan: Increasing access to health care. *Nursing Outlook, 38*, 260-263, 286.

Colling, J., Ouslander, J., Hadley, B. J., Eisch, J., & Campbell, E. (1992). The effects of patterned urge-response toileting (PURT) on urinary incontinence among nursing home residents. *Journal of the American Geriatric Society, 40*, 135-141.

Drummond, M. F. (1980). *Principles of economic appraisal in health care.* Oxford: Oxford University.

Eddy, D. M. (1991). Rationing by patient choice. *Journal of the American Medical Association, 265*, 105-108.

Garland, M. J. (1991). Justice, politics and community: Expanding access and rationing health services in Oregon. *Law, Medicine & Health Care, 20*, 67-81

Grace, H. K. (1990). Can health care costs be contained? In J. C. McCloskey & H. K. Grace (Eds.), *Current issues in nursing* (pp. 380-386). St. Louis: Mosby–Year Book.

Hadorn, D. C. (1991). The role of public values in setting health care priorities. *Social Science and Medicine, 32*, 773-781.

Haller, K. B., Reynolds, M. A., & Horsley, J. A. (1979). Developing research-based innovation protocols: Process, criteria, and issues. *Research in Nursing and Health, 2,* 45-51.

Hoffman, F. (1988). *Nursing productivity assessment and costing out nursing services.* Philadelphia: J.B. Lippincott.

Hoepelman, I. M., Rozenberg-Arska, M., & Verhoef, J. (1988). Comparison of once daily ceftriaxone with gentamicin plus cefuroxime for treatment of serious bacterial infections. *The Lancet, 1*(8598), 1305-1309.

Hu, T., Igfou, J. F., Kaltreider, L., Yu, L. C., Rohner, T. J., Dennis, P. J., Craighead, W. E., Hadley, E. C., & Ory, M. G. (1989). A clinical trial of a behavioral therapy to reduce urinary incontinence in nursing homes. *Journal of the American Medical Association, 261,* 2656-2662.

Hunt, S. M., McEwen, J., & McKenna, S. P. (1985). Measuring health status: A new tool for clinicians and epidemiologists. *Journal of the Royal College of General Practitioner, 35,* 185-189.

Jensen, D. M. (1988). Economic assessment of peptic ulcer disease treatments. *Scandinavian Journal of Gastroenterology, 23*(Suppl. 143), 214-224.

Kaplan, R. M., & Bush, J.W. (1982). Health-related quality of life measurement for evaluation research and policy analysis. *Health Psychology, 1,* 61-80.

Koeppen, C. J. (1990, July/August). Conference looks at nursing's effectiveness. *The American Nurse, 22,* 34.

McLoughlin, S. (1990, July/August). Framework to help develop standards, guidelines. *The American Nurse, 22,* 34.

Oregon Health Services Commission. (1991). *The Oregon health plan: Prioritization of health services.* Salem, OR: Author.

Peters, M., & Robinson, V. (1984). The origins and status of action research. *Journal Of Applied Behavioral Science, 20,* 113-124.

Rader, J., Semradek, J., McKenzie, D., & McMahon, M. (in press). Strategies for restraint reduction in Oregon's long term care facilities. *Journal of Gerontological Nursing.*

Riccolo, D. (1988). Institutional approaches to costing out nursing. In M. Johnson & J. McCloskey (Eds.), *Series on Nursing Administration* (Vol. 1). St. Louis: Mosby–Year Book.

Rooks, J. R. (1990). Let's admit we ration health care—then set priorities. *American Journal of Nursing, 90*(6), 30-43.

Rosser, R., & Kind, P. (1978). A scale of valuations of states of illness: Is there a social consensus? *International Journal of Epidemiology, 7,* 347-358.

Schoenbaum, S. C. (1980). Cost-effectiveness considerations in clinical trials. *Triangle, 19,* 103-106.

Spitzer, W. O., Dobson, A. J., Hall, J., Chesterman, E., Levi, J., Shepherd, R., Battista, R. N., & Catchlove, B. R. (1981). Measuring the quality of life of cancer patients. *Journal of Chronic Disease, 34,* 585-597.

Stewart, A. L., Greenfield, S., Hays, R. D., Wells, K., Rogers, W. H., Berry, S. D., McGlynn, E. A., & Ware, J. E. (1989). Functional status and well-being of patients with chronic conditions. *Journal of the American Medical Association, 262,* 907-913.

Watson, P. M., Lower, M. S., Wells, S. M., Farrah, S. J., & Jarrell, C. (1991). Discovering what nurses do and what it costs. *Nursing Management, 22*(5), 38-45.

Yin, R. K. (1989). *Case study research.* Newbury Park, CA: Sage.

CHAPTER 13

Beyond the Health Care Reform Decision: Future Implications of this Volume

John D. Crossley

The outcome of the health policy debate initiated as a major policy goal for the Clinton administration is unknown as this volume goes to press. Yet it is certain that the rationing of health care will continue as a centerpiece. We have now and will continue to have rationing, for there is no end to the demand for health care and no society rich enough to meet that demand. To meet the realities of a reformed health system, nurse executives must prepare their organizations, their staffs, and themselves for a capitated payment environment. They must expect a new emphasis on proactively managing the wellness of a client population. They must learn to transition away from the inpatient setting as the primary site of care. In short, nurse executives must take the lead in the massive revision of one seventh of the economy of the United States—the health care system.

All information has a half-life. Physicists among us remember that a radioactive element decays—loses its radioactivity—at a constant rate. The rate, or half-life, is stated as the time required for half of the initial radioactivity to disappear. That value may be an unimaginably small fraction of a second or a billion years. Elements with short half-lives are characterized as unstable.

Senior Vice President for Nursing, University Hospitals of Cleveland, Cleveland, OH 44106

Series on Nursing Administration—Volume 6, 1994

So it is with information. Some data have only the briefest value because they are unstable: the score of a game in progress, or the price of a share of stock at the moment a purchase decision is made. It is the score at the end of the game that matters, and what the share price does after you own it does not affect the original purchase decision.

The instability of the health care system in the United States and the arguments and discussions about its future came home to me as I read the chapters prepared for this volume. Most were written in late 1992. I was struck, as I reviewed them in May of 1993, at the absence of any mention of Hillary Rodham Clinton and her task group on health care reform and at the lack of discussion of the specifics of the health care reform debates, which are filling today's newspapers and trade journals. Today, the outcome of the debate is unknown. But by the time you read this, undoubtedly decisions will have been made, legislation will have been proposed and enacted, the regulatory process will have begun to creak in response—and the nurse executives of the United States will be evolving solutions for nursing in the changed environment.

This volume will serve you well in your endeavor. In spite of the lead time required to prepare a book, I see a long half-life for the content presented here.

It is inevitable that health care services in the United States will be rationed, probably by some combination of price rationing and non–price rationing. The politically correct term today for the former is *managed competition*, especially when spoken with an emphasis on *competition*. Non–price rationing is exemplified by the Oregon model. Nichols, Johnson, and Maas point out the fact of rationing for nurses. Haddad carefully differentiates between the "soft" rationing that nurses perform as caregivers and the "hard," logical, cost/benefit analyses that nurse administrators are called on to make as executives. The interpersonal nature of the delivery of care means, in the words of Maguire and McFadden, "it is nurses who will usually explain the decisions about rationing and other health care policies to the public and to patients." Nurse executives must keep in mind the immediacy of the problem for caregivers. Systems and words must support those who will be in the position of repeatedly saying that a service or amenity is not going to be provided even though it may be desired by both the patient and the provider.

Sharp insightfully addresses the reality of policymaking at the federal level. Nurse executives have their voice in Washington through various special interest groups that speak for nursing. In addition, we are each a constituent, with one member of the House of Representatives and two Senators vitally interested in our views. Take the time to express those views in brief, constructive letters that state your professional qualifications. Make your elected representatives part of your constituency. Remember that laws and regulations are promulgated from statehouses, county commissions, and city halls, as well as at the federal level. Sharp's direction and advice apply in these arenas too. Indeed, nursing administrators may find that involvement at the local level leads to success resulting in action at the federal level. Berkowitz and Capuzzi, in separate chapters, have described just such a state initiative in Oregon, a model that others may have adopted by the time you read this.

Wherever the policy discussion takes place, Merwin has emphasized that nurses and nursing need to be more accountable to the public. The essence of professionalism is this accountability, supraordinate to any employment situation. The creation of the Agency for Health Care Policy and Research (AHCPR) and the key role nurses are playing in its work on outcome measures demonstrate professional accountability. For nurse executives to translate AHCPR guidelines into consistent practice in their institutions will require accountability leavened with organizational and interpersonal leadership skills—and it will not be easy. Practitioners value their freedom to make decisions. Changing practice patterns for competent professionals can be compared with herding cats—quite possible in theory; quite difficult in the event.

We have the advantage that nursing respects data. McKenzie and Ray point out that research on clinical problems must include the cost effectiveness of the interventions under examination. Not to have done so in the past has been the norm; not to do so from this moment on is unprofessional and therefore not acceptable. In the debate over the cost of health care, our society is telling us that we are accountable for the cost of what we do and what we propose. Cost as a key variable in the clinical equation will be with us for the rest of the professional life of every nurse practicing today. Research and the application of research cannot speak of qualitative improvement alone.

Several authors have addressed the restructuring of health care and the effect various changes may have on nursing. Simmons raises an essential point: the uninsured are underserved only in preventive health interventions. The 36 (or 37 or 42—take your choice) million Americans without health insurance lack access only to preventive measures. They have access, at the time of crisis, to the entire panoply of high-technology, high-intensity interventions in our system. Of course no one wants to confront the fact that those services have to be paid for. The fact that the uninsured are denied preventive health interventions (which are relatively cheap) leaves them with no option but to wait until their condition deteriorates to the point that expensive interventions are necessary. It is not what they would choose. And it is not a model a rational systems designer would propose, since it is so terribly inefficient.

REWARD AND OPPORTUNITIES

The solution to the situation just described will offer expanded participation for nursing. Feather captures the issue in his discussion of the battle between episodic care and continuity in care. The uninsured are caught in an episodic series of exchanges with the health care system. Creating efficient continuity is what nurses are about. The images of the nurse as integrator or the nurse as the glue that holds the system together are easy to present because they resonate with the experience of every nurse, of every patient, of every physician. In this country in this century, nursing's roots are strongest in public health. Public health nursing is the strongest paradigm of what a managed care health system can be: ongoing professional involvement to educate and support individuals and their families in maintaining wellness and avoiding illness. Jones discusses various models of the delivery of nursing care in the acute care environment, and Falk and Bower define and describe managed care in the same environment.

But all indications are that we will be soon practicing in a reformed health care system that takes managed care at least one order of magnitude beyond anything we have seen. I find it interesting that health maintenance organizations talk not about the number of "patients" or "clients" they have in their plan but instead speak of "lives." Lives. They are saying that they are in the business of managing the provision of health needs throughout a human life. And they are paid a per capita fee to do so. Health reform will expand capitated models. As I write, the current term is "health alliances," or regional, vertically integrated provider groups who will contract to manage lives in relation to health care. Think about how the incentives will change for providers, especially hospitals, as health alliances bloom. In a fully capitated system there will be no cost shifting, since there will be no private insurers. There will be a stable patient enrollment or at least one that changes predictably over time or in consequence of contractual bidding. All providers will have the same financial incentives, because they are all employees of the health alliance. And the health alliance, like all insurers, will make its profit on the difference between what it charges in premiums and what it pays out in services over the life of its clients. What this means is that success will come by keeping covered lives as healthy as possible.

In a fully capitated model, every admission to the hospital is a financial loss. Every contact with the plan will involve a focus on health and wellness. Education in healthy life-styles will bring a financial reward to the system. There will be meaningful review of new technologies and of new treatment modalities for both efficacy and efficiency; and on completion of the review, an expedited integration of the improvement into the plan's clinical operation will occur. Because health alliances will compete with each other and enrollees will have a choice of plans, all must be done in a way to keep the members happy with the way their lives are being managed.

The opportunities for nursing are immense. Advanced practice nurses are more efficient providers of many services currently reserved for physicians. Advanced nursing practice will expand. The nurse as integrator in the inpatient environment will link with the home health role—seamlessly. The value of health education and the educated patient will be demonstrated as increasing wellness decreases resource use. Research will combine cost and clinical effects as coequal outcomes to be examined. The rewards seem endless for nursing and particularly sweet, since this model of patient- and family-centered wellness is one we have advocated as a profession since our earliest days.

CALCULATING RISKS

But there are risks. Nurse executives will be charged with reversing half a century's focus on inpatient nursing as the predominate model of our profession. It will always be needed, but inevitably in much smaller proportion. Executives will have to design and implement systems that make efficient use of nontraditional providers. If advanced practice nurses can replace more highly paid physicians, we can expect the same pressures to result in less expensive provider roles replacing highly paid nurses. Competency assessment and quality assessment and improvement will be more necessary than ever but will have to be achieved in multiple sites of care—perhaps in as many homes as there are subscriber families in a health alliance plan. Educators and researchers will have to adapt their products to the new environment and may well need help from the frontline nurse executive in that adjustment.

Maybe we should welcome the risks. They will come as we are given the opportunity to transform a health care system, the shortcomings of which we know intimately. Or perhaps we should curse the risks. They will disrupt everything we know—and are comfortable with—in the current imperfect system. Isn't there something about the devil you know being preferable to the devil you haven't met? It will be hard work to remake our world.

The one option foreclosed to us is to avoid the risks. We are here, and it is now. Nurse executives are in key positions in every health care enterprise in the United States. We have been prepared by education and experience for those roles. We are rewarded for those roles. We cannot avoid our professional and personal obligation to be an active, leading part of the effort to remake a system of overwhelming importance to our society. Our success will be the measure by which we are judged to have met nursing's obligation as a profession.

And I for one think it will be great fun to finally get it right.

Index